BURWELL

A History of a Fen-edge Village

BURWELL

A History of a Fen-edge Village

William Franklin

To the memory of my father, William Noel Franklin 1922–1998, who, throughout my childhood, encouraged me in my interests.

ISBN 0 9544456 9 4

Designed, Typeset and Published by
Heritage Marketing and Publications Ltd
Hill Farm, Great Dunham, King's Lynn, Norfolk, PE32 2LP
Tel: 01760 755645 Fax: 01760 755316
e-mail: sales@heritagemp.com

An extensive range of new and selected out-of-print books on archaeological and historical subjects is available on the Heritage Marketing and Publications website at:
http://www.heritagemp.com

Contents

Acknowledgements

To my wife who has put up with me spending hours in preparing this work and to my children who have encouraged me in continuing.

My thanks also go to the staff of Cambridge Record Office and Cambridge University Library for their patience and help, to Cambridgeshire Public Library Service for permission to use photographs from the Cambridgeshire Collection and to Mgr Paul Hypher for help with translation of latin documents.

Abbreviations used in notes:

B.L	British Library, London
C.A.S	Cambridge Antiquarian Society
C.R.O	Cambridge Record Office, Shire Hall, Cambridge
C.U.A	Cambridge University Archives
C.U.L	Cambridge University Library
P.R.O	Public Records Office, Kew, London
R.C.H.M	Royal Commission for Historical Monuments

FOREWORD

As a teenager I had the opportunity to wander the fields around my hometown of Rushden, Northamptonshire and took a great interest in the things I found there, whether fossils or man-made objects. My father encouraged my interest in all things old, by taking me further afield to visit a variety of historic buildings, including some of the countries finest churches. By the age of fourteen I was spending much of my summer in trenches on archaeological digs, in the autumn field walking and the winter Saturday mornings were spent in the local record office.

By the time I was sixteen, most of my weekends were either spent on excavations or field walking, but then as most of us do I discovered girls, alcohol and music. Despite this I kept an interest in archaeology greatly encouraged by David Hall, Chairman of the Higham Ferrers Hundred Archaeological Society and later field officer for the Fenland Project. In 1975 I commenced Nurse training initially continuing to work with the team when shift work permitted.

In 1982 my wife, Fe, and our young son Gareth moved to Burwell, a place steeped in history. Our first few years in the village were taken up by making our house habitable, working and family activities, especially as the family grew. Despite that on our walks around the Burwell countryside, my eyes noted the remnants of the medieval field system and I soon began to make regular visits to the Cambridge Record Office and later the University library, the Public Record Office at Kew and others in search of knowledge about my adoptive home village.

By the millennium, this book was taking shape. It has been a long time in the making and I have realised that in such an endeavour one can continue tweeking and adding to the text for as long as there are documents to decipher. I believe that in this work I have captured the most salient points in Burwell's history.

I am not alone in writing on Burwell's history. There are at least four books that have gone before, which all tell something of the past life of the village. The first was that by the antiquarian Mr Cole, who visited Burwell in 1743 and who gives his account of what he saw and some historical notes on the village. The second was a book called *The Fenman's World*, by Dr Charles Lucas. Dr Lucas, a General Practitioner published his book in 1930. As with Mr Cole, he describes much of what he saw or remembered, or what he was told about the history of the village. Not all of what he wrote was historically accurate and a few items in the book are quite fanciful.

The third account is not a book, but the writings of Mr Gathercole for the village magazine, *Clunch*. Mr Gathercole was a person with a clear passion for Burwell and its history, and not only gave good account of his recollections of the various parts of the village but also spent much time researching his articles, such as that on the history of the British School.

The fourth and most recent book is that written by Mrs Heather Richardson (1990), who drew upon her own knowledge of Burwell, that learned from Dr Lucas and Mr Arthur Gathercole and that gained from research.

So, why another book? What I hope I have achieved is the production of a work based on good historical evidence from surviving records and evidence in the local fields to show the history of the village from the very earliest times. I have unashamedly not written much about the twentieth century. Dr Lucas, Mr Arthur Gathercole and Mrs Heather Richrdson have all excelled in their respective parts of those years and I have not wished to repeat that.

Burwell is fortunate that a great wealth of historical documents survive relating to the village, including a large number of court rolls relating to the Ramsey Abbey Manor. I suspect there can be few villages in Cambridgeshire (excluding those in the former county of Huntingdonshire) that have such a wealth of historic documents, particularly of the medieval period.

William Franklin
Burwell
July 2004.

Glossary

Ad Opus	The term literally means "at work" and refers to the servile tenure held for the performance of labour services.
Ad Censum	Land held for labour services, which have been commuted to an annual money rent.
Advowson	From advow or advocare, a right of presentation to a church or benefice. He who possesses this right is called the patron or advocate.
Affeeror	Someone who gives assurance.
Ale-Taster	The ale-taster had the task of testing the ale of all of the village brewsters to make sure it was of proper quality and not watered down. Women could be fined for improper brewing if he determined that their ale was of poor quality. Often, even if it was not, they were fined – as a sort of unofficial licensing fee.
Amercement	Money extracted as a penalty.
Annate	One year's income of a benefice, paid to the Pope. From 1535 this was paid to the crown.
Arentata	Form of rental of land for a fee with no services being due on the Lord's land.
Assart	A piece of land, variable in size, recovered from previously uncultivated land, such as waste or marsh.
Assize of Bread	A national regulation of the baking trade, requiring that bread sold for consumption was of the proper weight and quality and that it was priced in accordance with current costs of the relevant grains.
Bailiff	A manorial official, frequently charged with collecting rents for the landlord or exercising other administrative responsibilities, including the oversight of the agricultural and pastorial activities of the manor. Sometimes a salaried employee in contrast to the reeve who was a villein and rewarded with rent reductions or a tenement.
Balk	A path or track across the open fields.
Beadle	The beadle was an officer of the manorial court. Subordinate to the bailiff and the reeve he helped to collect the rents as well as the fines levied by the manorial court.
Borough	A term (from the Old English *burh*) used to denote a place with urban characteristics and therefore likely to contain commercial institutions, including a market. The term originally indicated the defended character of the place but acquired additional connotations, including the distinctive legal customs, taxation rates and rights to representation enjoyed by the inhabitants of towns in contrast to those of the countryside.

Calendar	A published summary in English of the contents of a document or a series of documents. For example, the charter rolls are the manuscript record of charters granted by the king; they are written in Latin in a contemporary hand. The calendar of the charter rolls is a summary of their contents with some information, such as the witness lists, left out.
Capital Messuage	A Capital Messuage was the house (manor), of the Lord of the Manor, or similar large residence, also know as a mese.
Cellerer	A monastic official responsible for the provisioning of a monastery.
Charter	Document recording a grant. A royal charter is distinguished from other forms of royal instrument as it has a witness list and notifies specific groups of the royal act.
Close	An enclosure or garden.
Croft	A small piece of arable land sometimes, but not always, next to a house.
Croftman	Sometimes also called a cottar or cottager. These were people who rented a croft or a cottage with a couple of acres of land.
Curtilage	A small court, yard, or piece of ground attached to a dwelling-house and forming one enclosure with it.
Demesne	Land retained by a lord for his own use; royal demesne was the land retained by the king.
Demesne Overseer	One who oversees or superintends the land set aside for the Lord's table. A supervisor.
Distraint	The act of seizing and retaining, by court order, a piece of movable property from an individual as a means of enforcing compliance with an order. This distrained property is often referred to as a distress.
Escheat	The right of a lord to confiscate property held by a free tenant found guilty of a felony.
Fee Simple	Unconditional inheritance.
Feet of Fines	Also known as final concords, this was a means of settling a dispute, commonly with the purpose of conveying real property. The 'foot' was the copy of the agreement filed centrally, the others being kept by the two parties.
Ffeoffee	The holder of a fee, that is an estate in land held on condition of homage and service. Ffeoffees in the post medieval period were those who held land on behalf of a charity and ensured the profits derived were put to good use.
Firmarius	The Farmer. In medieval times the senior manorial official who regulated the rotation of fields and determined when services were to be provided.
Frankpledge	A court held annually by a sheriff in the hundred court in his circuit of the county, or especially by the thirteenth century, by a manorial lord including the right to oversee the activities of the members of local tithing groups and the enforcing of the assizes of bread and ale.
Fulsyngpounde	A manorial insurance scheme into which all tenants paid. If the villein was accused of having broken a bye-law he or she would only ever have to pay sixpence as paying into the fulstyngpound covered the remaining cost. The practice appears to have been almost unique to Ramsey Abbey.

Furlong	A measure of an area derived from the length of the furrow ploughed by a team of oxen before resting and turning the plough. As its Latin name indicates, the furlong was notionally 40 perches - 220 yards - in length. In reality, the size of the furlong would have been affected by the nature of the soil, the shape of the field, and other contingent factors.
Fyrd	The fyrd were working men who were called up to fight for Anglo-Saxon kings in times of danger.
Gersumarium	An entry fine, that is a payment by an incoming or outgoing tenant to the lord of the manor for permission take or release possession of a tenement.
Hayward	The hayward made sure the fences guarding the crops were good, fined people who let their animals into the fields (and impounded the animals), and made sure the seeds from the previous season were kept safe over winter until planting.
Headland	A piece of land – 120 acres.
Hide	An area of land comprising of 120 acres.
Holme	The term means marsh-meadow and was used to refer to meadows in general.
Hundred	A group of parishes, usually ten in number, each comprising 10 hides. These formed an administrative area with their own court.
Hythe	A mooring place for boats. In the fens this is usually associated with a wharf for unloading goods brought in by boat.
Infangthief	The lord of the manor's jurisdiction over a thief apprehended within the manor. The right of the lord of a manor to try and to punish a thief caught within its limits. (Outfangthief was the right of judging and fining thieves when outside of one's own jurisdiction).
Inquisition post mortem	When a tenant who held directly from the king died, an inquest was held to determine the nature and extent of his estates. The inquest was conducted by means of sworn testimony.
In Mortmain	An unlawful (without royal consent) alienation of lands, or tenements by sale or gift to a religious house or university college.
Joint Lay Subsidy	The tax levied in 1334. This replaced the previous system of direct tax on the wealth of individuals by a 'fixed quota' system in which every community agreed upon the sum it was to pay. Rural areas paid a fifteenth of their assessed wealth, whilst boroughs paid a tenth.
Leet	Manorial court at which rental business and the instigation of local bye-laws were conducted.
Leys	An area of arable land turned over to pasture.
Lode	A water course or drain.
Lollard	An early dissenter from the Catholic church. Lollards followed the teaching of John Wycliffe (b. 1330). The followers of Wycliffe formed a secret underground church and circulated handwritten copies of an unauthorised translation of the New Testament into English. Because of their need for secrecy they were said to whisper to each other. Hence they became known as Lollards, from an Old Dutch word for mumblers.

Messuage	A dwelling house with land and out-buildings.
Moiety	A share, usually of a possession.
Oratory	The private chapel of an abbot or bishop.
Pannage	A payment by tenants for the right to let their pigs forage in the woods.
Pipe Roll	Name given to the Great Roll of the Exchequer on account of its shape when rolled up. Records of the audit of the annual accounts of the sheriff of each county made in the Exchequer.
Rectorial Glebe	A piece of land serving as part of a clergyman's benefice and providing income.
Reeve	An official charged with responsibility for the economic and agricultural management of a manor, similar in function to a bailiff except that the reeve was of villein or servile status and was not usually paid a salary but was instead released from labour services and/or granted a piece of land.
Right of Gallows	The right of a manor to try and to hang its own population found guilty of a serious crime.
Right to Agist	The right to put animals out to pasture (agist = to pasture).
Senchal	Court official. A Seneschal or steward, a member of the lower aristocracy, often a knight or, if not, a monk. He was literate and acted as the lord's agent or factor – his deputy and chief administrator. The steward did not stay in the village and was not always even on the manor, but would appoint the bailiff.
Serf	A man or woman of servile status. Also called a villein or naif.
Sheepwalk	A field set aside for sheep.
Shire Reeve (Sheriff)	Principal agent of the Crown responsible for the administration and finances of a specific county.
Sokeman	A tenant who was free from certain burdens.
Tithe	One tenth of annual produce or earnings, formerly taken as a tax for the support of the Church and clergy.
Toft	A small house or homestead.
Virgate	A unit of land, usually a quarter of a hide or 30 acres.
Virgator	Sometimes called a Yardlander, virgators were the largest land holders among the peasants. They also tended to serve as the village officers (bailiff, jurors, ale-tasters, etc).

Introduction

Burwell is one of Cambridgeshire's larger villages. It lies next to the South Eastern edge of the Cambridgeshire Fenland, approximately 12 miles north-east from Cambridge and five miles north-west of Newmarket and within the East Cambridgeshire District Council area.

A village of great importance in the twelfth century, when it played its part in defeating the rebellious Geoffrey de Mandeville and ending the rebellion against King Stephen. The village now retains a mixture of old and new, and is a home to a thriving community, some of whom are employed locally, but many who commute to Cambridge or Newmarket.

Chapter 1

Topography and Archaeology

Burwell is a large parish covering 7011 acres. It is situated approximately five miles north-west of Newmarket and approximately 12 miles north-east of Cambridge. Geologically most of the parish sits on chalk of the Cretaceous period. This chalk is known locally as Clunch. Overlying the chalk is a bed of clay. Approximately one third of the parish is fen. Here peat deposited in the Mesozoic era overlies a greensand deposit. The level of the land ranges in height from 10ft above the Ordnance Datum to approximately 160ft above the Ordnance Datum at Newmarket Heath. The fen edge along which the village is built follows roughly a north-east to south-west axis.

Hundred

In keeping with the Midland Shires, Cambridgeshire was from about the tenth century subdivided into areas called 'hundreds'. Each hundred comprised of about 100 hides of land. These hundreds are considered to have been taxation units and usually comprised approximately ten villages. Burwell lies within the Staploe Hundred, along with Soham, Wicken, Fordham, Isleham, Kennett, Snailwell and Chippenham (including the former village of Badlingham). Until the mid 1800s, Exning was part of Cambridgeshire and also included in the hundred. In 1993, most of Landwade Parish transferred into Suffolk along with the southern end of Burwell (the heath south of the A14).

The hundred provided a convenient unit for calling out the 'fyrd', the local defence force, as well as for the collection of taxes. Meetings of the hundred court, which was concerned with the maintenance of law in the area, were held in the open air at regular intervals of four weeks so that everyone would know about them and there would be no need to issue a summons to appear. By the thirteenth century the role of the hundreds as courts was waning as most crimes were dealt with by either the manorial courts or the county courts, which from the reign of King Henry II occurred in most parts of the country, the king having established a system of paid professional judges who travelled around the country to try serious cases in courts held in the most important towns of each county. This appears to have been the case with the Staploe court, which from 1299 met twice yearly and continued to do so thereafter.

The name of the Hundred is derived from the name of the meeting place 'Stapel hoh', which means a spur of land with a pillar on it. Exactly where this meeting place was is not known. However it seems likely that the meeting place was in a Burwell field. Reaney[1], referring to the Cambridge Assize Rolls (1298) notes that 'the hundred is named from a place, Stapellhoo in Burwell'. It was mentioned in documents from 1086 and documents relating to Burwell and Exning refer to a trackway that led to it. Known as the viam de Stapelhoue in 1198[2], Stapilhamweye in 1451[3] and Stapillo wey in 1521[4], this trackway remained in existence in the fields of Burwell until enclosure. The section running through the Parish of Exning remains, albeit for the most part overgrown. Just off the present track is a small triangular field surrounded on two sides by the fields of Exning, so that it protrudes into Exning Parish like a spur of land, which may be the most likely location for the meeting place. The Burwell side of this field is bordered by a track, known today as Haycross Way, which comes off Ness road. On the other side of Ness Road this track is known as Howland Balk, a name that could mean that a track lead to the 'hoh land', the pillar land or the meeting place. This meeting place would have been remote from any of the villages in the Hundred as is the case across most of East Anglia.

In 1086, there were ten vills in the Staploe Hundred, of which three were assessed at 15 hides and three at ten hides. The others varied in hideage. Three of the parishes in the Hundred had royal manors in 1086. Burwell would have been the fourth had not its royal manor been given to the Abbey of Ramsey. From the twelfth century, Badlingham was incorporated into Chippenham.

The boundary of the Hundred forms the County boundary on its eastern edge, while the Devil's Dyke and the Reach Lode forms much of its western boundary. In 1954 part

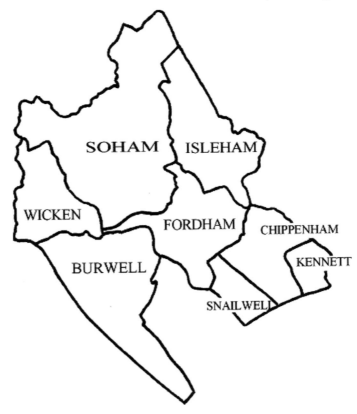

Map 1 *Map of the Staploe Hundred 1950.*

of this eastern edge, that around the two former vills of East Reach (Burwell Parish) and West Reach (Swaffham Prior Parish) with 436 acres were combined into one new Parish of Reach and transferred into the Staine Hundred. The northern boundary is formed in part by the river Cam, while much of its southern boundary was aligned to the Icnield Way, prior to the loss of Exning to Suffolk

Parish

The parish has undergone a number of changes in the last century, firstly (as noted above) with the loss of East Reach, which with West Reach amalgamated to form its own parish in 1954. The new parish comprised of 436 acres out of the parishes of Burwell and Swaffham Prior. Secondly as noted above, in 1993, the part of Newmarket Heath within the Parish of Burwell, transferred into Newmarket and the County of Suffolk. This change made the A14 Newmarket by-pass the new parish boundary to the South. For the purposes of this history of Burwell these recent changes have been ignored.

Geology of the Fenland

Burwell, like its neighbours the Swaffhams, is a parish that comprises three distinct topographical areas. To the north and east are the Fens whilst to the south and west are chalk slope, formed in the Cretaceous period and the heathlands, which comprise chalk outcrops overlaid with sand.

The fenland was originally part of a low basin, which was carved out by ice flows in the Pleistocene period. This basin stretches south to north, from Burwell to Lincolnshire, and east to west, from The Wash to Huntingdonshire. When it was created in the ice age the sea level was low, but as the ice flows receded, the sea levels rose. At the end of the last Ice Age it is estimated that the sea level was some 30 metres (100ft) lower than now. This meant that the fen basin was dry land. In this Mesolithic period the basin became covered by a deciduous forest. This forest was rich in flora and fauna, and a wide range of animal bones have been found in the peat over the past 150 years, including the skeletons of swans, deer, beaver, wolf and bear. Many examples of these can be seen displayed in the Sedgewick Museum, Cambridge.

Subsequently the sea levels rose and began to move up into channels created by rivers draining water from the uplands to the west. Peat formation commenced and as trees died they fell into the now boggy ground. The trunks of these trees (bog oaks) are often found. The fens continued to be drained by the former river channels but these became sluggish and many smaller channels developed.

By the third millennium BC, salt water covered most of the basin leaving areas of high ground as islands. A clay-like silt was deposited over the submerged areas. The absence of this silt shows that Burwell's fen area, while marsh, was not part of the submerged lagoon-like area.

Early Settlement

The earliest evidence of settlement within the parish is from the Mesolithic and Neolithic periods. This evidence is in the form of worked flints, including flint and

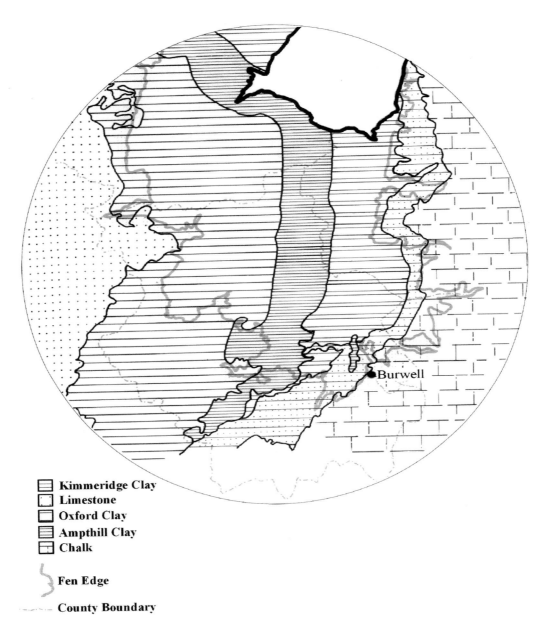

Kimmeridge Clay
Limestone
Oxford Clay
Ampthill Clay
Chalk

Fen Edge

County Boundary

Map 2. *The geology of the fenland.*

jadeite hand axes. (Wymer 1985)[5]. The principle settlement site identified from this period lies in Hallard's Fen (TL 570/675). This site, which is on chalk marl and gault clay lies between 5ft and 10ft above the ordnance datum, has revealed quantities of flint cores, flakes, axes, scrapers, arrow heads and polished stone axes. It is probable that this site was still in use in the early Bronze Age. Excavations in 1969 close to the weirs, where a hoard of bronze bowls was found, indicated another occupation site of the late Neolithic/early Bronze Age.

The Bronze Age

Evidence of Bronze Age activity has been found throughout the parish. Often the remains have been 'stray' finds; ie finds not associated with a settlement or burial site. Such finds have included small hoards, a Bronze Age torc (now in the Ashmolean Museum, Oxford) and bronze axe heads found on The Broads and other areas of the parish, including the churchyard of St Mary. There are a number of barrows (burial mounds) in the parish. At least ten are known to have existed into the nineteenth century including a number on Newmarket Heath but within the parish of Burwell. The ploughed out remains of the ring ditches of these barrows are still identifiable and at least 11 have been recorded by aerial photography. These are:

	Name/type	Map ref	Notes
1	Ninescore Hill Barrow	TL 6091/6304	700yd SE of Great Portland Farm. 65ft in diameter. It is shown as a barrow on the 1884 OS map but now only visible by aerial photography.
2	Ring Ditch	TL 6122/6358	730yd E of Great Portland Farm. It is shown as a barrow on the 1884 OS map but now only visible by aerial photography.
3	Ring Ditch	TL 6116/6352	40yd SW of no.2. It is shown as a barrow on the 1884 OS map but now only visible by aerial photography.
4	Ring Ditch	TL 613/633	300yd SE of no.2. It is shown as a barrow on the 1884 OS map but now only visible by aerial photography.
5	Ring Ditch	TL 6011/6885	200yd NW of Lark Hall. 100ft in diameter. Only visible by aerial photography.
6	Ring Ditch	TL 5960/6561	830yd SE of the church. 80ft in diameter. Only visible by aerial photography.
7	Ring Ditch	TL 5967/5655	930yd SE of church. 80ft in diameter. Only visible by aerial photography.
8	Ring Ditch	TL 5875/6539	700yd SSW of the church. 100ft in diameter. Only visible by aerial photography.
9	Ring Ditch	TL 5893/6535	230yd SE of no.8. 90 feet in diameter. Only visible by aerial photography.
10	Ring Ditch	TL 5937/6464	200yd SW of Lower Portland Farm. 60ft in diameter. Only visible by aerial photography.
11	Ring Ditch	TL 5830/6468	600yd NW of Ditch Farm. 40ft in diameter. Only visible by aerial photography.

Table 1 *Recorded ring ditches and barrows.*

Crop marks from Bronze Age settlements have also been noted on higher ground.

Iron Age

Adjoining the Devil's Dyke and spanning the parish boundary between Burwell and Swaffham Prior, is an Iron Age site that has produced a number of sherds of pottery. Further evidence of Iron Age activity was revealed during the excavations near the weirs.

Roman

The parish has a number of sites from the Roman period. These include a building or buildings under the site of Burwell Castle, noted during the excavations of 1935[6], but not excavated, and at least five settlement sites from this period[7], including:

1. A site north-west of Crownall Farm which has yielded glassware, pottery and roof tiles (TL 5806/6540).
2. A site near to the recreation ground which revealed pottery dating from the second to fourth century AD and ditches (TL 585/676).
3. A site 250yd west-south-west of Burwell Castle from which ploughing has revealed pottery, box tiles and roof tiles (TL 5854/6595).
4. A possible settlement site east of Ness Road of the second or third century AD (TL 5989/6805).
5. A possible settlement site found during the excavations of the Saxon cemetery between 1925 and 1929 (TL 5901/6651).

Amongst the finds of the Roman period from the parish is a Tankard handle found in 1846 in Burwell Fen. The handle, which dates the vessel to the first century AD, is decorated with the head of a boar or a horse. A lead cistern[8], one of about a dozen found in Britain (Figure 1), and a hoard of bronze bowls was also found.

Roman Lead Cistern

The lead cistern, which can now be seen in the Museum of Archaeology and Ethnology in Cambridge, is roughly circular and is approximately 75cm in diameter and 45cm high. Made from three sheets of lead, it has the capacity to hold about 45 gallons of liquid. The decoration on the sides was created during the casting of the two side panels, rather than after construction.

The cistern is believed to date from the fourth century AD. This date is based on the pottery found in the field where the cistern was discovered and is consistent with the date of other similar cisterns, which are thought to be associated with ritual ablutions. No building of the period is known to exist at the site.

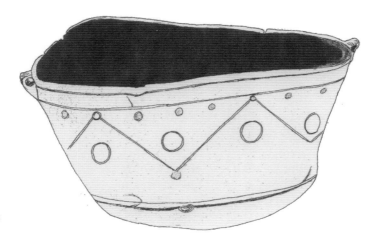

Figure 1 *Sketch of the roman lead cistern.*

Bronze Bowls

The hoard of bronze bowls found when preparing a field for ploughing in 1966. The hoard belonged to the fourth century AD[9] and comprised 18 objects, eight of which were bowls of 'Irchester' type (Irchester, Northamptonshire was a Roman fort and settlement where this type of bowl was first found), three cauldrons, a carinated bowl, a handled skillet, a hemispherical fluted bowl and two incised rings.

In 1969 the site was investigated[10] and revealed evidence of occupation from the late Neolithic/early Bronze Age, two ditch systems, one of the Iron Age, the other Roman and pottery and building debris suggesting a Roman occupation site in the proximity, dating from the second to fourth centuries AD. No structures associated with habitation were found.

The Dark Ages

Of the post Roman period, the Devil's Dyke is the greatest monument. This defensive earthwork stretches seven and a half miles from Reach to Wood Ditton. It comprises of a large bank and a deep dry ditch on its south-western side. It is the largest and longest of a series of dykes in the Cambridge area. Its precise date is unknown, but it is believed to be post-Roman in date. It forms the Burwell parish boundary from Reach to the A11 trunk road (formerly the Icknield way) at the south-western end of the parish. The north-eastern end of the dyke joins the Reach lode which was originally built by the Romans. The dyke at Reach was levelled in the thirteenth century to create the fair green. Over the centuries numerous cuttings have been made through the dyke. These cuttings are referred to as Gaps. Within the parish there are four Gaps as well as a cutting for the Cambridge to Mildenhall railway and, in recent times, the cutting for the A14 trunk road, although this was in effect a widening of an existing cutting through which ran the former Exning to Cambridge road.

In 1923–24 Sir Cyril Fox excavated[11] a section of the dyke near the cutting for the former Cambridge to Mildenhall railway. He was able to show that the bank was built upon ground covered by pottery of the second or third century. He concluded that the dyke was probably built in the seventh century as a defence by the East Anglians against attack by the Mercians under their King Penda. Other work by Fowler and Lethbridge (1933–35)[12], concluded that the dyke was later in date than the Reach lode which they knew to be Roman in origin. Lethbridge revised his theories in 1958[13] and proposed a late fourth century date, suggesting the dyke was part of a Roman military plan to block the retreat of Saxon invaders.

Further work undertaken at the time of the building of the A14 suggested that the dyke was probably of fifth or sixth century origin. It seems likely therefore that an accurate date for this great work of military defence may never be known but, on the best evidence so far, it appears to have been constructed somewhere between the fourth and seventh centuries and that its use as a defence was short lived.

Despite its short life as a defensive work, the impact of the dyke on the countryside has been spectacular. Not only in its visible presence but also on its effect on the organisation and farming practices of later generations. The Saxons both in Burwell and Swaffham Prior aligned their field systems to the dyke, rather than adopting the pre-existing field boundaries as they did in so many other places.

Map 3 *Identified sites in and around Burwell.*

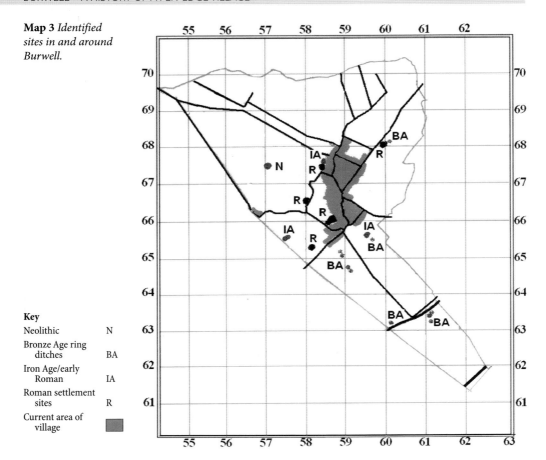

Saxon

The Saxons came to Britain from about the fifth century AD. By a century later they were well settled in East Anglia. It was during the Saxon period, probably in the sixth or seventh centuries, that Burwell first developed as the village we now know. However, despite four or five centuries of occupation in the area of High Town, we have little evidence of them by way of earthworks or archaeological finds. This is probably not surprising as most of the archaeological evidence for the period lies beneath later buildings and what remains there may be, will be of post holes from their timber-framed houses or domestic remains such as pieces of broken pottery. The chief remains of the period to have been discovered were those of a Saxon cemetery found in the late nineteenth century and the recent discovery of a Saxon farmstead on the former Tillotson's Factory site on Swaffham Road.

Saxon Cemetery

A Saxon cemetery was first noted in 1884 when a grave was found when the Victoria Lime Pits were being dug behind where the Crown Public House now stands. That is at the junction between Newmarket Road and the High Street. Further graves were discovered as quarrying continued. Adjoining the quarry was an allotment owned by the

Figure 2 *Skeletons in process of excavation. Burwell Saxon cemetery.*

local GP and antiquary, Dr Lucas, at whose request an excavation is said to have taken place. The excavation commenced in 1925 under the direction of T C Lethbridge[14]. The excavators discovered 127 graves between 1925 and 1929, and reported a further 14, which had been found during quarrying. The excavation of the site lasted for four seasons.

All except five of the burials were shallow graves of east-west orientation, suggesting Christian burials. Most of the people buried on the site were adults, and with one exception all had been carefully arranged in the grave at time of burial. Some of the graves contained artefacts. These included 12 knives, a *scramasax* (a short heavy one-sided knife or dagger), a bronze drum-shaped box (figure 3.), a gold disc pendant set with garnets, iron chains and buckles, beads and pins. No coffins or remains of coffins (eg nails) were discovered.

The cemetery, cut into the hillside and lying a short distance outside the northern end of the Saxon village, based upon the evidence gathered, can be dated to the sixth and seventh centuries.

Figure 3 *Bronze drum box found during excavations of the Saxon cemetery.*

Medieval

As with the Saxon period, most of the area of occupation of the medieval period is under the present village. The archaeological context of the site of Burwell Castle will be discussed here. The standing remains of the medieval period and the medieval field system will be discussed in subsequent chapters.

Burwell Castle

The mid twelfth century saw a civil war between King Stephen and Geoffrey de Mandeville, Earl of Essex. De Mandeville fell from power in 1143 and rebelled against the king. He took an army into the fens, capturing Ramsey Abbey, which he both desecrated and made his headquarters and from which he attacked the fenland towns and villages. To keep him in check, the king ordered a series of castles to be built around the fen edge.

Burwell castle is the best preserved of the remains of these castles and historically the most important (see Chapter 3.). What remains is an uncompleted castle and the site now comprises a rectangular ditch, 80–100ft in width, within which is a raised platform. This platform is uneven with mounds and hollows and there is a gap in one side leading into the moat. To the north and west, on the outside of the moat, are uneven mounds. The spoilheaps from the excavation of the moat were never taken away or levelled out. Up to about 1935 a section of walling, eight or nine feet high had remained. This however collapsed when the local fire brigade used it as a target on which to test their hoses.

The site overlies the remains of a former road and the house and close (garden). Remains of former dwellings that lay along the road can still be made out in the field.

Archaeological Investigation of the Castle

In 1935 the site was surveyed and partially excavated by Mr T. C. Lethbridge[15]. The excavation, considerably more rudimentary in its methodology than today, was carried out, in part, to test the theory that the mounds around the outside of the moat, to the north and west, were siege mounds, and that the mounds to the west were an assault bridge that was built to attack the castle. The assumption, derived from earlier surveys, was that the castle was complete at the time that it was attacked by Geoffrey de Mandeville in 1144.

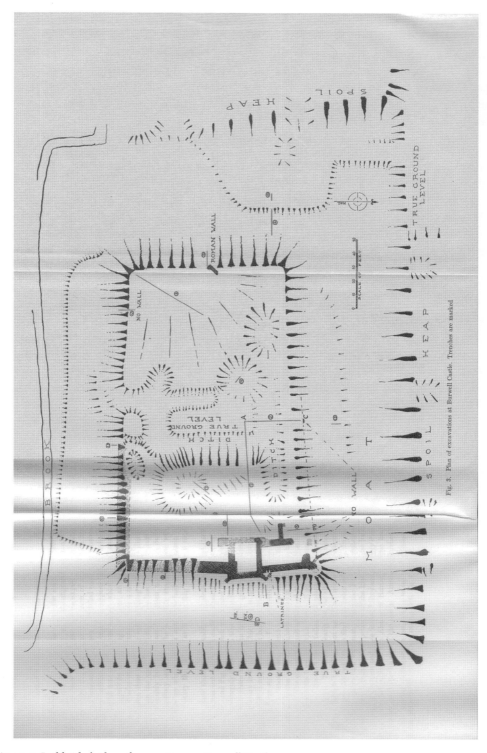

Figure 4. *Lethbridge's plan of excavations on Burwell Castle.*

No detailed search for documentary evidence appears to have been completed prior to the excavation and the excavators commenced their excavation with a trench in the moat next to the supposed 'assault bridge'. Here they discovered that the moat contained none of the silt deposits that would be expected of a water-filled moat '*It was soon seen that the moat had no fresh water muddy deposit in it at all.*' This was to be their first surprise. They then put a small trench in at the top of the mound that they assumed to be an assault bridge, Lethbridge wrote:

'*A trial hole was now cut on top on the assault-bridge. This proved to consist of unmoved chalk rock, as I might have guessed had I given it more careful thought, for it was covered with typical downland turf and flowers, very different from the lush vegetation in the moat itself. Very little work had now exploded part of our original theory.*'

The third surprise, which confirmed that the castle had never been completed, came when they started to excavate on the island, almost opposite the first two trenches. Here they discovered undisturbed chalk, where they had expected to find fallen walls, Lethbridge wrote:

'*It began to appear highly probable that Burwell was one of those things which we are warned never to expect in archaeology, namely, an unfinished work.*'

With these discoveries Lethbridge decided to concentrate on the island. He dug 12 trenches in total, either on the island itself or where it sloped down into the moat. Where footings were discovered these were traced along until they ended. How this was carried out is unclear from Lethbridge's report. He shows the location of his trenches on a plan as red lines. Largely, these do not correspond with the foundations discovered, and their size from the plan and description is unclear.

The foundations described appear to be those of a roughly square building, 21ft by about 15ft, which projected into the moat and a possible building abutting it to the north. The walls of this building, and a wall which went around the south side of the island, were 5 to 8 ft thick and constructed of clunch with an outer facing of flint. The building remains were thought to be the gatehouse of the unfinished castle. Glass and a piece of dressed clunch bearing the word 'MARIA', found on builder's spoil dumps near this building, caused some discussion about the possible use of these buildings after the castle building had been completed. The theory proposed was that the building was used as the abbot's manor house, and that the glass was that from his private chapel. Records show that the abbot was given permission in 1246 to construct a chapel at his manor in Burwell (see Chapter 4.).

The stone was ascribed to the fourteenth century, as was a piece of window frame. Whether or not this was used as the abbot's manor house, after its use as a castle ceased, Lethbridge was unable to say. He did however conclude that all of the building remains (ie their footings) were of the same period, namely that of the building of the castle in 1143–44.

Other medieval remains

Other than in the fields at Spring Close adjoining the castle site and the field between The Hall and Parsonage Farm, and some field remains such as the raised bank alongside The Causeway, there is little else remaining of the medieval landscape within the immediate area of the village. This is largely due to modern farming practices, in particular the switch from mixed farming to almost solely arable farming on most local farms. As Figure 5 shows, as late as the 1950s the clear remains of ditched enclosures or platforms of the medieval period existed in the fields adjacent to Spring Close. The same can be seen at East Reach and The Ness where modern ploughing has obliterated any medieval building remains that once existed, although at the Ness the silted up original water channel and some other earthworks have survived in a meadow.

In terms of surviving buildings, the village has a number of houses with medieval remnants within their structure and at least two almost complete medieval houses. These are Isaacson's House, a large house that was once part of a range of medieval buildings dating from the fourteenth century and no.69 North Street, a timber-framed hall house of the mid fifteenth century with a later upper floor. Burwell's finest medieval building, the parish church, will be described later.

References

1. Reaney, P H, 1943 *The Placenames of Cambridgeshire and the Isle of Ely*, English Place Names Society, Cambridge University Press, 187.
2. Rye, W (eds), 1891 'Pedes Finium (Feet of Fines), (Cambridgeshire)', *Cambridge Antiquarian Society*, **26**.
3. Reaney, P H, 1943 *The Placenames of Cambridgeshire and the Isle of Ely*, English Place Names Society, Cambridge University Press, 187.
4. *ibid*
5. Wymer, J J, 1977 *Gazetteer of mesolithic sites in England and Wales*. Council for British Archaeology. Res Rep 20, London.
6. Lethbridge T, 1936 'Excavations at Burwell Castle', *Proceedings of the Cambridge Antiquarian Society*, **36**.
7. RCHM, 1972 *An inventory of historical monuments in the County of Cambridge. Volume II North-East Cambridgeshire*. H.M.S.O. London.
8. Guy, C, 1978 'A Roman lead tank from Burwell', Cambridgeshire', *Proceedings of the Cambridge Antiquarian Society*, **68**, 1-4.
9. Gregory, T, 1970 'A hoard of Roman bronze bowls from Burwell', Cambridgeshires', *Proceedings of the Cambridge Antiquarian Society*, **66–67**, 63–80.
10. Browne, D M, 1970 'Excavations at Burwell Cambridgeshire', *Proceedings of the Cambridge Antiquarian Society*, **66–67**, 81–91.
11. Cyril Fox, Devil's Dyke excavations.
12. Fowler and Lethbridge, Devil's Dyke.
13. Lethbridge, Devil's Dyke 1958
14. Lethbridge, T, 1926 'The Anglo-Saxon cemetery, Burwell, Cambridgeshire', *Proceedings of the Cambridge Antiquarian Society* , **27**, 72–79.
15. Lethbridge, T, 1936 'Excavations at Burwell Castle, Cambridgeshire' *Proceedings of the Cambridge Antiquarian Society*, **36**, 121–133.

Chapter 2

The Development of the Village

To consider the development of Burwell from Saxon times to its present form, I have looked at the archaeological evidence and other evidence gained from fieldwork and records. These give a good idea about how the village developed, but they do not present the whole picture.

If the building development of the last 200 years is ignored, then the village can be seen to have a relatively simple form. It consists of a main street running approximately north to south and lying close to, and roughly parallel to, the fen edge. Throughout the period from the sixth century to the present this alignment has changed little. Some changes in direction did start to occur prior to the twelfth century, but the building of Burwell Castle stifled these. As a result the village development eventually extended out northwards along its north-south axis.

According to Reaney[1], the name Burwell means 'fort by a spring' (Burgh = A Saxon fortified township, Well = place for getting water). Despite the name there is today no evidence of a Saxon fortification. It is possible therefore that Burwell was not a burgh (fort), but a borough and the name may therefore be considered as Borough Well. This suggestion is not a new one. Reaney, in producing his work on place names in Cambridgeshire, drew on previous work produced by Skeat[2] who suggested both alternative meanings for the village name.

It has been suggested[3] that the earliest extent of the village was in the area between Stocks Green in the north and Issacson Road in the south. This area was built upon sometime between the sixth and eighth centuries A.D. By the tenth century this developed area expanded in a northerly direction (Map 2), probably to where, at the time of writing, a chemist shop stands. Two roads or tracks may have extended from the area of Stocks Green by the tenth century, the western road heading in the direction of Reach and the eastern in the direction of Fordham.

By the eleventh century the village had again increased in size and was expanding westward along the former road from Stocks Green to Reach (Map 3). At Spring Close, next to the earthworks of the castle, are the earthwork remains of garden enclosures of the former houses that lined this road. These were demolished to make way for the castle in the twelfth century. A very short section of a hollow way (a depression where the road once was) can also be seen along with the remains, in the form of low mounds and depressions, of two or three houses. From the earthwork remains at Spring Close, it appears that about ten houses were demolished to make way for the castle.

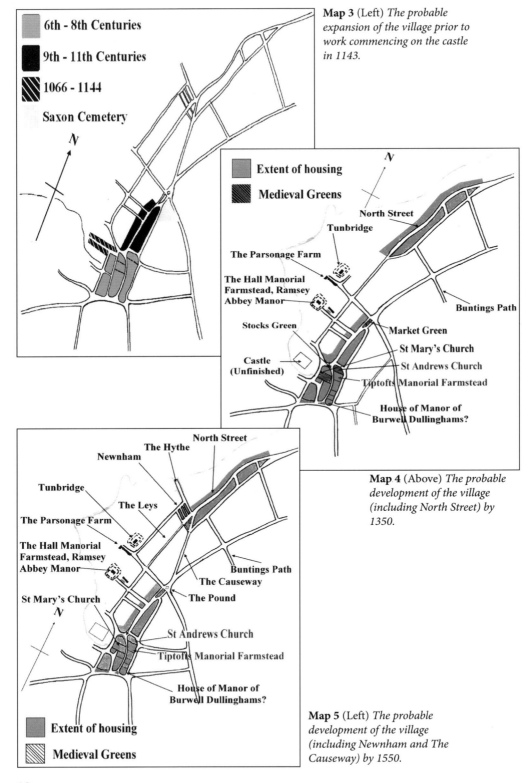

6th - 8th Centuries

9th - 11th Centuries

1066 - 1144

Saxon Cemetery

N

Map 3 (Left) *The probable expansion of the village prior to work commencing on the castle in 1143.*

Extent of housing

Medieval Greens

N

North Street

Tunbridge

The Parsonage Farm

The Hall Manorial Farmstead, Ramsey Abbey Manor

Buntings Path

Stocks Green

Market Green

St Mary's Church

St Andrews Church

Castle (Unfinished)

Tiptofts Manorial Farmstead

House of Manor of Burwell Dullinghams?

Map 4 (Above) *The probable development of the village (including North Street) by 1350.*

North Street

The Hythe

Newnham

Tunbridge

The Leys

The Parsonage Farm

The Hall Manorial Farmstead, Ramsey Abbey Manor

Buntings Path

The Causeway

St Mary's Church

The Pound

N

St Andrews Church

Tiptofts Manorial Farmstead

House of Manor of Burwell Dullinghams?

Extent of housing

Medieval Greens

Map 5 (Left) *The probable development of the village (including Newnham and The Causeway) by 1550.*

To assume that Burwell at this time was one settlement would be wrong. Burwell from at least the eleventh century comprised more than one area of settlement. The area described above was the main settlement area around what is now High Town. However it is known that two other smaller settlement areas existed and recent excavations on the site of the former Tillotson's Factory have shown that at least one farmstead of the Saxon period lay between the village and the Devil's Dyke.

The two other areas of settlement in the parish were that of East Reach (Reach was still two settlements separated by the Devil's Dyke) and a smaller settlement at The Ness. Each of these two smaller settlements were important; Reach because of the lode, built by the Romans, which offered navigable access to the river Cam and The Ness because of its watermill and its fishponds. It may also be possible that North Street was also a settlement by the eleventh century.

The Ness

The word Ness comes from the Saxon word *Naes*[1] which means 'a projection'. The Ness was linked to Burwell by the road to Fordham and (later?) by a track, which extended from church of St Mary, probably along the present footpath called the Leys, and then North Street and the Broads Way. This track, which ran parallel to the fen edge, probably ran alongside the former headlands and gave access to the fields. Recent excavations near Low Road found traces of the former track adjacent to the present Leys footpath, suggesting that part of this track may have been in existence in pre-Saxon times.

East Reach

The name Reach means an 'extension or strip of land', and was probably applied to the place after the building of the Devil's Dyke which formed a rounded projection extending out into the fen. Along either side of the dyke, the eastern being in the parish of Burwell and western being in the parish of Swaffham Prior, small settlements grew. The nature of the fen edge at Reach was such that East Reach had less room for expansion than West Reach, which may have contributed to its decline. However, in the fourteenth century it was also affected by the plague.

* * *

The Domesday Book[4], 1086, informs us that Burwell had four mills, and we know from twelfth century records that one of these was a watermill at The Ness and that it contained a millpond and other fishponds. Also included in Ramsey Abbey records of the twelfth century are details of rentals of properties at the Ness, including the mill and a house known as 'Long Croft'. A mill in the twelfth century and earlier would have been quite small, especially when compared to the eighteenth and nineteenth century watermills that remain in many parts of East Anglia. In a field at The Ness one can still see a silted up streambed, which may have been the original mill stream. This is banked on either side and is wider than the re-cut modern stream, which can be found a few yards away. Also visible in this field are other signs that might be the remains, perhaps, of the fishponds described in documents.

Just off of the end of the present Mill Lane, in the area now partly covered by the clunch quarry behind the Crown Public House, was the village cemetery of the Saxon settlement. This was partially excavated in the 1920s and revealed a number of burials some with grave goods[5].

It is likely that by the eleventh century Burwell had its two churches in existence. The church of St Andrew stood at the south-eastern end of the junction between the present School Lane and the High Street and St Mary's stood on the south-western side of the High Street, at its junction with Spring Close. The fact that Burwell had two churches by the eleventh century suggests the influence of two competing manors. St Mary's was, in all likelihood, always associated with the ownership of the manor by the Abbey of Ramsey, which commenced in the tenth century, and may be on the site of an earlier church built when Burwell was a royal manor. St Andrew's may have been associated with the lesser manor owned in pre-conquest times by Edeva the Fair, whose land was given to Count Alan after the Norman Conquest.

As previously noted, in 1144 the newly developing area to the west of St Mary's church was swept aside to build Burwell Castle. This was a momentous change, which had long-lasting consequences for the development of the village. Along with the destruction of a number of houses was the loss of the former Reach road, which probably went across the fields to the junction of the present Reach Road and Weirs Drove. In its place a new road to Reach developed outside of the village, using what was probably an existing road or balk giving access to Ditchfield and Reach Corner. In previous centuries this road, from its junction with the Swaffham road, was known as 'Scotred Lane'. This road and the pre-enclosure layout of the field, all aligned to the Devil's Dyke, suggest a Saxon field system rather than an earlier field system that was adopted by the Saxons, as found in many other places[6].

The building of the castle stopped all development in this direction and from 1144 the village commenced its development northwards. It is likely that development did not take place to the west of what by 1600 had become known as High Town due to quarrying in that vicinity. Quarries were in existence from a very early period, providing Stone for the building of Cambridge Castle in 1295.

The first developments in the northward direction were those of the Hall and Tonbridge, both of which stood within moated enclosures and may date from either the thirteenth or fourteenth centuries. Between the castle and The Hall there existed remains of other ditched enclosure platforms. However, ploughing has now destroyed these remains. Parsonage Farm also originated probably in the late thirteenth century. It was certainly in existence by 1307 when the land around it was referred to as *terram de persone* (land of the Parson) in the minister's accounts. North Street may have been developed at about the same time and was certainly in existence by the mid fourteenth century. These important houses seem to have assisted in ensuring that the old village, known from the eighteenth century onwards as 'High Town', did not develop further north into the gap between High Town and North Street until the nineteenth century.

Greens

The present green area adjacent to the post office is not a village green as such, but the southern end of The Causeway. The raised section, on which the footpath now stands, originated as a headland in the open fields. The soil has been raised by the action of ploughs turning over many years. From the point where this ends at the junction of

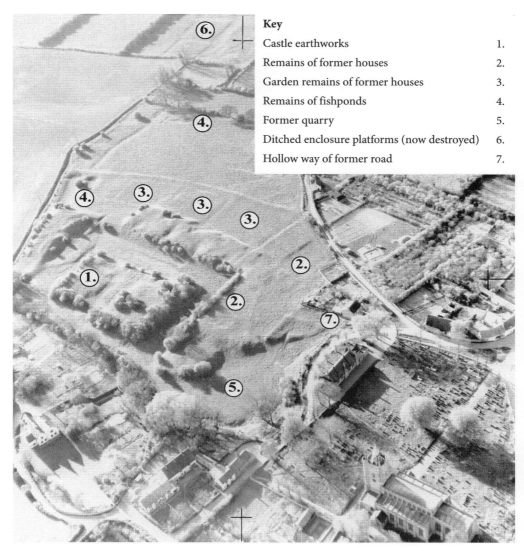

Key

Castle earthworks	1.
Remains of former houses	2.
Garden remains of former houses	3.
Remains of fishponds	4.
Former quarry	5.
Ditched enclosure platforms (now destroyed)	6.
Hollow way of former road	7.

Figure 5 *Burwell Castle from the air – prior to modern development.*

Parsonage Lane with the High Street to where, at the time of writing, the chemist and antique shops stand, there was formerly a village green, the largest of the four that appear to have existed. It was surrounded on all sides by roads and is therefore reminiscent of many market places throughout the country. It has been suggested that the small lane running north to south on its western side is possibly that known as Cuckolds Row in the early 1800s. The first reference to this name occurs in the enclosure documents of 1817. The road running north to south on the eastern side of the former green is the High Street, while the road at the northern end is Parsonage Lane. Nearby was the village pound, where stray or confiscated animals would have been kept, which is clearly shown on a map of 1806 but absent from the 1886 map.

It is likely, though not certain that this green was where a market and Whitsun Fair was held. A market was held from 1274[7] when Robert Tibetot (Tiptoft) was granted a licence to hold an annual fair at Whitsun and a weekly market, on Wednesdays, at his manor of Burwell. The Whitsun fair was still held in living memory adjacent to the area of the former green on Pound Hill. The market does not seem to have been particularly successful and no references relating to it appear to survive. This green, which survived until the early 1900s, was known as North Town Green in 1798 and is shown clearly on the first edition Ordnance Survey map of 1886 (Map 6). By the mid 1900s the green had disappeared and the site was occupied by the Burwell and District Bus Company and is now occupied by housing.

The other large green was at the southern end of the village, adjacent to the present

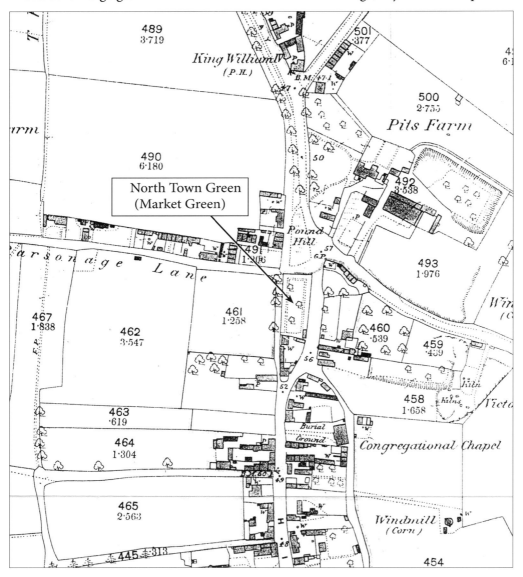

Map 6 *Section of the first Ordnance Survey showing the village green in existence in 1886.*

manor house. Unlike the former green at the northern end of the High Street, it was a long narrow green with two wider roughly triangular areas, one at each end, and a pond halfway along its length. It extended from Isaacson's Lane to the current Reach Road. This particular green was still in existence as a largely open area when the first Ordnance Survey took place in the 1880s.

The other two greens in the village were both smaller. One was a small triangular green near the Fox Public House. It is thought to have existed from the mid fifteenth century and is associated with the planned medieval development of Newnham. It appears to have been built over in the late seventeenth century.

The other was a very small green, just outside the north gate of the churchyard, at the intersection of School lane and the High Street. It was at one time known as Stocks Green after the village stocks, which were sited there. Such planned greens were common between the twelfth and fourteenth centuries, and were often associated with the economy of the village.

Northward Development

The position of the green at the northern end of the High Street and the location of important houses to the north-west of the village meant that any expansion could only occur at some distance from the main settlement. Ramsey Abbey, the principle landowner, appears to have allowed development in the former open fields in North Field. This development occurred on either side of a track, which probably ran alongside a headland and ran parallel to the fen edge thus giving access to the open fields.

By 1351 this track had become known as North Street at its southern end and

Figure 6 *North Street in 1900. The most distant building is the Anchor Public House. Four of the buildings shown have subsequently been demolished. Of those remaining, the third building in from the Anchor is a surviving medieval building of the mid-fifteenth century with a later gable end. (Cambridgshire Collection).*

Braddeye or Bradweye (Broad Way)[8] at its northern end. Initially the development of this area was sporadic, with more and more properties being built as time went on. This type of development is known as 'ribbon development'. The development of North Street over the former arable North Field probably coincided with the drainage of the broads, an area of fen land at the northern end of this tract and close to the Ness. This area of fen was being drained in the late 1200s as a document of 1294 refers to ditches in Le Brunde Fen (Broad Fen)[9]. Today this area is still known as The Broads. However it is possible that North Street represents an earlier, possibly pre-conquest settlement, within the North Field.

If old maps are considered then we can see a different pattern of drainage in The Broads and a few other fen areas, indicating medieval drainage patterns as opposed to eighteenth or nineteenth century drainage.

Once drained these areas of former fen were brought into use as arable land. The late thirteenth or early fourteenth centuries also saw the building of the first Burwell Lode, which was situated north of the present lode, emanating from Goose Hall. It was much smaller in size than the present lode, which was built in the seventeenth century.

Another area of land that was brought into cultivation in the thirteenth century was The Breach. Before the thirteenth century, this area to the North of the village, on higher ground around what is now Breach Farm, was uncultivated land such as either heath or woodland. Its name, Breach (Le Breche)[8] means 'newly cultivated land' and was first recorded in 1232.

That these areas of fen were drained and brought into use from a very early period can be deduced from the fact that their field patterns are different from that of the areas drained in the sixteenth to nineteenth centuries. Furthermore these fields were subject to tithes and shown as such by 1814, whereas the rest of the fen was not.

Newnham

By 1446 a planned development known as Newnham had taken place at the junction of North Street and the present footpath known as The Leys. The term Leys denotes an area used as pasture and it is likely that the present path takes its name from the use of the land across which it passes rather than from the former track. This points to a number of changes. Firstly, there was a change in use of the land here with former arable land being turned over to grazing, probably for sheep. That the land here had previously been ploughed is evident from the raised ground, formerly a headland, created by ploughing. This gave The Causeway its name. Secondly, a number of new roads had come into being, including Hall Lane, Parsonage Lane and Low Road.

The Causeway at this time was, at best, a track alongside a headland and is unlikely to have become a road in its own right until the late sixteenth century. At that time a better road to transport goods from the Hythe to High Town, Exning and Newmarket would have been required. The first record of The Causeway occurs in 1575[9] and in 1604 it is referred to as *le Causie*[11]. The former headland is the raised area along which the present pedestrian footpath runs. In the 1640s the raised ground of The Causeway was still grazed by cattle[12]. The Hythe, although in existence by 1486[13] was probably not a commercially viable area until the seventeenth century when the present Burwell Lode was constructed. The Hythe, approximately 600ft in length, was a common hythe

Figure 7 *Newnham at its junction with Low Road.*

that could be used by the people of Burwell, unlike the Tythehythe which was reserved for the transportation of the abbey's goods.

Newnham follows a typical grid pattern common to most planned medieval settlements, with four parallel streets and two intersecting streets to the east and west. Also to the east was a small triangular green, previously discussed, which was subsequently built over by the seventeenth century.

The development of Newnham may have also occurred at a time when the local topography was changing. In the twelfth century, when Burwell castle was being constructed, the water emanating from the springs adjacent to the earthworks would have taken a direct westerly route into the fens. At some time these were diverted along the fen edge to form The Weirs. This diversion may have taken place in the thirteenth or fourteenth centuries when the land immediately west of the fen edge was reclaimed. It is certain that The Weirs, which was diverting water into the newly constructed lode (Burwell Old Lode), was in existence in 1353 when it was referred to as *Wydeswereswater*[14].

Newnham presents a slight curiosity to the historical geographer in that it is a small, compact and planned area while North Street, developed at about the same time, is an example of sprawling ribbon development. North Street is over the North Field and appears to have been allowed to develop there by Ramsey Abbey, the principal landowner. Newnham could either be seen as a change of policy on the part of Ramsey Abbey, or it is a development brought about by another landlord. Given the proximity of Newnham to the moated medieval grange, now called Tonbridge and thought to be the former medieval manor house of the manor of St Omers, it is possibly a development of that manor.

Figure 8 *Casburn Lane, Newnham.*

At about the same time as North Street and Newnham came into being other new roads came into existence. Some of these have previously been noted[15]. They include:

- Buntings Path (*Buntynges Paath*), first mentioned in the *Liber Gersumarum* of Ramsey Abbey[16], 6 October 1399, although it may have been in existence before that time.

- Toyse Lane, which may be associated with land rented by John Toys in 1446 (John is first recorded as renting land at The Ness in 1398).

- Parsonage Lane (first mentioned in 1351).

- The High street, first referred to as *Heystrete* (1347).

In addition to these streets others, not known today, are named in documents of the period[17]. These include *Fyssher Street* (1440) or *Fysshestrete* (1423) suggesting a street where the fishermen lived and *Wodelane* (1425), possibly indicating a road leading to or adjacent to some woodland.

During this period it is also known that the village had a tithe barn, known as the *Tyceshous* (1398), and a hythe from which tythes were transported by barge to Ramsey Abbey, known as the *Tytheshythe* (1423). Both of these were probably in the vicinity of The Hall and the Parsonage, although right up to the dissolution of the monasteries much of the produce of Ramsey Abbey was taken either to Reach for transport to Ramsey or by road.

As well as these developments the village suffered some losses in the fourteenth and fifteenth centuries, principally due to the effects of the plague. While these losses are not apparent in the main village today they can be seen in the hamlet of Reach. It is generally assumed that the shrunken size of East Reach occurred around this time,

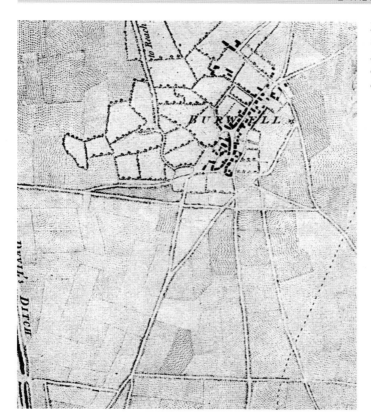

Map 7 *High Town, shown on the 1768 map of Newmarket Heath, showing the pre-enclosure fields, lanes and closes.*

probably as a result of the plague. A similar situation can be seen at The Ness, which appears to have been no more than two cottages by the end of the sixteenth century.

Seventeenth to nineteenth centuries

Village Expansion

The seventeenth, eighteenth and nineteenth centuries saw little change in the development of Burwell. The overall pattern of roads remained very much as we see it today. The period was one of consolidation, rebuilding and infill. However, this infill became problematic by 1582 as numbers of migrant poor were coming to the village, building dwellings and becoming entitled to a 'right of commons'. In 1582 the manorial court for the manor of Burwell Ramseys[9] put a stop to this by denying 'rights of common' where a dwelling had been constructed without consent. However this did not stop the existing residents from sub-dividing and subletting their premises. By 1613 the jury had restricted the 'right to agist' (to take in to graze for a payment) cattle to the rate payers of the town and forbade villagers to let houses to newcomers not already resident for three years unless they could provide surety to the wardens of St Mary's church that the person was not to become a burden on the parish, thus discharging the church of any cost.

These measures in the longer term did not stop growth because as part of this consolidation and infill, both of the remaining village greens were lost to development in the nineteenth century. The southern green was the last one to go with the building of the Railway Station in 1884. Despite the infill, for the most part the houses of the village were still largely confined to the medieval streets up to the end of the nineteenth century. The Causeway had no dwellings along it prior to 1830, as was the case with Ness Road and the area from the intersection of Ness Road and The Causeway to Parsonage Lane. By 1890 all these areas had dwellings on either side of the road.

Other areas such as Newnham and Scotred Lane developed in a similar manner in the mid nineteenth century. In the case of Newnham there were few dwellings along its narrow streets in 1806, but by about 1830 there were 30 dwellings and by 1861, 60. In High Town the number of dwellings increased from about 90 in 1840 to 125 in 1861.

Enclosure

The enclosing of Burwell's fields in 1815 brought about significant changes not only in the field pattern around Burwell, but also in the road system. Prior to 1815, the roads, trackways and paths in the parish had hardly changed in 400 years (Map 6). The enclosure however caused major changes. Most roads, tracks and paths were considered to be private and many were removed early on; for example Buntings Path beyond Ness Road was lost. Similarly Newmarket Way, a former road that went from the northern end of Isaacson's Road to Exning, was also lost. It is possible that Rayes Lane in Exning represents the eastern end of this road. Other roads were created, such as the present Heath Road. The westerly part of this particular road was already in existence but it originally led to a gap in the dyke and then into the parish of Swaffham Prior. Many of these changes will be dealt with in more detail in Chapter 8.

After enclosure in 1815 a number of farms were built in the High Street as well as on the former open fields in areas such as Warbraham, Ditch Field, Mill Field (Slate Farm) and The Breach. Despite this the village did not spread out and away from its tradition of houses lining the ancient streets until the mid twentieth century.

The expansion of the village was not without cost because, in the nineteenth and early twentieth centuries, Burwell lost its two main village greens, part of the southern green was lost to road widening and the Railway, and the Northern (market) green was lost partly due to Victorian infill at its southern end with the remainder being lost after it was sold to make way for the bus company depot. Other losses in the eighteenth and nineteenth centuries included the loss of the medieval guildhall, the gatehouse and other buildings, probably of medieval date, associated with Isaacson's House and the loss of St Andrew's church.

References

1. Reaney, P H, 1943 *The Place names of Cambridgeshire and the Isle of Ely*, English Place Names Society, Cambridge University Press, 187 – 189.
2. Skeat, W, 1901, 'The Place-Names of Cambridgeshire', *Proceedings of the Cambridge Antiquarian Society*, **5**, 36.
3. Taylor, C, 1983 Village *and farmstead: a history of rural settlement in England*, London.
4. Domesday Book.
5. Lethbridge, T, 1926 'The Anglo Saxon cemetery, Burwell, Cambridgeshire', *Proceedings of the Cambridge Antiquarian Society*, **27**, 72–79.
6. Hall, D, 1996 *The Fenland Project, number 10: Cambridgeshire Survey, Isle of Ely and Wisbech. East*

Anglian Archaeology, Cambridgeshire County Coucil.

7. Grant of Market.
8. De Windt, E B, (ed), 1976 'The 'Liber Gersumarum' of Ramsey Abbey: A Calendar and Index of B.L. Harley Ms. 445'. *Subsidia Medievalia* Toronto: Pontifical Institute of Medieval Studies, **7**.
9. P.R.O., Court Rolls for Burwell Ramseys. 1563 – 1587. Reference LR 3/8/2.
10. P.R.O., Ministers Accounts. 1398 – 1399. Reference SC 6/765/10.
11. Le Causie.
12. C.R.O, Court Rolls for Tiptofts Manor, 1643 – 1694. Reference R 56/6/1.
13. P.R.O., Court Rolls for Burwell Ramseys. 1487 – 1488. Reference SC 2/179/73.
14. C.U.L, Queens College Muniments. Reference QC Box 35: 39/3.
15. See note 1.
16. See note 8.
17. See note 8.

Chapter 3

The Period of Turmoil

Norman Destruction

Life in the period immediately after the Norman Conquest cannot have been easy for the population of Britain. Small rebellions probably took place in many areas of the country against the new rulers. One of the largest of these rebellions was that led by Hereward (in later tales referred to as Hereward the Wake). This is said to have taken place after Hereward returned to Lincolnshire, from abroad, in 1068.

The story of Hereward and his struggle is contained in a manuscript, called the *De Gestis Herwadii Saxonis* (The exploits of Hereward the Saxon). This document was written by Robert of Swaffham and survives to this day, in the library at Peterborough Cathedral. In 1895 a transcript of the Latin document with an English translation, was published by the Rev Sweeting[1].

The following is an excerpt from this document, which as well as documenting Hereward's struggle mentions an affray in Burwell and Reach. The leader of the king's guard who, with his men, was blockading the Devil's Dyke at Reach, relates the tale here to the king.

De Gestis Herwardii Saxoni – XXIII

Only yesterday I saw some men coming from the Isle, not a great number, no more than seven, in the dress of soldiers, and armed with proper equipments for war, all of whom except two were manifestly monks, and they were well acquainted with warfare, like the rest of the soldiers and claimed to exercise the rights of soldiers, set fire to the town of Burwell, and inflicted mischief in all directions, and not only they, but others also running about. And about ten of our men, ten in number before us all who were engaged in the blockade, hurrying without consideration to them, sought to capture them, because they were fewer in number than ourselves. At length they came up with them by the dyke aforesaid within distance of throwing lances. After long fighting our men at last succumbed, except one fine soldier, Richard by name, and by surname grandson of the Viscount Osbertus to whom by himself, apart from the main body, a man called Wenochus had stuck closely endeavouring to take him.

While these were long in fighting, and they who had come out of the Isle waited and could see neither prevailing, and observed a band of soldiers drawing near. Hereward, the leader of the soldiers caused them to be separated, and suffered no one to offer violence to Richard saying, that it was an unworthy thing for two or three to be fighting against one, and the he would, on no account allow such a thing to be done by his men; and this we learn from the mouth of the man himself. Finally we pursued them to their ships, and we killed one of their sailors with a spear, and caught another; and he recounted their dignities and who they were, adding their names.

Why this band attacked Burwell and how much damage was caused to the town in this affray is not mentioned in the document. However it can be surmised that the intention of the small band was in all probability to draw the soldiers from the blockade at Reach, thus allowing Hereward and his men to get to his ships there. The document makes no other reference to Burwell.

How difficult this period was for the people of Burwell is difficult to ascertain. However it was only about 70 years before the next turbulent event took place.

Burwell Castle and the fall of Geoffrey de Mandeville

Geoffrey de Mandeville was the Earl of Essex in the time of King Stephen (1135-1154). He was famous for his treachery and violent acts around the time of the civil war that waged between the king and the daughter of Henry I, the Empress Matilda. During this period he wreaked havoc and caused much suffering to the people of Cambridgeshire. The civil war of 1139-1153 is characterised by the greed and ruthlessness of many knights and gentry who declared themselves to be allied to either Stephen or Matilda but proceeded to wage war on whomever they could gain the most, whether it helped either of the main protagonists or not.

Stephen, the nephew of Henry I, had opportunistically seized the throne with the help of his brother, the powerful Bishop of Winchester, immediately after the death of his uncle. However, Henry had persuaded his barons to swear an oath in support of Matilda, his only surviving legitimate heir. However, it was not a hard decision for many of the barons to renege on their oath to support Matilda and transfer their allegiances to Stephen instead; Matilda had spent most of her life in Germany, she was a poor diplomat, she was married to an Angevin (an unpopular alliance as far as both the English and the Normans were concerned) and she was a woman.

Stephen might have avoided much bloodshed during his reign had he not made a big mistake in the way he dealt with Roger, Bishop of Salisbury whom he suspected, perhaps not unreasonably, of being in league with Matilda. Roger had experienced a meteoric rise in fortune during the reign of Henry. The king is said to have discovered Roger in France where he had been impressed at the speed at which the clergyman could read a mass. He was appointed chancellor and Bishop of Salisbury and was quickly elevated to justiciar - making him the second most powerful man in England after Henry himself.

During Stephen's reign, Roger had established a powerful dynasty with his son as chancellor, his nephew Nigel as Bishop of Ely and another nephew as Bishop of Lincoln, who were all building or strengthening their own castles and garrisoning them and ostentatiously taking large retinues of armed men about with them wherever they went. Stephen used a street brawl involving Salisbury's men as an excuse to seize Salisbury, his son and the Bishop of Lincoln and to chase Nigel of Ely to Devizes. After a siege lasting three days Salisbury's mistress, who feared for the safety of her husband and son, betrayed Nigel. The king now had all the castles of Salisbury's family and had badly abused the legates in his custody. This action proved to be disastrous for Stephen. The Church was appalled at the way in which Stephen had treated the clergymen and, consequently, the king found many of his supporters switching to Matilda's side, including his own brother, the Bishop of Winchester.

Stephen was a fearsome soldier. His chivalry and misplaced generosity, however, could be said to have been excessive and detrimental to his cause. His downfall at the Battle of Lincoln in 1141 can be attributed to behaviour that was typical of him. Towards the end of 1140 one of Matilda's supporters, Rannulf the Earl of Chester, seized the castle of Lincoln. Instead of attempting to punish Rannulf, Stephen gave him the not only the castle but also the city of Lincoln and a number of other castles. It was complaints of harsh treatment by the citizens of Lincoln that caused Stephen to rush to the city to deal with Rannulf. However Rannulf had slipped away to get reinforcements among the desperate knights who had lost everything they possessed fighting for the empress.

The Battle of Lincoln took place on the 2 February 1141. The forces of the king easily defeated some scouts sent by Rannulf to impede his progress and gained a good tactical position. Obeying his fatally chivalrous nature, Stephen took his men from easily defendable high ground to a marshy plane by the city of Lincoln to meet the earl's rabble in a fair fight. His cavalry failed to ward off frenzied attacks of the disinherited knights who had nothing to lose and everything to fight for. Stephen fought fiercely until both his sword and axe were broken and, having been knocked down by a flying stone, he was forced to surrender to Robert of Gloucester.

The king's cause was now left in the hands of his shrewd queen, also called Matilda, who stood her own Cambridgeshire estates as collateral for a loan from the London justiciar, Gervase of Cornhill. She repurchased the support of Geoffrey de Mandeville who had transferred his allegiance to the empress when things started to go wrong for Stephen. She also won back the support of Stephen's brother, the Bishop of Winchester whose support Stephen had lost after he mishandled dealing with Roger of Salisbury.

In November of 1141 Stephen was released in exchange for Robert of Gloucester, an important ally of the empress who himself had been captured by Royalist forces whilst fleeing a defeat at Winchester. Unchastened by his experience with the Earl of Chester, Stephen heaped rewards and privileges on the treacherous Geoffrey de Mandeville on top of the payment already made to him by the Queen. De Mandeville became sheriff and justiciar in three separate counties. He was made Constable of The Tower - a role that effectively put him in charge of the City of London but in which he evidently earned the loathing of the people of the city. The proof of the Londoners's hatred of de Mandeville exists in a document which points to his ultimate treason (that is, before he turned into the sadistic monster of the fens). He changed his allegiance back to the empress, drawing up a charter in which he dictated that she should make no peace with the Burgesses of London without his consent 'because they are his mortal foes'. He continued to attend court and feign friendship with the king even though it was generally known that he was in league with Stephen's enemies. Eventually his arrogance was too much and he was arrested in St. Albans in 1143. As punishment for his treason he was given the choice of execution or giving up the Tower and his castles in Essex. He chose life and decided to take out his vengeance on the people of Cambridgeshire!

De Mandeville fled to the marshy swamps of the fens with an army of mercenaries and ruffians. He seized and occupied much of the Isle of Ely, using it as a fortress and he then drove the monks out of Ramsey Abbey and used it as a headquarters for his mob. From here he plundered, ransacked, and burnt property. He employed every type of torture conceivable to extract crippling ransom from anyone unfortunate enough to fall into his hands. Cambridge itself was ransacked and burnt. No one, regardless of age, sex or profession was safe. Over a stretch of 20 or 30 miles of countryside there was not an ox or plough to be seen. A serious famine resulted to add to the already large death toll. King Stephen was unable to get an army through the impenetrable fens to rid the area of the evil earl leaving de Mandeville free to carry on at will. Stephen therefore set about building a series of castles around the fen edge, including one at Burwell. Before the castle was complete de Mandeville attacked and, in the affray, he was hit by an arrow. He was carried from the battlefield and taken to Mildenhall, where he died on 14 September 1144. The story of the de Mandeville's plundering, including his attack and wounding at Burwell is recorded in the Ramsey Abbey Chronicles, a translation of the section relating to this attack and de Mandeville's death at Mildenhall is set out below.

The Death of Geoffrey de Mandeville
– a literal translation from the Ramsey Abbey Chronicle

Count (Geoffrey de Mandeville) listening with little patience to this (what the abbot had to say?), agreed many terms with him (the abbot) for giving him back his property; but he did not ever fulfil his promise, such that he seemed rather to delude him, than to wish to restore the stolen property to him. As a result the poor abbot, miserably afflicted by a fear of death, wished he had already released the debt. But the common saying is true: 'When grief is greatest, consolation is close.'

Listen! A miracle. When that profane count falsely and deceitfully, as it is said, had betrayed the simplicity of a good man, a little later with his army in order to attack a castle which had recently been built at Burwell and going around it with his helmet raised in order to pick a weaker section of it for the attack, he finally took up position on a piece of land, close to the castle, which belonged to the monastery at Ramsey, and still belongs to them up to the present day, when a most worthless Archer from among those who were within the castle, struck the count a lethal wound in the head.

It is believed therefore that this had been done on St. Benedict's estate, so that all could understand that God, the Lord of all revenge, had done this to atone (?) for the hate and to vindicate (?) the harm which the sacrilegious Count had brought to the monastery of St. Benedict.

When, at Mildenhall, he (the count) was oppressed by the narrowness of death, the Abbot, hearing this, forewarned (?) rushed over to him with the greatest haste.

When he had arrived there, there was neither sense nor voice to the Count; however his servants, greatly grieving for their lord, received the Abbot well and immediately sent him on with the count's own documents to his son, Ernaldus of the Great House, who himself had built a certain castle at Walton, so that he might make restitution of the monastic property without delay.

Finally and unwillingly, after some delays and not without difficulty, he (Ernaldus) did this; for he had loved that place and its environs very much.

So the profane soldiers withdrew with their unjust retinue; the Abbot received a worthless possession, polluted by harlotry, full of filth and abandoned by any goodness, lest he should with any part of it from the first day feed his household or live in it.

Translation by Monseniour Paul Hyper

It should be noted that theft of church property was a great sin and sacrilege at this time and de Mandeville's servant as well as his son would have wished for the monastery to have been returned as quickly as possible to ensure the count got to heaven. The delay in dealing with this at Walton, was probably due to negotiations relating to de Mandeville's body and repararations for damages. While it is not clear about payments for damages, de Mandeville was buried in accordance with his status as a count in the Temple Church, London.

With the death of de Mandeville the revolt ceased and for the people of Cambridgeshire normality returned. For the rest of England the anarchy slowly abated over several years.

References

1. Sweeting, R, 1895 *De Gestis Herwadi Saxonis*, Peterborough.
2. CHRONICON ABBATIAE RAMESEIENSIS, 1886 *Chronicles and Memorials of Great Britain and Ireland during the Middle Ages (Rerum Britannicarum Medii Aevi Scriptores): The Rolls Series*, London.

Chapter 4

Manors

Estates were organised as manors by the Saxons and the Normans. In the simplest of cases a manor would be coextensive with a parish and consist of a village and its fields, while in complex cases a village could comprise four or five manors. Within a manor everyone held land from the lord and even freeholders paid nominal dues and acknowledged the lord at his local court. Burwell is an example of a village where there was more than one manor.

In Saxon times the Crown held the principal manor in Burwell while a lesser manor was held by Edwin, son of Othwulf. In about AD940 Edwin gave five hides of land to Oda, Archbishop of Canterbury. Oda then gave these in about AD970 to his cousin Oswald on his founding of Ramsey Abbey. According to the cartularies of Ramsey abbey[1], written in the eleventh and twelfth centuries, King Edgar (AD944–975) gave a further five hides of land in Burwell to the Abbey of Ramsey on its foundation. Ramsey's founder and abbot, (St) Oswald, was not only the cousin of Oda, Archbishop of Canterbury, but also Bishop of Worcester. At the same time as he made the gift to Ramsey, the king also gave one hide of land to the nuns of the Abbey of Chatteris. In addition to these gifts, the abbey also received three and a half hides from Aelfgar[2], and another estate owned by Aelfsige of Landwade and his wife. Abbot Aelfwine (1043–1080) allowed the heir of Aelfsige, Godwin to hold this land at farm for life. At the Norman Conquest it was taken by Earl Ralph and never recovered by Ramsey Abbey, leaving the abbey with its original ten hides.

Immediately prior to the Norman Conquest Burwell's second manor appears to have been owned by Edeva the Fair.

The Norman Conquest brought mixed fortunes for the Anglo-Saxon clergy. They had played no active part in the resistance against King William and so were for the most part allowed to keep their estates in the early conquest years, at a time when many who supported King Harold lost their lands.

The Domesday Survey 1086

In 1086 William the Conqueror ordered that a survey be undertaken for taxation purposes. This record, known as the Domesday Book, is the oldest financial assessment of any European country. It records the names of the owners of the land held in 1086, the amount of land held, and other details about undertenants and the values of meadows, woods and mills. Often the owner in 1066 is also given.

The entry for Burwell records four owners; The Abbey of Ramsey, Count Alan, Hardwin de Scalers and The Abbey of Chatteris.

The Abbey of Ramsey

The Abbey of Ramsey was a large landowner in Cambridgeshire and Huntingdonshire, and held lands in Hertfordshire, Norfolk and Suffolk. Most of these lands had, like Burwell, been given in the lifetime of St Oswald by either Aethelwin, Ealdorman of East Anglia, or by his foster brother King Edgar.

The entry in the Domesday Book reads:

'The Abbott of Ramsey holds BUREWELLE. 10 hides and 1 virgate. Land for 16 ploughs. In lordship 3 hides and 40 acres; 4 ploughs there.

$42^1/_2$ villagers with 12 ploughs.

8 slaves; meadow for 10 ploughs; pasture for the village livestock; 2 mills at 6s 8d.

The total value is and was £16; before 1066 £20.

This manor lies and always lay in the lordship of St Benedict's church.

The abbey was the largest of the four landowners in 1086, holding approximately 1230 acres of land (one hide is equal to 120 acres and one virgate is equal to 30 acres or 0.25 of a hide), 400 acres of which were in the manorial demesne.'

Count Alan

Alan Rufus (1050–1093), second of at least seven legitimate sons of Count Eudo, Regent of Brittany from 1040–1070, and Agnes alias Orguen his Angevin wife.

Alan was called Rufus to distinguish him from his younger brother, Alan Niger. His father Eudo was a brother of the Breton Duke Alan III: their mother was an aunt of William the Conqueror. Eudo's status entitled his legitimate sons to bear the title *comes* (count).

In 1066 a Breton contingent, probably including Alan and his younger brother Brien, played an important role at Hastings. Brien was given lands in Suffolk and, later, in Cornwall after helping to defeat an attack on Exeter by the sons of Harold II in 1069.

Alan was already a rich and powerful man when in 1070, following the northern revolt, the honour of Richmond and much of Lincolnshire was given to him. In 1075 he acquired the lands of Ralph de Gael in Cambridgeshire, Suffolk and Norfolk, following the fall from power of Ralph who revolted against King William. Thus East Anglia was dominated by Alan and two of his men, Aubrey de Vere and Hardwin de Scales. By 1086 he was one of the richest and most powerful men in England with considerable holdings in Cambridgeshire, much of which had formerly been held by Edeva, known as Edeva the Fair.

At the time of the Domesday survey, Count Alan's lands in Burwell were held by tenants and the entry reads:

'In BURUUELLE Alan holds $2^1/_2$ hides from Count Alan. Land for 5 ploughs in Lordship 2.

4 villagers have 3 ploughs.

4 slaves; 2 ills at 6s 8d; meadow for 3 ploughs; pasture for the village livestock.

Value £4; when acquired £3; before 1066 £6.

2 Freeman held this land under Edeva; they could withdraw without her permission. One of them found escort of 4d in the Kings service.'

The entry continues:

'In the same village Geoffrey holds 1 hide and 1 virgate from Count Alan. Land for 2 ploughs; they are in lordship, with 3 villagers; 2 slaves.

Meadow for 1 plough; pasture for the village livestock.

Value 40s; when acquired 30s; before 1066 40s.

1 Freeman held this land under Edeva; he could withdraw without her permission.'

Alan or Alan de Burwell, was a juror in the Staploe Hundred. His position in the list of jurors identifies him as an Englishman, though his personal name is Breton. It is thought that he may therefore have been a relic of the pre-conquest Breton settlement associated with Ralph the Staller.

Geoffrey, or Geoffrey de Burgh, was probably another Breton. According to Domesday scholars he took his name from Burrough Green where his successor, by the early twelfth century, was Thomas de Burgh. This same Geoffrey is also listed as a tenant of Count Alan in Isleham.

Hardwin De Scales (Deschalers)

Hardwin was probably a Breton, although some historians have suggested that he was Flemish. His earliest holdings were in Cambridgeshire where he was a major tenant of the Abbey of Ely. He was also a tenant of both the king and Count Alan. At his death at sometime after 1086 his lands were divided between his sons Richard and Hugh. He had one other son, Robert.

The Domesday entry for Hardwin reads

'Hardwin holds ½ Hide from the King. Land for 4 oxen; they are there. Meadow for these oxen.

Value 20s; when acquired 16s; before 1066 20s.

Thork, the Abbott of Ramsey's man, held this land; he could not withdraw without his permission; however he found either escort or 4d in the Kings service.'

The Abbey of Chatteris

Like the Abbey of Ramsey, King Edgar had given the Abbey of Chatteris its holdings in Burwell about AD966. However, unlike the Abbey of Ramsey, the nuns of Chatteris never sought to buy additional land and so, at the time of the Domesday Survey, their land was as given by King Edgar.

The Domesday entry for the Abbey of Chatteris reads:

'In BURUUELLA the nuns of Chatteris hold ½ hide.

Land for ½ plough; it is there.

Meadow for 2 oxen

The value is and always was 10s

This land is and was always of the Church's Lordship.'

The Domesday entries are quite informative and we can see that in 1086 the value of land, livestock, mills etc in Burwell was £20 70s 0d, and that the recorded population was 46½ villagers and 12 slaves. The half villager was not a mistake. In all probability it was a villager living between villages.

The terms 'villagers' and 'slaves', cover those aged 12 and above and is therefore somewhat short of the total population which probably numbered between 200 and 300 persons.

The village at this time had four mills, most likely watermills. Windmills were not generally in use in Britain prior to the thirteenth century.

Of the four landowners, the Abbot of Ramsey was the chief landowner and therefore held the largest manor. This was a position the Abbots of Ramsey continued to hold up to the dissolution of the monasteries.

The Manors

It is likely that by 1086 at least one house, suitable for one of its visiting lords such as the Abbot of Ramsey, Count Alan or Hardwin de Scales, would have existed. These are not described in the Domesday Book and the exact location of any of these may never be known. However from existing records, field studies and archaeological evidence it is possible to identify a great deal about the post-conquest, post-Domesday manors.

The Manor of Ramsey

By the end of the eleventh century Norman tenants-in-chief were gradually replacing the Anglo-Saxon secular and ecclesiastical aristocracy. In addition a number of lesser Normans were pressing to acquire properties by the payment of rents or services. This combined with new Norman laws led to a period of unrest that was to last for two generations. In this period the Abbey of Ramsey, like all the other Anglo-Saxon monasteries, found themselves out of favour as the new Norman aristocracy had their own ecclesiastical allegiances. This changed slowly over time as the Anglo-Saxon abbots were replaced by Norman ones.

During this period of change, King William and his successors issued a number of charters which set out the roles of the population, whether abbot, knight or freeman. As part of their role of tenant in chief, those holding estates had to provide for military service. The Abbot of Ramsey held six and a half hides in Burwell, which required him to provide a fee for one knight. The fee would have probably included both an allowance and a house and land for the knight. Thus the abbot had to cede land to a Norman knight 'for love of the king'.

In the early twelfth century a change in the administration of the holdings of abbeys occurred. Their estates were separated out into farm and the abbot's holding. This appears to be associated with the Norman aristocracy gaining control over the abbeys, as most senior ecclesiastical positions would have been held by persons whose background was from the ruling classes (see Chapter 5.).

The farm was operated by the *firmarius* (farmer) and its role was to provide food and some income for the abbey, while the manor provided for the abbot. In Burwell a charter of Abbot Aldwin informs us that there was a full farm (farms are described as full or half farms) and its value was £17. Like the abbot the *firmarius* was usually a person from a middle or upper class background, and we know from the Ramsey Cartularies[1] that in the early twelfth century Widone was the farmer at Burwell. This Widone was one of the lesser Normans referred to above who had seized land on a number of manors throughout the Fens.

The farmer was the most important person in the management of the farm and the order of cultivation. The management of the manor, however, was the responsibility of the reeve, the demesne overseer and his deputy the beadle. Furthermore, each county also had a reeve, the 'shire reeve' or sheriff. They had the power to fine individuals and carry out punishments in respect of the manorial courts, which were held regularly throughout the year.

It is known that by this period the Abbot of Ramsey had a manor house in Burwell. Initially this may have been somewhere close to St Mary's church or even on part of the castle site. The civil war (1139-1153) caused havoc to the Abbey of Ramsey; Geoffrey de Mandeville occupied and ransacked the abbey buildings at Ramsey, including the church, and used it as his base for attacking the fenland towns and villages. King Stephen sought to construct a series of castles around the fen edge to contain de Mandeville. Burwell Castle was one such fortification and a complete street was demolished to make way for its building. The remains of the yards of houses can be made out in the field adjacent to the castle mounds (Chapter 2).

While the castle was being built de Mandeville launched his attack and was mortally wounded[2] (see Chapter 3). The castle was never completed and even though the land was returned to the abbey, the abbot did not seek to complete the castle or build upon the site. The rebuilding of the abbey was the most immediate task. The occupation and desecration of the abbey, and in particular the abbey church, by de Mandeville had cost the abbey a considerable amount of money in repairs and rebuilding. To assist in this rebuilding Abbot Walter (1133–1161) sold land to provide funds. His successor Abbot William also sold land in Burwell for this purpose.

It is likely that at this time the manor house was moved to the site currently occupied by The Hall. It is referred to as the capital messuage (manor house) in official documents which, unfortunately, do not state its location. The first reference to the capital messuage is in 1646 when the manor was surveyed for the Crown[3]. At that time the capital messuage was The Hall. What form the early house took is uncertain. However it would have been large enough to hold the abbot and his entourage on the occasions when they visited. In addition most monastic manor houses or granges of the late twelfth or thirteenth centuries would have contained a chapel for the private worship of the abbot or prior when visiting. The abbot, like all priests and monks, was required to spend much of his day in worship.

It is evident from documentation that in the first instance the manor house did not have such a private chapel and the use of St Mary's church for the purpose of the abbot's private prayer was considered unsuitable. As a result a licence to build an oratory or private chapel was sought in accordance with law from the Bishop of Norwich, in whose see Burwell fell because Ely was not a Cathedral at this time.

On 29 September 1246, Walter Bishop of Norwich gave a licence to the Abbot of Ramsey to construct his oratory, 'in the Manor of Burwell'[1]. This document reads:

'To all the faithful in Christ who shall see or hear these letters. Walter by the grace of God, Bishop of Norwich, greeting in the Lord.

We; minding that religious, especially when they ought to be present in the divine offices, should be entirely separated from worldly turmoil, to whom, in parish churches owing to the frequent concourse of the populace in multitudes, matters tend to become no less irksome than perilous; and willing to provide for honourableness, do, to the best of our power, of our special grace,

- grant free faculty to the venerable and discreet man, the Abbot of Ramsey; of constructing an oratory in his manor of Burwelle, in our diocese, in which it shall be lawful for him or his monk, when they shall arrive there, to celebrate divine service, for the use of him and his retinue, with the consent of the rector of Burwelle, the right and indemnity of the before mentioned church being saved in all things.

In witness whereof we have caused our seal to be appended.

Dated at Suthelingham, the third Kalende of October, in the second year of our pontificate.'

Since the excavation of part of the castle site by Lethbridge in the 1950s it has been suggested that the remains of a small stone structure within the castle moat was that of the oratory[4]. This may be the case although it remains more likely that the oratory was part of the manorial complex (the hall) and it is known that when, in the early 1900s, a wing of the Hall was demolished, a large 'perpendicular' window of the type found in churches and chapels was found. At that time it was believed that this might have been a fragment from the abbey that was thought to have existed close to Parsonage Farm and which had been built into the later house. It does however remain a possibility that this wing, which is known to have been medieval in date, contained the aforesaid oratory. It is doubtful that the oratory would have stood alone within the moated enclosure of the castle site, in other words, in a muddy field.

Today The Hall still retains some medieval parts and stands within the remains of a moated enclosure. The moat around the enclosure was, according to the Royal Commission for Historic Monuments[5], originally 40ft wide. It is likely that The Hall was built at the time when the abbey was starting to recover from the financial burdens, which occurred after the devastation caused by de Mandeville. Therefore the buildings, the moat and the timing of the licence for an oratory all point to the mid thirteenth century as the time when the abbey once again started to pay attention to its Manor of Burwell.

The moat around The Hall is consistent with this date. Many manors in Cambridgeshire and surrounding counties were protected by moats at this time for fear of attack by rebelling peasants (the peasants rebellion), and indeed some Cambridgeshire manors were attacked. The same may be the case for that around Tunbridge Farm, which is considered to be of similar date, type and size.

Manorial Land Values

During the late twelfth century and into the early thirteenth century, the Abbots of Ramsey sold a good deal of land in their manors. This, with cash from sales of produce and donations, allowed them to rebuild the abbey after the devastation caused by Geoffrey de Mandeville.

In addition to these sales, both Abbot Walter (1133–1161) and Abbot William (1161–1179) ceded lands to themselves for 'Baronial Administration'. Usually the taking of such land happened with the permission of the abbey. However both the abbots took land in Burwell without permission. Abbot Walter ceded one virgate of Demesne land and two virgates of land outside of the demesne and Abbot William ceded three and a half virgates and three crofts.

The abbots were not the only people lining their own pockets because, at the same time, the *firmarius*, John, took one virgate out of farm production for his own use.

Yet despite all these changes the abbey saw its land values and income rise, to £37 15 6 by 1170[6].

Period	Value (£)
Pre-Domesday	20
Domesday – 1086	16
1095	17
1140	30
1170	37 15s 6d

Table 2 *Abbey holdings – land values.*

By 1201 the manor and the farm were being valued separately. The manor was valued at £10 but no value was given for the farm.

Much of this increase in value can be explained by the increase in rentals, which was achieved by sub-dividing previously cultivated land as well as increasing the amount of land in production. The land around Breach Farm was brought into cultivation in the thirteenth century. The Broads and other shallow areas of fen were drained and brought into cultivation in the thirteenth or early fourteenth centuries. The population was rising and the demand for land was growing.

In adition to the increase in land rentals, the value of produce was increasing and, while there is no data for Burwell, it is known that the value of assets such as mills on other Ramsey estates tripled in the 15 years since the Domesday Survey. In the case of Burwell, the abbey not only increased the value of its assets, but also increased the number of such assets, including mills. It owned two of the four mills in Burwell in 1086 but by the late 1100s it owned four of the six mills in the parish. One of these was the mill at The Ness, purchased from Robert de Ness. Unfortunately, the location of the other is not known. What is clear, however, is that this was a new mill, not one purchased from another manor.

During the thirteenth century the manor appears to have continued to increase in value. The demand for land, referred to above, continued and the farm started to diversify, increasing the numbers of sheep on its land from the middle of the century. By the close of the thirteenth century the farm was able to produce more wool than the abbey required and surplus wool was being sold from the farm.

By the late thirteenth century the holdings of the abbey were no longer split between the farm and the manor but had reverted back to one entity. This appears to have occurred during the time of Abbot William of Godmanchester (1268–1285). However this did not stop the abbot spending as if he still had the income of the manors because his successor, John de Sawtrey, had the unusual experience early in his term of office of the monks holding a sit down strike in the abbey church in protest over his debts and their effects on the abbey.

The fourteenth century continued much as the thirteenth century had ended. But this was soon to end. In 1349 the Black Death (Bubonic Plague) struck. In this region it started at Cambridge and was recorded as arriving at Cambridge Friary at Eastertide and lasted throughout the summer. This plague and the successive ones had a devastating effect on the abbey and its manors.

Initially the abbey sought to minimise the effects by adjusting the way it ran its

Table 3 *Lords of the Principle Manor of Burwell*[7].

The Crown		Up to 933
The Abbey of Ramsey	Abbot	(933 – 1539)
	St Oswald	
	Aednoth	993 - 1006
	Wulfsy	1006 - 1016
	Withman	1016 - 1020
	Ethelstan	1020 - 1043
	Aelfwine	1044 - 1079
	Wilsi	1080 - 1087
	Herbert Losinga	1087 - 1091
	Aldwin	1091 - 1102
	Bernard	1102 - 1107
	Aldwin (2nd term of office)	1107 - 1111
	Reginald	1114 - 1130
	Walter	1133 - 1161
	William	1161– 1179
	Robert Triariel	1180 - 1200
	Eudo	1200 - 1201
	Robert of Reding	1202 - 1206
	Richard	1214 - 1216
	Hugh Foliot	1216 - 1231
	Ranulph	1231 - 1253
	William Accolt	1253 - 1254
	Hugh of Sulgrave	1255 - 1268
	William of Godmanchester	1268 - 1285
	John of Sawtrey	1286 - 1316
	Simon Eye	1316 - 1342
	Robert of Nassyngton	1342 - 1349
	Robert of Shenyngton	1349 - 1378
	Edmund of Ellington	1378 - 1396
	Thomas Butterwyk	1396 - 1419
	John Tychemersch	1419 - 1434
	John Crowland	1434 - 1436
	John Stow	1436 - 1468
	William Witlesey	1468 - 1473
	John Warboys	1473 - 1489
	John Huntyngdon	1489 - 1506
	Henry Stukeley	1506 - 1507
	John Lawrence de Warboys	1507 - 1539

farms in order to avoid the underemployment of land. This had some effect but was insufficient, so the abbey created a new type of land rental, the *arentata*, to encourage artisans and other landless persons to take up a holding. This rental appealed to many ordinary peasants as it did not entail having to provide services and customs associated with the traditional *ad opus* form of rental.

Despite these measures the Manor of Burwell went into debt, as can be seen from the extents of the manor between 1351 and 1359 (Table 4).

Year	Amount of Debt
1351	£3 7s 2d
1352	£1 5s 2d
1358	£12 14s 9d
1359	£13 09s 4d

Table 4 *Manorial Debt 1351–59.*

From 1351 the abbey decreed that the reeve should make up the debt in staged payments over a number of years. This obviously caused the reeve considerable difficulty as in some years, such as 1358, no payment was made and by 1360 the debt had risen to £63 11s 8d. During that year (1360) the payments were set at £10 2s 6d.

By 1370 the situation had not improved. In fact it had deteriorated further. To resolve the situation the abbey set up a reorganisation of its estates and their administration. These measures included the abolition of heavy food quotas to the cellarer of the abbey. The cellarer received instead cash payments and villeins were encouraged to take up longer leases, including lifelong leases on properties. Unlike the situation on many other manors, the villeins on the Ramsey manors were not subjected to large increases in works and services.

These measures together may have helped not only in easing the debt on the manor, but also appears to have helped in lessening any discontent in the manorial population. Thus in Burwell, as in other Ramsey manors, there were no disturbances against the abbey during the peasant revolts of 1398. This was in complete contrast to the situation on other manors in Cambridgeshire, such as at Guilden Morden where the revolting peasants destroyed the manor house of Thomas Haselden, the steward of John of Gaunt.

Whether due to the effects of the Peasant Revolt or due to other reasons, by the late fourteenth and early fifteenth century the Abbots of Ramsey, like those of many other monasteries, had stopped travelling between their manors, preferring to remain in their abbeys. The manor house, like those in most Ramsey manors, was rented out.

That the abbot's manor house in Burwell was rented out can be seen in a number of instances in abbey documents such as the *Liber Gersumarum* of Ramsey Abbey[8]. The first is a record of 1410 when it is recorded that 'the capital messuage' is rented with some land to John Kent.

By 1413 things become less clear because there are two rental entries that record the rental of the capital messuage, suggesting that the house might have been divided into more than one tenement or residence.

'*Thomas Rower: the capital messuage of one tenement of 15 acres once held by John Kent, for 20 years, rendering annually as did John. Gersumarum: six capons*

Laurence Skenale: the capital messuage of one tenement of 20 acres recently held by Simon Calvysbane and now held by William Gell, and one tenement of 8 acres, for 20 years, rendering annually for the capital messuage 2s and for the eight acres 8s with 2d as common fine and with obligation to rebuild the insathous on that messuage within the next 2 years on penalty of forfeit. G.: six good pullets.'

In a subsequent record of 1417 it is recorded that the capital messuage reserved to the lord is rented out to John Clerk, alias Blaunteyn, for 20 years for the sum of 16 shillings and the fulfilment of customs and services. At no other time are there entries suggesting more than one tenant.

In another record for the same court (1417) it is also noted that a croft is reserved for the lord. Possibly indicating that should the abbot visit, this croft is where he would have stayed. None of the tenants seem to have rented the manor house for long as it is recorded six years later that the capital messuage was rented out, along with some land, to John Notwyn and his wife Maria for 40 years. The Notwyns were charged the sum of two shillings and six pence per year for the house alone.

Early records concerning the manor house or capital messuage inform us that it consisted of a house and buildings. In 1325 and 1400, a kitchen is referred to. Immediately surrounding the manor house itself was a moat and in the fields outside it were a vineyard, an orchard and fishponds. The present sunken area in between the modern houses in Hall Close is all that remains of a fishpond and is shown as such on early nineteenth century maps. Medieval fishponds were often larger or grouped together, and this may be the remains of one of a number of such ponds on the site. The Hall, as would be expected of a large manorial complex, also had a large range of barns built around a separate enclosure. This range of buildings remained until the mid 1900s when they were demolished for housing developments. The manorial complex also contained its own vineyard. The extents of the manor of 1277 and 1298[9] record that,

Figure 9 *Picture showing the manorial farm buildings at the Hall prior to demolition. (Cambridgeshire Collection)*

as part of their customary dues, a number of tenants were required to make an annual payment for the vineyard.

The Manor house had a gate, as the following rental record of 1418 tells us, 'half croft once held by John Sparwe next to the gate of the manor'. What form this gate took will probably never be known.

From these early tenancy records we can get a picture of the layout of the land directly attributable to the manor, the demesne, which included most of the land adjoining the Devil's Dyke, 'Dychefeld', land adjoining what later became North Street, 'le Nethfeld' (North Field) and land near to Bunting's Path, referred to as 'Estfeld' (East Field) up to the fifteenth century, but known in the eighteenth and nineteenth centuries as Mill Field.

In accordance with common practice the manor held its own courts regularly, to both administer justice and to let properties within its jurisdiction. The Court of Jurisdiction, which let out property, is referred to as the 'Leet'. There are a number of surviving records from Ramsey Abbey, which record these events and which contain records regarding Burwell.

The renting out of the manor house was to be but one of a number of changes that took place in the fifteenth century. Probably the biggest change was the severance of the villeins from the demesne in the late fifteenth century.

At the beginning of the century the villein class rented land and continued to provide works and services to the lord (the abbey), usually work on the manorial demesne. However during the fifteenth century the long leases that had commenced in the late 1300s increased in number and the ability of the abbey to enforce the customs and services decreased, so that by the end of the fifteenth century it had become all but obsolete.

This had a direct effect on the abbey's income for it is clear from canonical visitations carried out by the Bishop of Lincoln in the years 1518 and 1530, that the affairs of Ramsey Abbey were in a poor state[10]. There were about 30 monks and novices in the community, some of which were in the smaller cell of Ramsey at St Ives. The fabric of the monastery was in a dire condition, with such serious leaks in the church roof that when it rained water poured in over the high altar. Similarly the dormitory of the brothers had leaks in its roof, causing the monks to become wet when it rained. This situation prevailed in St Ives and probably also existed in most of the abbey's properties.

In 1534, the Act of First Fruits and Tenths transferred to the Crown those taxes known as annates and tenths, which had previously been paid to the Pope by new incumbents of benefices. Commissioners were sent out to survey and value all benefices, including religious houses and Oxford and Cambridge colleges. Subsequently in 1536, the Court of Augmentations of the King's Revenues was set up. The role of the court was to deal with the lands and revenues of the dissolved houses that had come to the Crown. The court operated until 1553 when it was absorbed into the Exchequer. Ramsey Abbey surrendered to the Crown and was dissolved on 22 November 1539. From this date the Court of Augmentations was in charge of the former Ramsey Manor of Burwell. The former tenants of the abbey now became tenants of the Crown through this court.

All of the monks were offered a pension, usually £5–£8 per year, and those that had been ordained were also offered a parish. Those not ordained were usually offered a pastorial assistant role.

Four of the monks, including the last Abbot of Ramsey, John Lawrence de Wardeboys, abbot from 1508 until his resignation, came to Burwell. On his death in 1542, three years after the dissolution of the abbey, John was buried in St Mary's church where his grave is marked by a monumental brass showing him in clerical gown in surplice and almuce rather than that of an abbot (Figure 2.). His will[11] of 29 February 1537, states '... *My body be buryed in the church of Sainte Mary at Burwell ...*'. At his funeral he was attended to by three of his former monastic colleagues. He had attended most of the meetings called to consider the dissolution of the monasteries and had supported the dissolution of the smaller monasteries. He also gave oath in 1534 accepting the king as the head of the church. As a result he was awarded a very handsome pension. This was recorded in records of the Court of Augmentations[12] for the dissolution of Ramsey Abbey on 22 November 1539, which states:

> 'John Lawrence, Abbott, £266.13s.4d (besides the house of Bodsey, 100 loads of wood yearly out of Bottnall, Buckyse grove and Warvyswood, one hundred mark of Swans with the profit thereof, and one 'bootegate called the subcellarers bote gate, with the hylke and pertinences belonging to the same).'

Bodsey house was the former manor and grange of the abbey near Ramsey. The 'Bote gate' was probably a private landing place for boats, with a gate (a boat gate) or possibly a lock or weir with fishing rights.

Given the average pension for a monk this was a very handsome pension. John however died less than three years after his surrender of the abbey. In that time he lived in the former manor house of the abbey, The Hall, which may be the 'Hylke' and its pertinences referred to in the pension award. It is possible that this gave rise to the myth that the area between The Hall and Parsonage Farm was the site of a monastery. Parsonage Farm was known into the 1960s as the old priory. His companions in this time, which he referred to as his chaplains, were John Faunte, John Pawmer and George Marshall and they lived their lives as a small community, a sort of miniature Ramsey Abbey. On his death John bequeathed to each of his companions '*the prests that were of the house of Ramsey*', 6s.8d.

John Faunte remained in Burwell after John Lawrence's death and was recorded in 1553 as parish priest of St Andrews, Burwell and after 1556 he was rector of Pickwell in Leicestershire. George Marshall left Burwell after the death of John Lawrence and become rector of Long Stanton, before moving in 1554 to become rector of Cookley where he stayed until 1557. In 1556 Queen Mary reconstituted Westminster Abbey as a monastic institution and George entered its cloisters in 1557 with two other former Ramsey monks. As for John Pawmer, nothing is recorded after 1542, and as he does not appear in the review of monastic pensions in 1551, it is likely he died before that year.

Given that John Lawrence was given the former abbey's considerable house at Bodsey it is not clear why he chose to retire in Burwell. It may have been due to his links with Cambridge University with which, as a Doctor of Theology, he held close links.

The post-medieval manor

In 1541, two years after the dissolution of Ramsey Abbey, Sir Edward North, knight and Treasurer of the King's Court of Augmentations, purchased from the king large amounts of land in Burwell, Stetchworth, Haddenham and other parishes, much of which had formerly been lands owned by the monasteries of Ramsey, Ely and Fordham. The sale document[13] for these states;

> '[The King] sellith unto the said Edward Northe to his heirs and assigns for ever all those his meases londes tenements mylles medowes marshes pastures fedynges woodes underwoodes glebe londes pencious tithes oblacious wastes commons warrens waters fisheings rents fee farmes annuytyes knights fees etc.'

The document does not detail as to how much land was purchased and whether this included the full manor and its lands. The document does include in the sale to Sir Edward,

> 'the manner of Burwell with all and singular his rightes members and appurtenances in the said Countie of Cambrige And the advowson gift and patronage of the parsonage and parish church of Burwell in the said Countie of Cambrige And an annual rent or pencion of fourty shillings going out of the parsonage of Burwell.'

A separate record in the state papers[14], states that the sale was a grant in fee and that part of the deal included manors and advowsons already in Sir Edward's holding. This document, while much shorter, does tell us that the purchase by Sir Edward included not just the Ramsey manor but also the manor of Dullinghams in Burwell. According to the record of Sir Edward's acquisition of the manor of Burwell Ramseys in 1541, all the lands of the Ramsey Manor were in the tenure John Whetlye of Fulbourn.

Sir Edward split the manor into two. The former manor of the Abbey of Ramsey was retained as the Manor of Burwell Ramseys. While the lesser part, the advowsons of the parsonage and of the parish church, the right to choose the vicar of St Mary's, and the vicarage were formed into a second manor, known in later years as the Manor of Burwell Rectory. This manor probably included with it the lands formerly owned by the Abbey of Chatteris and the Priory of Fordham, but not the advowson of St Andrews.

In 1544 Sir Edward North was given a grant *in mortmain* to give the Manor of Burwell Rectory to the University of Cambridge. At about the same time, according to early writers such as Lysons, Sir Edward gave back some land to the Crown, including the Manor of Burwell Ramseys. What actually happened was the manor was returned to the Crown partly in exchange for other lands. While such exchanges were common in this period, this exchange appears to have been largely due to large sums being missing from the coffers of the Court of Augmentations of which Sir Edward was treasurer.

The Manor of Burwell Ramseys in its new form comprised the manor house, 251 acres of land and various houses etc. most of which were rented or leased out as in medieval times. However the lessees were now monitored by Stewards appointed by the Crown. These were appointed by grants of stewardship and documents[15] survive for at least three such grants. For example in 1553, in the first year of Queen Mary, the steward was George Freville, esquire, who took into stewardship a number of Cambridgeshire manors, including Burwell:

> 'Grant for life to George Freville esquire of the following stewardships with further grant for the exercise of the same in respective yearly fees against each of the manors of Over, Graveley, Woodehuste, Oldehurste, Lyttle Stukeley and Burwell in the counties of Cambridge and Huntingdon, lately parcels of Ramsey Abbey. Yearly fee £8.6s.8d, the manors of Over charteres and Burwell charteres, county of Cambridge, lately parcels of Charteres Abbey. Yearly fee 40s.............to receive the said fees from the revenue of the said lands.'

This document tells us that the previous steward was one William Coke, who had recently died. The lessee of the manor at the time of Freville's appointment was one John Bennet, who was in occupation of (leasing) the manor in 1551.

As well as payment from the Crown for each manor held in stewardship, the lessee had to provide accommodation, food and entertainment when the steward visited. This can be see from a lease agreement in 1563, in the sixth year of Queen Elizabeth I, when the manor was leased to Henry Whitney for 21 years. The lease to Henry Whitney includes the stipulation that he provides entertainment for the Queen's Steward and the Surveyor coming to court or to survey the manor. On taking up the lease, Henry paid an admission fine of £66, and yearly rent of £20.

The Whitneys leased the manor for less than five of the twenty-one years for it was again leased by the Crown on 27 May 1568 to one John Gardener. The lease to John Gardener is more detailed than that of Henry Whitney and allows for the quarrying of Clunch, then referred to as '*Le Clowthe*'. The lease also shows us that the manor was leased out prior to the dissolution of Ramsey Abbey and that the manorial buildings were in a state of decay. The document reads:

> '*Lease for 21 years to John Gardener of the site and demesne lands of the manor of Burwell in the county of Cambridge, once of the monastery of Ramsey, in the county of Huntingdonshire and afterwards parcel of lands of Edward Northe, knight, Lord Northe, exchanged with reservations, from Lady day last; yearly rent £20; the lesee may have on the premises sufficient of the stones called 'le clowthe' for his use; the lesee to provide entertainment for the Queens Steward and surveyor coming to hold courts at the manor or to survey the same. In consideration of the surrender by Gardener of an indenture, 15th April, 28 Henry VIII whereby John Abbot and the convent of the said monastery lease the premises to John Whetelye of Fulborn in the county of Cambridge, with reservations, including ground for quarries and the right to take therefrom 'clowth' stones except those which should be the farmers, for 40 years from the termination of the interest of John Bennett, the occupier of the manor; at a yearly rent of 42 quarters of wheat from the fields of Burwell at a rate of 6s.8d. a quarter to be delivered to Reche, in the county of Cambridge in which indenture there are about 13 years to run; also because certain buildings in the premises are in such decay that the farmer shal spend great sums on their repair as appears by certificate of the surveyor of the county of Cambridge; and for a fine of £20 paid at exchequer.*'

Calendar of Patent Rolls of Elizabeth I

The reference above to the Queen's Steward and Surveyor coming to court is but one indication that manorial life appears, at first, to have continued much as in the medieval period. Instead of the monastery officials visiting and holding the manorial court it was the crown officials and as during the medieval period the majority of disputes were minor. One dispute however did seem to get out of hand. In 1586, during the reign of Queen Elizabeth I, the attorney generals office investigated a dispute over the right of commons on the Devil's Dyke. The case became, 'The Queen v. Andrew Pearne, Dean of the Cathedral Church of Ely, along with Elizabeth Edwards, William Cook, John Ruse, Francis Tuthill, John Chambers, and others', these being the lords, tenants, and inhabitants of Swaffham. The issue that sparked the dispute was the impounding of the cattle grazing on the dyke. These animals belonged to the people of the town of Swaffham and the Manor of Knights in Swaffham. During the case the people of Swaffham Prior claimed that the Dyke was in their fields and not in the fields of Burwell, stating therefore that the right of commons was theirs alone. The reeve, the people of Burwell, and the Manor of Burwell Ramseys claimed otherwise.

A further dispute taken to court in February 1609 but this time the issue was to do with the rights of four copyholders of the manor, Thomas Pampling, John Chapman, Godfrey Rogers and William Gilbert.

The first mention of the manor house of the manor of Burwell Ramseys comes in 1623 when, during the reign of King James I, the manor house was leased out to Justinian Povey for 21 years. The document setting[16] out this lease survives in the Public Record Office. It has the title, the 'Site of the Manor of Burwell', and gives a brief description of the house and its appurtenances, which included the house, stables, barns, gardens, an orchard, fishponds and fisheries (*Fisheings*).

A better description of the manor house is given in a survey[17] for Parliament conducted in January 1649 following the execution of King Charles Stuart and Queen Henrietta This reads:

'by virtue of a commission granted uppon an act of the Commons assembled in Parliament, for the sale of honours, manors, and lands heretofore belonging to the late King, Queen and Prince, under the hand and seale of five or more of the Justices in the said act.'

This survey shows the capital messuage, as the manor house continued to be called at this time, was named as *'Burwell Hall*, in the possession of Justinian Povey, leasehold tenant. In fact, The Hall was actually sublet to Richard Gilbert who is described as the occupier of the house. The survey lists all the tenants of the manor, the lands they hold and their values. It also states that the manor house consisted at that time of:

'an olde farmhouse consistinge of a hall, a parlour, a kitchen and a buttery with two other necessary rooms below stayres, and fower chambers above stairs, with a barne and stable, and some other outehouses, a dovehouse and an orchard planted with olde appletrees and some other fruits.'

Elsewhere in the document reference is made to fishponds and fisheries in its possession. The full transcript of this document is given in Appendix 2.

Lessee	Leasing	From	To
John Lawrence, former abbot	Manor House	1539	1542
John Whetlye of Fulbourn	Lands	1537	1551
John Bennett	Full Manor	1551	1563
Henry Witney	Full Manor	1563	1568
John Gardener	Full Manor	1568	1578
Clement Stonard Gent	Full Manor	1578	?
Justinian Povey	Full Manor	1623	1649

Table 5 *Post-medieval period – Lessee Lords of the Manor.*

The Commonwealth

During the Commonwealth period when the country was under Cromwell's protectorate, the estates of the Crown were put up for sale. In the case of the Manor of Burwell Ramseys the estate was put up for sale in 1649. Justinian Povey bought The Hall and the land pertaining to it, while portions of the estate were purchased by Richard Ashfield, Thomas Herrick and others. The same men appear to have bought land in a number of manors. As the sitting lessee Justinian Povey claimed the manor. According to an earlier indenture, he or his children were entitled to hold the manor for sixty years, should they live that long. The earlier indenture was a grant from Queen Henrietta, the wife of Charles I, to Justinian, the Auditor General to the Queen as well as the holder of a variety of other posts.

With the return of the monarchy, the sales were overturned and crown manors that

Table 6 *Copyholders and other lessees of the Manor of Burwell Ramseys 1649.*

Name	Tenancy	Acres	Roods
? Chapman	Copyholder		
Amos Ginings		03	00
Ann Fuller	Copyholder		
Barnaby Gardner		01	02
Benjamine Paine		16	02
Cornelius Pamphlin	Copyholder		
Danyell Wilkin	Copyholder		
Edmund Gardner	Copyholder		
Ezechiell Perkins (the elder)	Copyholder		
George Carrowe	Copyholder		
George Clarke	Copyholder		
Henrie Clarke	Copyholder		
John Baron		06	02
John Bridgman	Copyholder		
John Buntinge		6	00
John Casborne	Copyholder		
John Clark		090	00
John Flawtrer		13	00
John Fuller		39	02
Mary Izackson	Copyholder		
Oliver Pamphlin	Copyholder		
Philip Fyson	Copyholder		
Richard Gilbert	Under lessee of the Hall	221	0
Robert Casborne	Copyholder		
Robert Wilkins	Copyholder		
Stephen Palmer		39	00
Steven Paine (Manorial Bailiff)	Copyholder	10	02
Thomas Castborn		21	00
Thomas Izatson		32	03
Thomas Paine	Copyholder	25	03
Thomas Palmer		13	03
Thomas Pratt	Copyholder		
Thomas Vice	Copyholder		
William Fuller	Copyholder	18	00
William Hinde	Copyholder		
William Ransdell		11	00
William Rogers	Copyholder		
William Spearman		31	02
William Wilkin		33	00

had been sold were again returned to the Crown. Little happened locally from that point on. The land continued to be rented or leased and the feudal model of land management and justice continued through the manorial court. A number of post-medieval documents exist which demonstrate this. For example;

Document Desription	Date	Reference
Court Minutes	1560 – 1565	Huntingdon RO
Admissions	1728 - 1821	L21/21 - 27
Admissions	1756	R52/9/5/19
Admissions	1763	R52/9/5/23
Admissions	1766	R52/9/5/25
Admissions	1771	R52/9/5/26
Admissions	1777	R52/9/5/30
Admissions	1779	R52/9/5/31
Admissions	1783, 1795	R52/9/5/37-39, 45
Admissions	1816, 1837, 1856	R52/9/5/50, 65, 75, 76

Table 7 *Documents and references – manor of Burwell Ramseys.*

The Manor of Burwell Tiptofts

As noted earlier, at the time of the Domesday Survey Burwell had two manors. The second of these, originally owned by Edeva the Fair who rented it out to three sokemen, was given to Count Alan in 1066. Alan split this into two and rented it out to lesser knights. The larger of these two new manors, comprising 2½ hides of land was rented to Alan and later became the Manor of Burwell Tiptofts.

At sometime after 1201 and before 1213 Lord Ralph de Cameys acquired the manor, probably through marriage. The Cameys were barons by tenure of Flockthorpe Manor in Norfolk and held the knights fee in a number of manors across East Anglia, including Woodditton, Kirtling and Cheveley. In addition by 1242, Ralph de Cameys was sheriff of the Counties of Surrey and Sussex.

In 1258 Ralph died leaving the manor to his son, also called Ralph, who carried on much as his father had done. Ralph married Ascelina, daughter and heiress of Roger de Torpel of Torpel (in the parish of Ufford) Northants. They had two children, John and Ralph. Like his father, this second Ralph was a knight and during his career he fought against the Welsh and joined with Simon de Monfort against the king, for which he was later pardoned (1267).

On his death in 1277 his son John, then aged 27, succeeded him. John sold a number of their Cambridgeshire manors although he retained Woodditton. One of these manors was Burwell, which he sold sometime between 1277 and 1279 to Robert Tibetot (Tiptoft).

Despite having sold the manor John appears to have retained the knight's fee in the manor. The fee seems to have been retained because in 1316 John's son, Ralph Lord de Cammoys, was certified pursuant to writ as being lord of a number of manors including Burwell. After 1316 there are no records of any association between the Cameys and Burwell.

Robert de Tibetot (Tiptoft) who acquired the manor between 1277 and 1279, was an important knight. He had been on crusade, he was Governor of Nottingham, Carmarthen and Cardigan and, as Lieutenant for Wales, he had defeated Rees ap Meredeth in battle and took him to York to be executed.

The Tiptofts, like the Cameys before them, were a powerful family and it is therefore unlikely that they spent much time in Burwell. Their manor house would probably have been a modest affair, a manorial farmstead, maintained by a steward on behalf of the lord, and it is likely that the land was purchased for its rental income rather than a place for the Tiptofts to live. In 1279 when Cambridgeshire was surveyed for taxation[18] purposes Robert de Tiptoft had 30 tenants in Burwell. All paid rent and were obliged to provide customary service (Table 8). Some also paid a fee to the Honour of Richmond.

Robert's income from this land was £2 15s 6d. This may not seem much today but in 1279 this was a good income. Some of the tenants, such as Adam de Nes, were renting land and houses from both Robert Tiptoft and Ramsey Abbey. In Adam's case this amounted to two messuages and 26 acres.

Robert and his successors provided a knight's fee in the village. This usually meant that the knight holding the fee was resident, living in a house provided and deriving some income from the land provided with the fee. In the case of Burwell the knight was John de Cameys. Both his father (Ralph who died age 64 in 1277) and his grandfather (Radulph, who died in 1254) had previously held this knights fee in Burwell.

The house was probably on a site adjoining the former St Andrew's churchyard, which in the 1800s was still known as the Old Tiptoft Manor. Charles Lucas makes reference to this in his description of the former guildhall. He refers to the guildhall being *situated on the north-east side of the church and on the border of the churchyard opposite the Old Toptoll Manor House*[19]. Manorial buildings associated with the manor of Burwell Tiptofts were first mentioned in the period 1300-1330[20].

While the Tiptofts bought much land in Cambridgeshire, by the later half of the thirteenth century Burwell had become their largest holding in the area and commensurate with this Robert applied for and was granted a licence by charter to hold a market and fair at Burwell. The fair could be held for 15 days from Whitmonday each year while the market was held weekly on Wednesdays. It should be stressed that this market and the fair is not that held at Reach. The fair at Reach was already in existence, having been granted in 1201 to the Burgesses of Cambridge and the Prior of Ely.

Robert Tibetot died in 1298 leaving the Manor of Burwell, along with his other estates, to his son and heir Payn de Tybetot. Payne, like his father, was an active knight who also would have spent little, if any, time in Burwell. He was Governor of Northampton Castle and spent much of his time in Scotland quelling the Scots, for which he was made 1st Baron Tiptoft. He was mortally wounded at the battle of Bannockburn in 1314.

The manor, along with the other Tybetot manors, remained in the estate of Payn's widow Agnes. She was married in 1315 to Thomas de Vere who then owned the manor until his death in 1329. In 1334 John Tybetot, son of Payn, reached adulthood and successfully reclaimed the manor.

John, 2nd Baron Tybetot, became Governor of Berwick on Tweed. He died in 1367, during the reign of King Edward III. He had three sons by his wife Margaret, daughter of Bartholomew, 2nd Baron Badlesmere. Robert, the eldest, inherited the title and most

Name(s)	Property Rented	Rent
Gilbert son of Nicholas and John Mildelton	1 messuage and 26 acres	6s. 8d plus 2s to Honour of Richmond
Andrew de Collingg	30 acres	6d
Henry son of Fulcon	1 messuage and 30 acres	6s 8d plus 9d to Honour of Richmond
Adam de Nes	1 messuage and 2 acres	3s
Hugh son of Elye	1 messuage and 2 acres	1d to Honour of Richmond
Thomas Bunting and Robert Son of Watt	28 acres	10s
Peter Afkil	2 acres	3s
George de Arpisfeld	1 messuage and a croft	2s
William le Elk	1 acres	6d
Walter de Bonenfant	1 messuage and a croft	3s plus 1d to the Honour of Richmond
Richard Sweyn	1 messuage and a croft	2s plus 1d to the Honour of Richmond
Robert Prior	1 Croft	3s plus 1d to the Honour of Richmond
Radalf Mercator	1 messuage and 9 acres	2s 8d
Thomas Mersh	1 Toft	6d
Elena, widow of Symois son of Peter	1 Messuage and a Croft	16d plus 1d to the Honour of Richmond
Elena Ordiner		
Radulf Styward	1 Rood	24d
6 villeins held	15 acres (7 acres of which are marsh)	6s 8d plus 6d to the Honour of Richmond
7 Cottagers held	3 Roods	2s plus 1d to the Honour of Richmond

Table 8 *Tenants of Robert Tiptoft in 1279.*

of the estates but not the Burwell manor, which by 1373 was in the possession of his third son Payn, who held it until his death in 1413. Payn also had three daughters, Margaret, Millicent and Elizabeth by the time of his death.

In 1413 the manor descended to Payn's son John, who became Baron John Tiptoft from about 1426. This John was succeeded in 1443 by his heir John Tiptoft who was probably the most notorious member of the family to have anything to do with the manor. Born in 1427 at Eversden, John was educated at Oxford. He became Earl of Worcester in 1449 and by 1452 was Treasurer of the Exchequer. On leaving that post in 1456 he became Lord Deputy of Ireland. In 1457 he went on Pilgrimage to the Holy Land and then spent two years in Rome where it is said he ruined many libraries by purchasing books which he later gave to Oxford University. In 1462 he returned to England and became Constable of England.

He was said to be a man of both great learning and of great cruelty and in his role of Constable he persecuted, sentenced and put to death many of the Lancastrian leaders. When Henry VI re-ascended to the throne, the Lancastrians who hated him and referred to him as 'the butcher of England', seized their opportunity and John was tried at the Palace of Westminster and was subsequently executed on 15 October 1470. He will probably be best remembered in literary circles for his translation of Cicero's *De amicitia*, which was printed by William Caxton in 1481.

John, although executed, was not stripped of his title and lands so these were left to his only son and heir, Edward. When Edward died childless on 12 August 1485 the Tiptoft line ended with him. Initially the manor remained in the hands of John's widow Elizabeth, who held it until her death in 1498. She had remarried after 1470, to Sir William Stanley, but like her first husband he was executed (in 1495). At this time the earldom reverted to the Crown.

At some time between 1498 and 1513, the manor passed to Sir Thomas Lovell, who had married Isabel, the eldest daughter of Philippa, Earl John's sister. Sir Thomas died in 1524 without a male heir and by provision of his will the estate went to Francis Lovell of East Harling in Norfolk, who was the younger son of Sir Thomas's brother Gregory. Francis died in 1552, leaving the estate to his son and heir Thomas Lovell, knight, who when he died some 15 years later in 1567 left the estate to his widow Elizabeth and his son Sir Thomas Lovell. Sir Thomas owned it until his death in 1604 when it passed to another Francis who was to be the last of the line to hold the manor. In 1607, Sir Francis Lovell, son of Sir Thomas, sold the manor to William Barrow of Westhorpe, Suffolk.

William Barrow died six years later in 1613 and was succeeded by his youngest son Maurice. It would appear that his widow Elizabeth remained associated with the manor because in 1624 she acquired the underlease of the Manor of Burwell Ramseys. Maurice Barrow retained the Tiptoft manor for 19 years and then sold the manor in 1632 to the Marsh family.

A document in the Cambridge University Library[21] informs us that in 1629 the manor comprised 796 acres of which 280 acres were in the manorial demesne. This was made up of 240 acres of arable land and 40 acres of meadow. The remainder comprised 9 acres of 'stangnant lande' (marsh) and the rest rented out to 36 copyhold tenants (Table 9). The list refers to arable, pasture, meadows and woods of which there were 14. In some cases the woods were listed under pasture indicating their use as such.

It is obvious from the text at the bottom of the page that there was some uncertainty about the actual amount of land in the estate and that this related to the land being rented by Chapman (Figure 10).

This uncertainty is probably due to the document being from a source other than the manorial records. It is one of three sides of paper concerning Burwell contained in a folio of letters and miscellanea to Cambridge University.

In 1643 the manor was in the possession of Thomas Marsh. Thomas died in 1657 and the manor remained in the possession of his widow Margaret until her death in 1678. In 1677, during the period of Margaret's tenure, she acquired 276 acres of land, including fen for use as '*Sheepwalks*', and its manorial rights. Sir Thomas's grandson sold the manor in 1679 to Samuel Clarke of Snailwell.

Samuel commenced the break up of the Tiptoft manor in 1681 when he sold 180 acres of land and the 100 acres of the fenland and sheepwalks that had been acquired by Margaret Marsh. He did however retain the remainder of the manor up to his death in 1719 when his son, Sir Robert Clarke, succeeded him.

In about 1730, Charles Seymour, the Duke of Somerset acquired the Manor of Burwell Tiptofts. He died in 1748 leaving his estates to his daughters and in 1763 it appears to have passed to Charlotte, the wife of Heneage Finch, Earl of Aylesford. Heneage was

	Arable	Pasture	Meadow	Woods
Ye manor itself	240		40	
Jo: Pooly Esq	40		0	
W Rogore	13	8G	10	3
I Roll	10		0	
Jo: Chapman	70 or 10		5	
Thos Bunting	12		0	
Dan Wilkins	40	3	0	
Tho Fuller	2	0		
Hen Chapman	5	1		
Luke Woodbridge	2		1	
John Mordon	1		0	
Tho Wenham	2		0	2
Tho Chapman	2	2	0	
Tho Browne	1		0	
Willm Turner	0	2	0	
Ed Naper (name difficult to read)		0	3	3
Sam Stinton	0	2	0	
Jo Causeburn	34		2	
Tho Barron	20		0	
Jo Barron	4		0	
Robt Causeburn	30		0	
Jo Causeburn	22			
Tho Causeburn	12		4	
Tho Malmow	4			
Jo Butcher	1			
Hen Ffuller	4			
Ezukill Perkins	36		0	2
William Leifechild (name difficult to read)	3			
Stouer Palmer	1		1	1
Cornel Pamplin	23		2	
Stagnant Lande	9			
Jo Wilkins	6			
Willm Beyton	2			
Widdow Baron	1			
Jo Bridgman	20			
Jo: Bette Hoynes (name difficult to read)	3			
Willm Hinds				3
Tho Pamplin Gent	60		1	

Table 9 *Tenants of the Manor of Burwell Tiptofts – 1629.*

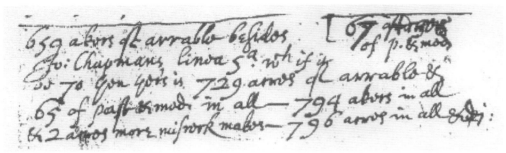

Figure 10 *Section of the 1629 document relating to the Manor of Burwell Tiptofts.*

Table 10 *Lords of the Manor of Burwell Tiptofts.*

Lord	From	To
Edeva the Fair	?	1066
Count Alan (rented out to Alan)	1066	
Lord Ralph de Cameys	1201–1213	1258
Lord Ralph de Cameys (2nd)	1258	1277
Lord John de Cameys	1277	1277–1278
Robert Tibetot	1279	1298
Payn de Tybetot	1298	1314
Thomas de Vere	1315	1329
John, second baron Tybetot	1334	1367
Payn de Tybetot	1367	1413
John Tiptoft	1413	1443
John Tiptoft	1443	15th October 1470
Edward Tiptoft	1470	12th August 1485
Elizabeth Tiptoft	1485	1490
Sir William Stanley	1490	1495
Sir Thomas Lovell	1495–1513	1524
Francis Lovell	1524	1552
Thomas Lovell	1552	1567
Sir Thomas Lovell	1567	1607
William Barrow of Westhorpe, Suffolk.	1607	1613
Maurice Barrow	1613	1632
Thomas Marsh	1632	1657
Margaret widow of Thomas Marsh	1657	1678
Samuel Clarke of Snailwell	1679	1719
Sir Robert Clarke	1719	1730
Charles Seymour, duke of Somerset	1730	1748
Heneage Finch, Earl of Aylesford	1763	?
Heneage Finch, Earl of Aylesford	?	1812
John Harwood of Exning	1812	1815
Mary, Ann and Elizabeth Harwood	1815	1834
Admiral, Richard Thomas Hancock	1834	1850
Richard Hancock	1850	?

succeeded by his son, another Heneage, who was an artist and whose works still feature in well-known galleries such as the Tate to the present day. It is unlikely that the earl spent much time in Burwell and it is likely that the manor as land was rented out.

In 1812 this Heneage Finch sold the manor to John Harwood of Exning, who already owned 650 acres of land in Burwell including 120 acres of fen. When John Harwood died in 1815 his daughters, Mary, Ann and Elizabeth succeeded him. Neither Mary nor Ann Harwood married.

By about 1830, the manor comprised 338 acres, which included 166 acres of fen. Elizabeth married in 1834 to Captain, later Admiral, Richard Thomas Hancock. Richard and Elizabeth were succeeded by their two surviving children, Richard and Jane. In 1850 Richard received two thirds of the estate while Jane and her husband William Hussey received one third. The Hancock portion from 1908 to the 1920's belonged to Edward Kinver Hancock.

A number of court rolls and other documents survive in the County Record office or other locations, including:

Document Description	Date	Reference
Court Roll Extracts (Document in Bodlean Library)	1242	Bodl.11653,f113 (Rawl.3.319)
Rentals (Documents In Northumberland Record office)	1474	
Court Rolls	1580 -1586	R55/7/81
Deed for the Manor	1607	L73/1
Court Roll for the Manor	1643 - 1694	R56/6/1-10
Surrenders and Admissions	1649, 1668	R52/9/5/2,3
Manorial Documents	1680 - 1684	R51/25/1
Manorial Documents	1684 - 1925	R51/25/6 a) – l)
Admissions	1697	L21/28
Court Books	1726 – 1757	R51/25/6 (j)
Manorial Documents	1823 – 1923	R51/27/7 a) - c)
Letters, memos etc re Burwell manors, but mostly relating to the Manor of Burwell Tiptofts	1845 - 1945	R51/25/22

Table 11 *Manor of Burwell Tiptofts – documents and references.*

Lesser Manors

From quite an early period Burwell had a number of lesser manors. Generally these comprised lands purchased by a wealthy owner and were given the name of the principle manor of the new owner.

The Manor of Valence

One of the earliest of these lesser manors was the Manor of Valence, Valence being the Manor of the Countess of Pembroke in Exning. The name Valence originated from the family name of the countess's husband, Aymer Valence. In the thirteenth century the Valence family had purchased land in Burwell, in this case from John of Castle Martin, Pembrokeshire, who in 1342 had acquired 54 acres of land in Burwell. John's purchase was probably from the Abbots of Ramsey at the time when they were selling land.

Prior to her death the countess bequeathed her lands to the college she had founded in 1347 in Cambridge, which was then known as the House or Hall of Valence Marie.

The college was to derive income from such lands to support its Master and Scholars. The Patent Rolls[22] of Richard II record the licence for this on 20 June 1392, 22 years after the death of Mary.

> 'Licence for 10 marks paid to the king by the Master and scholars of the hall or house of Valence Marie, Cantebrigg, for the alienation in mortmain by Richard Moreys, clerk, John Rodby, clerk and William Bateman, of one messuage, 47 acres of land and 4 acres of meadow in Burwell and Wykes, not held in chief to the said Master and Scholars and their successors, in aid of maintenance.'

While this record does not describe the foundress as deceased, a subsequent record made two years later does. This subsequent record, again for the grant of a licence, was more concerned with the Manor of Valence in Exning, the Manor of Jardyns in Exning and,

> 'One weir, three acres of meadow, 2s 6d of rent and view of frankpledge of the hamlet of Reche with appurtenances in Burwell and Reche in the county of Cambridge....'

These grants of licence, and another dated November 1409, ensured the continued ownership of the land by the college and detail those involved in the colleges efforts in this. Land in medieval times could be owned by individuals, the religious communities (in the name of the abbot or prior) or by the king. Colleges, such as that of Pembroke Hall, had not yet been granted that right and to avoid the land being escheated they had to constantly re-affirm their right to it, lest it fall to the crown or the current tenant.

In a record of 1409 Richard Yate, is said to have 'surrendered his right' to the same land referred to in the 1392 and 1394 references. At that time the land was being held by Drogo Barantyn, a citizen and goldsmith of London.

From 1780 Salisbury Dunn leased the Manor of Valence from Pembroke College.

The Manor of Burwell, Badlinghams, later St Omers

It is not clear when the Manor of Burwell Badlinghams was created but it might have been as early as the thirteenth century. In 1320 John le Waleys acquired the manor in marriage. According to the details of its sale in 1325 to William Wigmore, Robert Beverlay had been the previous owner. On the death of William Wigmore it came into the possession of Bertram de St Omer on whose death it was passed to his father, Sir William de St Omer of Norfolk. Sir William was succeeded by his eldest son, Sir Thomas de St Omer, who died in 1364. Sir Thomas had no male heir but he had two daughters, between whom the manor was given as coheirs.

In 1406 one of the daughters, Catherine, widow of Sir John de Burgh gave St Omers manor to endow her chantry in Burrough Green church. Until its suppression in 1547, the manor belonged to the chantry and provided it with an income of 10 marks. At that time, the manor comprised lands in Burwell belonging to Ramsey, Dullinghams and Chatteris manors. In the early 1540s all the land that had been endowed to the chantry was rented out to John Chapman prior to the suppression in 1547. After that time the chantry lands reverted to the former manors. The rental document survives in the Public Records Office.[25]

On 4 May 1553 John Butler of Woodhall, Herts, a knight and Thomas Chaworthe a gentleman purchased the manor, along with much of the former chantry land, for £1,072. 13s 5½. The sale is recorded in the patent roll for that date and reads:

'The Manor called Seynt Thomas in Burwell, in the county of Cambridge, and land there in tenure of Thomas Bailey and Hugh Chatterton, which lately belonged to the chantry of Borough in the county of Cambridge.'

It was again recorded in 1562 as being in the possession of John Butler, knight, and his wife Grizel. In that year they sought a licence to alienate the manor and its lands in Burwell and Reach to Thomas Fookes. Fookes (or Folkes) had also acquired the rectory of St Andrews in 1570, which had previously been sold by the Crown in 1564.

Fookes died sometime between 1584 and 1588 and was succeeded by his daughters Agnes and Anne. Agnes was the wife of Theodore Goodwin of Reach and Anne was the wife of John Grange of Swaffham Bulbeck. Theodore Goodwin appears to have held the manor and on his death probably passed it on to his son Thomas, who probably sold it because, on his death in 1623, it is not recorded in his possession. In 1639 another Goodwin, not the heir of Thomas, sold the manor to Walter Clopton.

Walter Clopton sold the manor in about 1646 to William Russell. The Russells had previously purchased the former St Andrews rectory lands, which had been sold to them in 1600 by Theodore Goodwin and John Grange jointly. They sold them on to Issac Barrow of Spinney whose son had given them to Cambridge University and who were in 1646 leasing them back from the University. William Russell died wilfully intestate in 1663. The manor was claimed by Sir William Russell's elder brother Sir Francis Russell of Chippenham against their younger brother, and expected heir, Gerard Russell. Sir Francis's younger children appear to have acquired it by 1678 and in 1711–1712 Stephen Isaacson of Burwell purchased it from five coheiresses. The Isaacsons were of a longstanding and well-established Burwell family, and Stephen had ten sons and daughters. On his death in 1736 the land was divided between them. One daughter, Mary, was assigned the title of the Lordship of the Manor of St Omers and was also given the Manor house and 30 acres. The Manorial sheepwalks and heathland comprising 100 acres were given to Stephen's eldest son John.

Mary Isaacson did not marry. Manorial courts were held for her for the period 1738 to 1758. Her sister Diana, who also never married, succeeded her. Courts were held for her in the period 1764 to 1791. In 1806 the manor house, with the lands of Mary, Diana and Hanna, passed to Hanna's son William Sandiver, surgeon of Newmarket. It is from his time that the manor house became known as the Doctor's House.

William Sandiver sold the lands of the manor and the titular Lordship to John Harwood in 1813, after which it was incorporated with the manor of Burwell Tiptofts.

Document Description	Date	Reference
Court Books	1703 – 1912	R51/25/5 a),c)
Court Minute Books	1845 – 1912	R51/25/5 d),e)

Table 12 *Documents of the Manor of St Omers in Cambridge Record Office.*

The Manor of Burwell, Dullinghams

The Manor of Burwell Dullinghams was created, like the Tiptofts manor, by Count Alan sub-dividing the land, formerly owned by Edeva the Fair before 1066, into two manors leased to knights in his service.

The manor in 1086 comprised 1½ hides of land in the possession of Geoffrey. What happened between 1086 and 1235 is not known, but in 1235 it was in the possession of

Henry son of Robert, a knight of the Burgh family of Burrough Green. In 1275 Henry's Burwell demesne covered 180 acres of land. In that year half of it was given for life to Henry's son, Robert. By 1316 it was in the possession of Thomas son of Henry.

It then passed in marriage to John Dullingham in 1339. John died in 1349 and what followed is not clear. However by 1377 the lordship and its lands were acquired for Maurice Tove of Bottisham. When he died in 1396 a Nicholas Tove conveyed the lordship with 200 acres for William Vaux, whose heir granted it in 1443 to John Lord Tiptoft. It is referred to in the indenture of John Lord Tiptoft dated 14 August 1493[23].

Here however the Patent Rolls tell a different story. An inspection of letters patent in 1507 records this licence:

> 'Inspeximus of letters patent dated 20th May in the tenth year of Richard II granting licence for the Prior and convent of Ely to aquire in mortmain lands to the yearly value of £24 and licence in pursuance of the same for Robert the Prior and the said convent to aquire the manors of Dolynghams and Hington and a messuage, 220 acres of land, 9 acres 3 roods of meadows, 10 acres of pasture, 3 weirs with their fisheries and 20s of rent in Burwell, Haddenham, Thetford, Wentworth, Ely and Leveryngton in the county of Cambridge of the yearly value of £10 as appears in an Inquistition taken before Edward Mynskyp escheator.'

This appears to indicate that in 1387 a licence was granted for the acquisition of land by the prior and convent of Ely. This was *in mortmain*, that is, given forever. Like so many medieval documents the licence was granted well after the event and merely ratified what had already taken place. Included in the acquisition of land was the Manor of 'Dolynghams'. This suggests that either the acquisitions by the Vaux and Tiptofts were rentals of the manor from the prior and convent of Ely or the prior and convent wished to give that impression. Ely retained the manor until the surrender of the abbey in 1539.

As with the Manor of Ramsey Abbey, the Ely Manor of Dullingham, along with its land in Burwell, was sold to Sir Edward North and was subsequently returned to the crown with Ramsey manor and lands. It remained as Crown property for 80 years after the dissolution of the monasteries.

The Dullinghams manor and its lands, like those of the Ramsey manor, were leased or rented out prior to the dissolution and they continued to be leased out afterwards. By 1561 (2 March) Dullinghams was being leased to Lord Keeper Sir Nicholas Bacon who sublet it to local men. The entry for this lease in the Calendar of Patent Rolls reads:

> 'Lease for 21 years, by advice of the treasurers etc. for a fine of £83 paid at exchequer, to Nicholas Bacon, knight, councillor of the great seal, of the site and capital messuage of Burwell called Dullinghams, in the county of Cambridge and lands (named) thereof in Burwell now in the tenure of John Wyat and John Gryme.'

In 1582 it was let for life to Henry Warner but by 1597 it was in the possession of John Bosome, who sublet it from Warner. An amendment to his lease signed on 2 October that year survives, listing 3 manors included in his lease. The record in the letters and papers of state reads,

> 'Lease in reversion with provision for tenants, to John Bosome, for 30 years, of the site of Laystonhall manaor, of Dullingham in Burwell manor and of Whitley Park and other lands and tenements in the counties of Northampton, Suffolk, Cambridge and Surrey; Rent £50,7s.0d. Fine £302.2s.0d.'

In 1600, Warner conveyed his interest in the manor to Isaac Barrow of Wicken. He appears to have continued the trend of subletting and by 1613 Dullinghams was sublet by the Goodwin family.

The Crown sold the manor to Edward and Robert Ramsay in 1626. The Ramsays were speculators who in turn sold it on, sometime before 1648, to the Cropley family of London. The Cropleys were London merchants. In 1682 Sir John Cropley was recorded as Lord of the Manor. On his death in 1713 he left all his lands to his friend Thomas Micklethwaite, who is referred to as lord in 1715. On Thomas Micklethwaite's death in 1718 the lordship went to Thomas's brother Joseph, who in 1727 became Viscount Micklethwaite. On his death in 1734 his property was left to Anne Ewer who had been the mistress of both of the Micklethwaite brothers. From 1734 to 1739 she was known as the Lady of Dullinghams. With her death the manor passed to her nephew Anthony Ewer, who sold it in 1747 to the Duke of Somerset. The Duke gave it in joint ownership to his younger daughters and their husbands. As with the Tiptoft manor, also owned by the Duke of Somerset, it was sold to John Harwood in 1812.

Document Description	Date	Reference
Court Books	1681 – 1921	R51/25/4 a)- c)
Rentals	1739 – 1915	R51/25/8 a) - g)
Court Minutes	1562 - 1563	Huntingdon RO
Manorial Documents	1823 – 1923	R51/27/7 a) - c)

Table 13 *Manor of Burwell Dullinghams – Documents and References.*

The Manor of Burwell Rectory

As noted earlier Sir Edward North, Chancellor of the Court of Augmentations purchased the Manor of Burwell Rectory after the dissolution. Sir Edward originated from a middle class background and appears to have been intent on increasing his fortune. He held a position of power in which he could purchase former monastic properties at a good price and sell them on for a profit later. This he did in the case of the newly created Manor of Burwell Rectory. This comprised the church lands of both St Mary's church and St Andrew's church, other lands added by Sir Edward, and the pensions due to the vicars of both churches.

The University of Cambridge, intent on providing income for its fellows, bought a number of properties in this period including the Manor of Burwell Rectory. Such manors gave them a steady income from the land that was let out to tenants. In addition where the manor included the patronage of the parish church the University could ensure positions for either fellows or suitable postgraduates.

For Sir Edward to be able to pass on the Manor of Burwell Rectory to the University he required the permission of the king. This was granted on 25 November 1544. The grant reads,

> 'Sir Edward Northe, Chancellor of Augmentations. Mortmain licence to grant the advowson of the parish church of Burwell St Mary, Cambridgeshire, Norwich Diocese; to the University of Cambridge for ever. Two thirds of the cost of the repair of the chancel and the pension of 40s to the abbot of Ramsey to be borne by the University and the remaining third by the vicar for the time being.'

This grant, although two years after the death of John Lawrence, suggests that an agreement had been made between the former abbot and Sir Edward North to give the advowson of the church to the University. Sir Edward, it would appear, had honoured this agreement. It is also of note that at the time when the submission had been made (prior to John Lawrence's death), the former abbot was still known as the Abbot of Ramsey, and was also drawing the pension of the rector of the church of St Mary.

With the University holding the advowson, it was only one year before a deal was struck between Sir Edward and the University for the sale to the University of the remainder of the newly created manor. The lengthy document of indenture for the sale of the Manor of Burwell Rectory by Sir Edward North to the University of Cambridge for £600 on 10 October 1545 survives.

This indenture of sale states,

'that the said Chancellor, Master and Scholars shall have granted by the same letter patents to them and ye successors forever, the advowson and right of patronage of ye vicarage of Burwell aforesaid: And that before the feast of the Nativity of Our Lord, He the said Sir Edward North, his heirs or assigns, shall discharge the said Parsonage and Church of Burwell, and every part and parcel thereof, of all and every incumbent and incumbents of all former Advowsons, and all manner of leases, made by the consent of the Parson, Patron and Ordinary…'.

The indenture also sets out the pension arrangement for the current incumbent (vicar) at that time and his successors, 20 shillings per year, coming out of the income of the parsonage or the church. In addition the former pension, given to the last Abbot of Ramsey, was to be awarded between the vicar and chancellor and the University of Cambridge. An earlier document of 1541 tells us that the pension to the last abbot, and included in the sale to Sir Edward Northe, was 40 shillings.

As with Burwell's other manors, the Manor of Burwell Rectory was leased out. This is apparent from a document in Cambridge University Library, dated 21 October 1629, in which the University asked Sir W Russell, knight, to surrender the lease of Burwell Rectory and any underleases to them. The document states that they were offering to re-lease the manor with the advowsons of both vicarages for two hundred pounds per annum payable in two instalments. The lease offered was for 80 years and contained fines for late payments and other stipulations, including that he should repair the chancel (St Andrews?) within two years, repair and re-edify St Andrew's church, give the alms, tenths, subsidies etc. due to the poor, be hospitable to visiting dignitaries such as the vice-chancellor of the University of Cambridge and provide board with Saturday night and Sunday lunch meals for them.

Sir W Russell was also charged with holding the regular manorial court in a fitting manner and ensuring the court roll was correctly recorded.

With the incorporation of St Andrew's in 1640, the university-owned manor had all the tithes of the village and a rectorial glebe of 83 acres of arable land and 17 acres of closes. Sixty-two acres of these had been recorded in 1600[24] as being attached to the Parsonage. Parsonage Farm continued to be used as the farm for the estate, the lessee being resident there until the nineteenth century. In 1922 the University sold Parsonage Farm with 53 acres to the County Council. In 1628[25] it is recorded that there were two tithe barns at Parsonage Farm of which one survives today.

Queens College

The college of St Mary and St Bernard, Queens College acquired land in Burwell in the sixteenth century. Terriers of Land in Cambridge University Library suggest that by 1678 the college owned 46 acres of arable land. Queens College lands after enclosure were those of Lark Hall Farm, which it sold to the County Council in 1913.

Manorial Buildings

Excluding the Castle site, Burwell possesses six possible 'Manorial sites'; Tunbridge, Pembroke Farm, The Hall, Isaacson's House (sometimes called the Doctor's House or the Old Manor House), the building currently known as the Manor House and Crowland Farm. According to the Royal Commission for Historic Monuments two of these represent known manorial sites of medieval manors. It should be remembered that all of Burwell's manors were owned by absentee landlords They leased the principle house of the manor to a retainer with whom the lord would stay should he pay a visit. As a result none of Burwell's manorial sites are particularly large nor are their remains spectacular. All but two of them are farmsteads on the High Street.

Tunbridge – According to the Royal Commission for Historic Monuments[5] Tunbridge was the Manor house for the medieval manor of St Omers although evidence from tenure suggests this may not be the case. It is however a site of manorial quality, the house standing within the remains of a thirteenth or fourteenth century moated enclosure. According to English Heritage, this moat was originally about 40 feet wide.

Pembroke Farm – also known as Castle Martins, was the site of the Manor of Valence given by the Countess of Pembroke to the newly founded Hall of Valence Marie (Pembroke College) in 1392. The present house upon the site dates from the nineteenth century and was the principal farm of the college in Burwell.

The Hall – according to lease documents of the sixteenth and seventeenth centuries, was the former manor house of the Manor of Ramsey Abbey. It lies within a large moated enclosure, one side of which is still filled with water. The Royal Commission for Historic Monuments suggests that the moat is consistent with other moated enclosures from the twelfth or thirteenth centuries. Documents mentioning the manorial buildings exist from the early fourteenth and early fifteenth centuries although they lack much detail. However the sixteenth and seventeenth century lease descriptions are consistent with some of the descriptive texts of the early medieval period confirming that The Hall is the original manor house of the Abbots of Ramsey. It is in close proximity to Parsonage Farm and the former Hythes of the Manor.

Documentary evidence described above tells us that around the end of the fourteenth century the manor house was rented out along with much of the manorial demesne. This rental continued through to the dissolution. We also know from documentary and visible evidence that, despite having rented out the manor house, the abbots took a keen interest in Burwell and, in particular, St Mary's church. Furthermore it would appear that accommodation was available for the abbot should he visit. We also know from fifteenth century records that the abbot's manor had a gate (house?) adjacent

Figure 11 *The Hall. (Cambridgeshire Collection)*

to which was at least one dwelling (a croft) and fishponds. In addition seventeenth century records describe the ponds and an orchard that was already 'very old'.

The present mostly seventeenth century house contains some medieval remains and is smaller than it originally was. A medieval wing had been pulled down in the early nineteenth century. This wing is said to have included a 'perpendicular' window of the fifteenth century and this may indicate the site of the abbot's oratory.

***Isaacson's House*–** is known as such after the family that lived their for many generations. This house has also been referred to, at times, as 'the Doctor's House' (still referred to this by some older local people) after it was the residence of a surgeon and ' the Old Manor House'. This building dates to the last years of the fourteenth century and is of a type constructed in the period to house visiting dignitaries. It is known to have been the principle building in a range covering a 'D'-shaped area and on nineteenth century maps it appears to have a gatehouse and other attendant buildings. Charles Lucas, although not the most reliable of historians, does mention the demolition of this gatehouse in his book, *The Fenmans World*.

Writing in 1930, he states: '*There was until quite recently a gate-house at the east end of the house, and when it was pulled down a stoup was found*'. In 1886 the first Ordnance Survey map of the village was produced. This showed buildings still standing but slightly altered from the earlier maps.

One theory regarding this house is that it was the original house of the Manor of Burwell Dullinghams. Its period of construction is approximately consistent with the acquisition of the Manor of Dullinghams by the abbot and convent of Ely on or before 1387. The type and quality of the building are also consistent with this theory. Such a building would have been useful to the monks of Ely, and would have ensured they had a safe refuge in Burwell and would not have been waylaid, as was Prior Crauden

Figure 12 *Isaacson's House.*

earlier in the fourteenth century. The only documentary evidence relating to buildings associated with the Abbey of Ely's Manor of Dullinghams relates to a building east of North Street that might have been their manorial farmstead. A building of the fifteenth century, possibly a chapel, is described in Charles Lucas's book, which might have been part this farmstead.

An alternative theory is that Isaacson's house was the principle house of the Manor of St Omers. This is largely based upon its association with that manor and the Isaacson family who occupied it in the early 1800's.

Royal Commission for Historic Monuments describes the remaining building, built

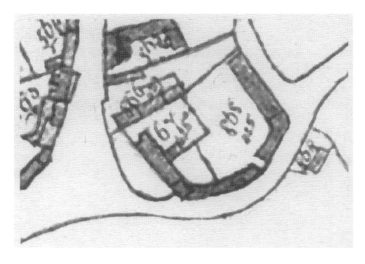

Figure 13 *Detail of a map of High Town, showing the present Isaacsons house with its attendant buildings, which were demolished at the end of the nineteenth century. The undated map is believed to date from between 1830 and 1843.*

Figure 14 *Crowland Farm, nineteenth century house on the site of the Tiptofts Manorial Farmstead.*

in clunch, as being the surviving range of a large domestic group. The view we now see of the building from the road is very much an eighteenth century view. During that period the medieval buttresses were removed and the medieval windows either blocked or replaced with large casement windows.

The Manor House – The present building known as 'The Manor House', which is located at the southern end of the High Street, has probably only been known as such in the past 150 years. The present structure on the site dates from the seventeenth century and was probably never a principle house of any of the medieval or immediately post medieval manors.

Crowland Farm – The site of Tiptofts manorial farmstead is on the opposite side of the High Street from St Mary's churchyard and adjoins the site of St Andrew's church, for which the manor was the principle benefactor in medieval times. The present house on this site was built in 1830 by Stephen Gardiner, a builder, for the sum of £200. There are a number of farm buildings on its southern and eastern sides and an early nineteenth century pigeon house with nesting boxes for about 690 pigeons. The Tiptoft manor association with this site ended in the nineteenth century.

References:

1. CARTULARIUM MONASTERII DE RAMESEIA, 1884 *Chronicles and Memorials of Great Britain and Ireland during the Middle Ages (Rerum Britannicarum Medii Aevi Scriptores): The Rolls Series,* London.
2. CHRONICON ABBATIAE RAMESEIENSIS, 1886, *Chronicles and Memorials of Great Britain and Ireland during the Middle Ages (Rerum Britannicarum Medii Aevi Scriptores): The Rolls Series,* London.
3. B.L., Survey of Manor 1646, Add 2718(2).

4. Lethbridge, T, 1936 'Excavations at Burwell Castle, Cambridgeshire', *Proceedings of the Cambridgeshire Antiquarian Society*, **36**. 121–133.

5. R.C.H.M., 1972 *An Inventory by the Royal Commission on Historical Monuments, North-East Cambridgeshire*, HMSO, London.

6. Raftis, J, Ambrose, 1957 *The Estates of Ramsey Abbey, a study in economic growth and organisation*, Pontifical Institute of Medieval Studies, Toronto.

7. B.L., Ramsey Abbey, Co Hunts, List of Abbats 970 – 1532, Add. 33451 f. 51.

8. Dewindt, E B, 1976 *The Liber Gersumarum of Ramsey Abbey: a calendar and index of B.L. harley MS.445*, Pontifical Institute of Medieval Studies, Toronto.

9. P.R.O., 1277, 1298, Extents of the Manor of Burwell, C133/16/9, C133/85/3.

10. Thompson, A H, (Ed) 1947 'Visitations in the Diocese of Lincoln, 1517 – 1531, Vol. 3', *Lincoln Record Society*, **37**.

11. P.R.O., London, PROB 11/29, q.11, folios, 86v – 87r. Will of John Lawrence Abbot of Ramsey, witnessed 12th December 1541, probated 7th November 1542.

12. H.M.S.O., 1898, Pensions awarded to monks of the Abbey of Ramsey, Transcripts of letters and papers foreign and domestic, 31 Henry VIII.

13. Bodelian Library, North MSS Cat p 5 – 6, 1541, acquisition of lands by Sir Edward Northe.

14. H.M.S.O., 1898, Grant in Fee to Sir Edward Northe, Transcripts of letters and papers foreign and domestic, 31 Henry VIII, Vol 16, 1540 - 1541.

15. H.M.S.O., 1898, Caledar of Patent Rolls Series of Elizabeth I.

16. Lease to Justinian Povey

17. Survey 1646, Add 2718(2).

18. Illingworth, W, & Caley, J, Rotuli Hundredorum temp Henry III & Edward I. Record Commission, 1812 – 1818.

19. Lucas, C, 1930 *The Fenmans World: Memories of Fenland Physician*. London. 128.

20. P.R.O., London, C 3/413/147. Chancery Pleadings, Russel vs Chapman: Cambridge.

21. C.U.L., West Mss Add.23f24v. Document relating to acreages and copyholders of the manor of Burwell Tiptofts, 1640,

22. H.M.S.O., 1898, Caledar of Patent Rolls Series of Richard II.

23. C.U.L. Queens College Muniments, Indenture of Lady Ingoldisthorpe and Lord John Tiptoft Earl or Worcester, QC Box 35.

24. P.R.O., London, C133/85/3, C134/37/10, C135/11/13.

25. C.U.A., Doc. XVI. 13A, 75, 119.

26. P.R.O.. SC 12/6/4.Rental of Lady Katherines Chantry.

Chapter 5

Medieval Life

Life for most people in the medieval period was difficult. Not only were conditions harsh but most people were also tied to land they rented from powerful lords. That rental as we will see from documentary evidence meant that a fee and a service was paid and in addition strict rules about how the land was managed had to be adhered to. The early medieval period was also perilous, due to war and pestilence.

We can see from visible evidence in Spring Close that village life was perilous. There, in the field surrounding the castle earthworks, are the remains of the closes (gardens) of a number of houses that lined a road heading in the direction of Reach. These houses were on Ramsey Abbey land and would have been rented out. In 1144 there was the need to build a castle to defend against Geoffrey de Mandeville, who was headquartered in and ransacking Ramsey Abbey. The houses were flattened and the work on the castle commenced. We do not know what damage was caused to the rest of the village when de Mandeville attacked, but it is likely that there may have been some.

Documents

As noted in previous chapters, there are a number of medieval documents relating to Burwell that give a good picture of life in the village for the ordinary person. The majority of these documents are surviving manuscripts of Ramsey Abbey. Unfortunately there is little early documentation from the other Burwell manors. The Ramsey Abbey documents are some of the most complete and well-studied medieval manorial records to have survived and consequently we can learn a great deal about life in the early medieval period from them. Later medieval documents of the abbey are less complete.

In these Ramsey Abbey documents, the Manor of Burwell features alongside the other Ramsey manors. For some of the manors there is a greater wealth of information than for others. Where Burwell appears, the data from Burwell for goods such as produce is comparable to the other Ramsey fen edge manors. Thus where there are gaps we can surmise that Burwell would have been similar to those Fen edge villages where data does exist.

The extent of the Manor

By the late twelfth or early thirteenth century, the manor of Burwell was managed as two separate units. Manor and the demesne lands were organised to provide a living for the abbot while the remainder, the farm, was used to provide for the monks and their guests, including the infirm.

The first detailed account of the manor that gives an indication into life in medieval Burwell is an extent of the manor carried out during the reign of King Henry III (1216–1272) as part of an inquest into the holdings of Ramsey Abbey. This is part of a series of abbey documents, known as the *Ramsey Abbey Cartularii*[1], which relates to the abbey and its manors. The inquest only concerned itself with the Ramsey holdings and not the other manors in the village. Further extents were carried out in 1277, 1298, 1315 and 1328 in response to various aspects of mismanagement. However, some of these have not survived in anywhere near such a complete state.

As well as informing about the holdings of the abbey and the demesne, this early extent also gives information about the land being rented, the names of those renting land and the services and customs associated with such rentals in the late thirteenth century.

From this extent (see Appendix 1 for a full transcript) we know that the abbot held the church of St Mary and six hides and three virgates (810 acres) within his demesne. The six hides are described as being at his table while the three virgates are at a place known as 'Hinlandes'. The term 'Hinlandes', refers to High Lands, an area in the North Field. In addition St Mary's church had one virgate (30 acres) pertaining to it.

The abbey employed at that time a man named Gilbert as the reeve, a clerk named Geoffrey and a shepherd who is not named. Each of these men was renting 15 acres of the abbot's demesne. The reeve was the local person who upheld the law and had the power to bring people to justice. He was also the overseer of the manorial land, the demesne and separate from the *firmarius* who was the person in charge of the manorial farm. Each manor had its own reeve as did the county (the shire reeve or sheriff).

As previously noted the abbey's holdings were split at this time into two groupings; the manor assigned to the abbot's chamber and the manor assigned to the convent of the monks. The manor assigned to the convent is identifiable in the extents where tenants are said to receive their land 'by the gift of the Steward' or 'by the gift of the Cellarer'. In the Burwell extent there are a number of records relating to the rental of land 'by the gift of Reginald the Cellarer' whereas those renting land from the abbot are shown as renting 'by the gift of Abbot William'.

Burwell was one of eight manors of Ramsey Abbey that was recorded as being a 'full farm', the others being half farms etc. This term did not relate to the size of the farm but what it produced. In the early years the full farm sent all of its produce to the abbey, not all at one time but at four times in the year. In October, for example, parts of the farms (that is, part of the produce) of Weston, Elton (both Huntingdonshire), Burwell and Therfield were due along with some produce from half farms. The produce received was meant to last a fortnight but, by the time of the extent, it was being used to supply the abbey for four weeks. It is thought that the extension from two to four weeks resulted from Geoffrey de Mandeville's occupation of the abbey. The remainder of the Burwell produce was due in January, February and July.

The list of what each full farm was expected to supply the abbey in a single year can be seen in Table 14.

Burwell also delivered five cartloads of hay and also had to give, in cash, £4 per year.

Item	Description	Value
Bread		
	12 quarters of ground wheat to be used for the monks and their guests	20s
	2000 loaves (Vokepanni) for servants	12 Marks
Ale		
	50 mittae of Barley	32s.
	25 mittae Malt	26s.
Other		
	24 mittae of Fodder	
	10lbs Cheese	
	10lbs Lard	
	2 treiae of Beans	
	2 treiae of Butter	
	2 treiae of Bacon	
	2 treiae of Honey	
	10 Fressings	
	14 Lambs	
	125 Hens	
	14 Geese	
	2200 Eggs	
	1000 Herrings	

Table 14 *Supplies from a full farm to the Abbey of Ramsey.*

The total value of the produce and the cash was, therefore, £17. This, however, was not all that the abbey received, because added to this were certain 'presents' made from the manor, including that made (compulsorily) by the *firmarius* who paid five shillings less one penny each year in food and at the three festivals, Christmas and Easter. In addition ,at various times the church of St Benedict was 'presented' fixed amounts of cheese, butter, eggs, wheat, malt, barley and a number of hens. Once a year the *firmarius* was also required to provide 36 men to work in the vineyard and customary tenants were required to cut the Hall straw. The Hall fen referred to as Hallode in Maresco in 1419, and still known today as Hallard Fen, provided very good quality sheaves of sedge and reed. In 1399 it is recorded that 8000 sheaves were cut by customary tenants for the abbey.

While the income to the abbey kept the monks well fed the ordinary people of the village, the villeins (sometimes referred to as *virgators*), cottagers and croftmen (or toftmen), had much less. The very poor would receive little by way of charity and each Ramsey manor was only required to provide 16 pence per year for the poor, probably all the poor, in the parish. This was given on Maundy Thursday and was raised from the eleemosynary or Maundy acre. This was a piece of land whose rent covered this expense.

The extent shows that a few people received food as part of their wages, for example. *'The Shepherd of the Sheep ......and food by the year'*. In some cases land was set aside for the specific purpose of providing food for wages, for example Clariz and Robert de

Clervaus, Walter de Bamville and Ralph de Osdene held (rented) a fishery and had *five acres of arable land towards the food of the Fishermen*'.

The majority of people were of servile class. They rented lands and provided customary services to either the farm (the abbey) or the abbot. The extent contains many good examples of different types of service, including:

> *'Alan Ruffus holds twenty four acres, with his croft. And he ought to work (on the lords land) from the feast of St Michael to Pentecost for one day each week. And to plough on rood and a half, except twelve days at Christmas, and in the Easter week, and in the Whitsun week, and this is fifteen acres. And from Pentecost until the day of St Peter ad Vincula to work for two days in each week, and to plough one rood and a half. And from the day of St Peter ad Vincula until the Nativity of St Mary he ought to work for three days in each week. And moreover, at these biddings he ought each day find one man. And moreover he ought to mow three half acres; but he ought to have three loaves with companage. And he ought to lead three cart loads of wheat and three cart loads of oat. And he ought to collect the Abbots hay with the villate and bring it to the court. And from the Nativity of St Mary until the feast of St Michael he ought to work for his days in each week.'*

These services were assigned to the land or property being rented. If the tenancy was given up then the new tenant would take on any services that the previous tenant had to perform as part of the rental agreement. The following example from the *Liber Gersumarum* demonstrates this:

> *'Johanna widow of Robert Barow: one tenement of 15 acres once held by Wakelyn, and another tenement of 15 acres once held by John Barow, one cote once held by Helywys, with the croft reserved to the lord, two crofts at the land of the rector, four acres of demesne land, and one cotland at Ness called Longcroft, for 20 years, rendering annually 43s, ploughing, suit to court and leet, and all other services and customs rendered by John.'*

The rental agreement usually comprised the customary services, a money rent and, additionally, a tenth (a tithe) of the produce to be given to the abbey.

By the fourteenth century the manorial farm was less reliant upon work provided by its tenants and for much of the work on the demesne it employed permanent staff including, a shepherd, a cowman, a swineherd, a carter and four ploughmen.

The *Liber Gersumarum* of the abbey[2] is a record of court events such as admissions to the manor and fees for permission to marry. From this document we can see the amount charged in money rent over a period from the mid 1400s to the dissolution of the abbey in 1539.

Few people in the early medieval period were wealthy enough to pay tax. This statement is supported by another early document in which Burwell features, the *Rotulii Hundredorum*[3] (Hundred Rolls). In 1279 a survey was carried out for the king. Known as the Hundred Roll this survey survives for Cambridgeshire. It lists the major landholders and the people from whom they rented land (Table 15). It is clear from this that by 1279 a good deal of subletting of land was taking place. However, despite this the two principal landowners were the Abbot of Ramsey and Robert de Tibetot (Tiptoft). Robert had 30 tenants while the abbot had 98. The rents listed in this document vary in amount from people such as Peter de Mildelton who rented one messuage and 24 acres from the abbot at eight shillings and eight pence per year to lesser tenants such as Peter Afkil renting one messuage and adjacent croft whose rent was 'to carry the abbot's goods as required'. At the very lowest level of society were the unnamed villains, some

30 of whom were renting 35 acres between them for 46 pence per year, or in the case of a further 12 villeins who rented eight acres for 12 horseshoes.

The medieval class system is very much in evidence in this document. The total number of tenants comprised 43 freemen, 49 villeins, 59 cottagers and 22 tofters making a total of 173 persons renting in the village. The actual number of people in the village would have been considerably more than this as such documents only consider the tenant, usually the senior male in the household.

Another document detailing early rentals, dated 1307, records the tenants of Burwell and their rentals. Forty-eight tenants are listed in this document, which, like the Hundred Roll, only lists important persons in the village.

After the early 1300s there is little in the way of detailed extents of the village or any of its manors that details the numbers of tenants until the early seventeenth century, when documents recording, for example, hearth tax appear.

Manorial Court

In the medieval period certain aspects of the law were vested in the lord of the manor. This was administered through the manorial court or leet court. The word leet first occurs in the Domesday Book and refers to a territorial or jurisdictional area. The manorial court was administered for the profit of the lord of the manor rather than what we normally consider as judicial matters. However, this court could deal with breaches of local law and the reeve would oversee punishment. The court could also set new bye-laws to be upheld in the manor and levy fines for those who broke them. We are fortunate in that a number of records of the manorial courts (court rolls), which contain entries for Burwell, have survived although the condition and readability is variable.

Each manor held its own court, usually a leet court. Ramsey Abbey claimed *infangthief*, the right of taking and fining a thief within the boundary of one's own jurisdiction, in the late thirteenth century using a forged charter of King Edward the Confessor to show its right as principal manor. It was granted this and was able also to hold a view of frankpledge, by which members of a group of households or small village were held responsible for one another's behaviour, and hold the assize of bread and ale. This was confirmed by King John and was to be held in the presence of the king's bailiff. In 1256 the rector of St Mary's agreed that his tenants attend the abbey's leet rather than one held by the rector. It is known that views of frankpledge and assizes were held in 1270 and 1299.

In the fourteenth and fifteenth centuries the court usually met only for two leet sessions each year, which enforced the assizes of bread and ale. This was a practice that continued into the seventeenth century.

The Manor of Burwell Tiptofts claimed *infangthief* in 1299 and, like Ramsey, was granted this and the Right of Gallows. The manor of Dullinghams appears to have only held assizes[18].

The Ramsey and Tiptoft manorial courts could clearly meet out levels of punishment from small fines to death by hanging. The regular leet court held at the manor, and the less frequent full manorial courts, mostly dealt with small fines for breaches of bye-

Table 15 *Freemen and other important tenants as listed in the Rotilii Hundredorum (Hundred Rolls) 1279.*

Name	Position	Rental	Tennant of	Rent
William de Kennet	Priest and secretary of Cambridge Court			
Alan Evilchild	Boatman			
Elyas Affaryefen	Boatman			
Fulco Lovel	Rector of St Mary's	24 acres		
John Appilfeld	Freeman	1hide + 1 messuage	Abbot of Ramsey	5s
Bartholomew son of Bartholomew	Freeman + Juror	1 messuage + 26 acres	Abbot of Ramsey	5s
Alexander de Erdwyk	Freeman	1 messuage + 26 acres	Abbot of Ramsey	20s
Peter de Mildelton	Freeman	1 messuage + 16 acres	Abbot of Ramsey	8s 8d
Thomas de Benwyle	Freeman	1 messuage + 16 acres	Abbot of Ramsey	8s 8d
John de Clervaux	Freeman	— 1 messuage + 16 acres	Abbot of Ramsey	8s 8d
Andrew Coling	Freeman			
Walter Richer	Freeman	1 messuage + 9 acres	Abbot of Ramsey	6s
William de Swaffham	Freeman	1 messuage + 24 acres	Abbot of Ramsey	2s + he shoes 2 horses and makes 1 load of iron per year.
Adam de Nes	Freeman	1 messuage + 24 acres	Abbot of Ramsey	£1
Peter Afkil	Freeman	1 messuage + an adjacent croft	Abbot of Ramsey	5s + he provides stone for the abbey
John De Cameys	Knight		Robert Typetot	
Gilbert son of Nicholas	Freeman	— 1 messuage + 13 acres	Robert Typetot (fee of Richmond)	2s
John de Mildelton	Freeman			
Andrew Colingg	Freeman	30 acres	Robert Typetot	6d + 2 wagons for use of the lord
Henry Fulcon	Freeman	1 messuage + 30 acres	Robert Typetot	6s 8d
Adam de Nes	Freeman	1 messuage + 21/2 acres	Robert Typetot	3s + 1 wagon
Hugo son of Elye	Freeman	1 Messuage + 2 acres	Robert Typetot	2s 6d + 1 wagon
Thomas Bunting	Freeman			
Robert Watt	Freeman	— 28 acres	Robert Typetot	10s
Peter Afkil	Freeman	2 acres	Robert Typetot	3s + 2 wagons
George de Arpisfeld	Freeman	1 messuage + an adjacent croft	Robert Typetot	2s + 2 wagons
William Le Elk	Freeman	11/2 acres	Robert Typetot	6d
Walter de Bonenfant	Freeman	1 messuage + a croft	Robert Typetot	3s + 1 wagon

Table 15 *Freemen and other important tenants as listed in the Rotilii Hundredorum (Hundred Rolls) 1279 (Continued).*

Name	Position	Rental	Tennant of	Rent
Richard Sweyn	Freeman	1 messuage + a croft	Robert Typetot	3s + 1 wagon
Robert Pior	Freeman	1 croft	Robert Typetot	3s + 1 wagon
Radulph Mercator	Freeman	1messuage + 9 acres	Robert Typetot	2s 8d + 2 wagons
Thomas Marsh	Freeman	1 toft	Robert Typetot	8d
Elena, widow of Simon, son of Peter	Freeman	1 messuage + a croft	Robert Typetot	16d + 1 wagon
Elena Ordiner	Freeman	1/2 acre	Robert Typetot	6d
Radulph Styward	Freeman	5 roods	Robert Typetot	14d + 1 wagon
Walter Redking	Freeman	1 messuage + 16 acres	Abbess of Chatteris	17s
Robert Le Vere	Freeman	1 messuage + 9 acres	Abbess of Chatteris	6s 4d
Thomas Wyger	Freeman	1 messuage + 9 acres	Abbess of Chatteris	4s
Gilbert Nicholas	Freeman	16 acres	Abbess of Chatteris	6s
Stephen Blangmong	Freeman	1 messuage	Abbess of Chatteris	2s
Henry son of Odon	Freeman + tenant of Robert de Burgh in the village	1 messuage + 29 acres	Honour of Richmond	1 pair gilded spurs + 6d + a donation of 13s 4d to the prioress of Swaffham to pray for Robert de Burgh
Ida De Spalding	Freeman	1 messuage + 4 acres	Henry Odonis	4s 6d
Baldwyn St George	Freeman	1 messuage + 15 acres	Henry Odonis	£1
Elena Aubrey	Freeman	1 messuage + 15 acres	Henry Odonis	£1
Alexander de Erdwyk	Freeman	9 acres	Henry Odonis	12d
Robert Giru	Freeman	1 messuage + 15 acres	Henry Odonis	2s
Nicholas Deubenege	Freeman	5 roods	Henry Odonis	3s 4d
Laurence Giru	Freeman	21/2 acres	Henry Odonis	4s
Alan Le Flemigg	Freeman	21/2 acres	Henry Odonis	3s
Matilda Grey	Freeman	5 roods	Henry Odonis	3s 4d
Gilbert	Freeman	2 acres	Henry Odonis	12d
William de Stevichworthe	Freeman	1 messuage + 4 acres	Henry Odonis	17d
William Alfretun	Freeman	1 messuage + 1 acre	John Arpisfeld	3s

Table 16 Tenants and their tenancies in Burwell 1307.

Tenant	Tenancy
? Hammond	15 acres + 1 croft
Agnes le Bere	15 acres
Agnes wife of Henry	24 acres
Alberic le Maleys	15 acres
Alice in Woodland	24 acres
Alicia le Wyse	15 acres
Basil Hering	20 acres
Basil Waleys	1 croft
Christina de Macham	15 acres
Daniel le Orymere	24 acres + 1 croft
Godfrey de Holm	15 acres
Godfrey de Reche	20 acres
Godfrey Edward (Reeve)	24 acres +20 acres +15 acres + 1 croft
Henry Kantelyn	15 acres
Henry le Wyse	24 acres + 1 croft
Hugh Edward	24 acres
John Ardayne	8 acres + 1 croft
John Edward	1 croft
John Inlop	20 acres
John Kantelyn	1 croft
John Lawrence	1 croft
John le Waleys	8 acres
John le Were	20 acres
John Machner	1 croft
John Milward	15 acres
John Morite	1 croft
John Pope	1 croft
John Sene	8 acres
Lawrence le Wynner	1 croft
Mabel Helewys	20 acres + 1 croft
Margaret de Macham	15 acres + croft
Matilda Morite	15 acres
Michael Godfrey	1 croft
Ormond Fedde	8 acres
Radulph Kantelyn	20 acres
Radulphus Miller	1 croft
Richard Edward	8 acres
Robert Ardayne	8 acres
Robert de Macham	15 acres
Robert Martmot	1 croft
Thomas Carlewayn	15 acres + croft
Thomas Edryth (Beadle)	15acres + 8 acres + 1 croft
Thomas le Milner	15 acres + 1 croft
Thomas Ungent	20 acres +24 acres +1 croft
William Ardayne	1 croft
William le Millwyn Jr.	15 acres + 1croft
William le Milwyn, Sen	15 acres + 1 croft
William le Wynner	15 acres + 8 acres

laws etc. More serious crimes were occasionally dealt with and the gallows were used during the early medieval period. Burwell's gallows were sited on the Devil's Dyke at *'Galewhyll'*[17]. The right to a gallows was conferred to the Abbey of Ramsey by King Henry III[18] and the name Gallows Hill is first recorded in 1396, along with a tumbrel (an instrument of punishment) and the punishments charged[19].

William Carlewayn et Edm	Simon Le Carte	**Table 17** *Persons listed in the lay subsidy roll for Burwell in the reign of King Edward III – 1327–1377.*
Basil Cateline	Agnes Le Lacey	
John Cotoun	Rado Le Rower	
John Crable	Thomas Le Swyn	
Elena de Holm	William Le Swyn	
Isabell De Paer	Matilda le Wite	
William De Southo	Dulcia Le Wyse	
Reginald De Sutton	John le Wyse	
John de Swafham	John Le Wyse Jr	
John Ffedde	John Morice	
De Roberto Ffrend	Thomas Parch	
Batholomew fit Bathi	Andrew Poul	
John Fit Nicholas	Galfro Pposito	
John fit Petri	John Rolf	
William Gatele	John Rolf Jr	
Henry Gernon	Thomas Rolfe	
Hugo Glenewed	Robert Squill	
Alexander Godfrey	Thomas Waleys (the Quarrier)	
John Hankyn (The Chaplain)	William Wyngeperie	
Peter Hankyn	Gilbert Wynnock	
Mabilia Helewys	Elena Wynnok	
Robert Helewys	Nicholas Wyrel	
Thomas Helewys	Robert Ydeyn	
Gilbert Kateline		

In respect of the assizes of bread and ale, from the end of the thirteenth century, up to the seventeenth century ale-tasters were appointed by the Ramsey manor court. In Burwell as in most of the Ramsey Manors, a number of 'officials' were appointed, including a reeve and a beadle (constables), jurors and, from 1350[20,] fenreeves who had responsibility for fen issues such as drainage. It is also likely that in keeping with other Ramsey Manors an affeeror, an officer responsible for assessing manorial amercements and fines, a hayward responsible for the protection of hedges and other constables were appointed as required.

In the early days of the manor all the officials were appointed by the 'whole homage'. By the fifteenth century appointments such as the beadle, reeve and other constables were appointed by the jurors. The people filling all these posts were all local people and it was considered to be an honour to be appointed. However failure to accept the post always resulted in a fine as did a failure to carry out the job properly. The earliest record of the Jurors of Burwell is in the Ramsey Abbey Cartularies of 1114–30[1] (Table 17.).

1114–1134		1134–1160	
Name	Trade	Name	Trade
Morin		Rainoldi	
Alanus son of Bertae		Alanus son of Bertae	
Alfgarus de Elsworthe		Alfgarus de Elsworthe	
Godwin Corvesarius	Cordwainer	Godwin Corvesarius	Cordwainer
Arnaldus Camerarius	Servant (of the Chamber)	Ernaldus Camerarius	Servant (of the Chamber)
Ricardus et Imecan coci	Cook	Ricardus et Imecan coci	Cook
Haraldus Braceator	Brewer	Haraldus Braceator	Brewer
Gosfridus son of Everardi		Gaufridus son of Everardi	
Thomas Fabri	Builder	Thomas Fabri	Builder
Godricus Fabri	Builder	Godricus Fabri	Builder
Robertus Cementarii	Stone Mason	Robertus Cementarii	Stone Mason
Richardus Cementarii	Stone Mason	Richardus Cementarii	Stone Mason
Osburnus Vitrarius	Victualler	Osburnus Vitrarius	Victualler
AEdnothus de Biri		Ednothus de Biri	
Warinus Vinitor	Vineyard Worker	Warinus Vinitor	Vineyard Worker
Hereberus Marescallus	Marsh Worker?	Hereberus Marescallus	Marsh Worker?
Ernaldus de Begavilla		Ernaldus de Begavilla	
Ricardus et Ingelramnus son of Thurstani		Ricardus et Ingelramnus son of Thurstani	
Warin Cepel			
Ricardus Pistor	Baker		
Alfstanus de Heithmundegrave			

Table 18 *Jurors of Burwell 1114 – 1160 (from Ramsey Abbey Cartularii).*
Note: the texts in the Cartularium are not usually dated and the date ranges equate to the reign of the abbot referred to in the text, rather than actual years served as juror.

However, as noted above much of the business of the manorial courts was related to minor infringements and manorial management issues such as admissions, surrenders and other rental matters. Gaining the ability to rent a house or land in the manor was not easy because a person had to apply to the court for admission to the manor. This required a fee known as the *gersumarum*. The fee to the lord varied considerably. Sometimes it was a monetary fee as shown in this court entry for the 11 October 1400,

> *'John Peytour: One plot with building with 15 acres of land once held by Robert atte Brygge, in bondage for 20 years, rendering annually 16s as rent at the customary times, and in all things as did Robert. Gersumarum.: 6d.'*

Alternatively the *gersumarum* could be a fee in kind such as this entry for the same court where two capons are paid as the following example shows.

> *'Thomas Schipwreyght; one tenement with one building and 15 acres previously held by Alexander Sparwe in arentatio from the previous michaelmas for 10 years, rendering annually 20s, with 4d for capitagium, at the customary times. Gersumarum.: two capons.'*

In a few cases the court could waive the fee. This is seen in the case of Thomas Bosoun, a chaplain, who also presented at the court on 11 October 1400.

'Thomas Bosoun, Chaplain: eight acres of demesne land lying at Le Nesse, four acres of demesne land at 'Bynnges' and 'Rebynes Hanedlond', four acres of demesne land at Estfeld (East Field) previously held by John Walden, two acres of demesne at Ayllyhanedlond recently held by John Walden, two acres of demesne in Dychfeld at Galowhyll (Gallows Hill) and one rod of demesne in Northfeld (North Field) at Braddeye (The Broads) touching upon Gyllescroft, and three acres of demesne in Le Braach, (The Breach) from the previous michaelmas for 20 years, rendering annually 20s 6d at the customary times. Gersumarum.: excused by the senchal.'

The leet court also levied similar scales of fees for people withdrawing from the rental agreement, known as a surrender, as this example from 1413 shows,

'Robert Chapman, for the surrender of one tenement of 15 acres once held by William Swynedd, to the use of John Rolf Jr., for 30 years, rendering annually 23s. at the customary times and all other services and customes owed therein. G.: excused because of rent increase.'

Clearly here the rent increase had made the rental of this land by Robert Chapman unviable and, as he was unable to pay the *gersumarum,* he was excused.

In Burwell and a few other Ramsey manors we have the unusual occurrence in the records of a payment being made by villeins to the abbey in case they performed a misdemeanour. This is seen in the thirteenth century extents where as part of customary duties a payment was levied to *fulstyngpounde.* For example:

'Alan Rufus....... And sixteen pence and one farthing to fulstyngpounde.'

When a misdemeanour was committed the accused paid only six pence to the court either at the beginning or the end of the trial and no more, or they could withhold payment pending the judgement and pay twelve pence. Thus the payment to the *fulstingpounde* acted like an insurance against having to pay more if the villein ended up in court.

The court, as well as dealing with entries, surrenders and misdemeanours, also gave permission for people in the servile classes to marry. Again a fee was usually levied as can be seen from this example from the court of 2 August 1398.

'Helena, daughter of Thomas Sparwe and naif (native) of the lord, pays 5s for the licence to marry whom ever she wishes.'

As with the land *gersumaria,* the amounts of fine varied, based upon the ability to pay, so that it appears that a pauper presenting for permission to marry paid nothing, as this example from the court of the 6 October 1398 shows.

'William Westmorland pays 8d for licence to marry Agnes, daughter of Thomas Swyn and naif of the lord. And he pays no more because he is a pauper.'

The following is an example of a common fine from the court of 1413.

'John Poket: all lands and tenements recently held by John Plumbe, from Michaelmas for 18 years, rendering annually as did John Plumbe, with a rent increase this year of 12d., and common fine, the reaping of one acre of wheat and one acre of Barley, and the carrying of grain. He will repair and maintain the property at his own expense. Pledges: William Poket and William Jay. G.: six capons.'

When a court levied a fine it was the personal responsibility of the reeve and/or the beadle to collect it. If they failed to collect the fine they were responsible for it and it could be taken from their personal assets. Consequently across most Ramsey Abbey manors in the early fifteenth century the majority of debt owed to the abbey is listed as debt owed by the reeve or the beadle. In the example of John Poket he had to provide two guarantors to ensure that the fine was paid, in this case it was for work to be carried out, so that the reeve or the beadle did not become liable for it.

Fines for breaking bye-laws in Burwell were originally kept by the lords of the manors but, as a record of 1412[11] shows, in that year profits were split three ways. One third went to Ramsey Abbey, one third to the lord of the Tiptoft Manor and one third being split between the two parish churches. Dullinghams, while holding its own court, did not enter into this arrangement. This may be due to its possible ownership by the monks of Ely by this time.

Table 19 *Tenants of the Ramsey Abbey Manor appearing before the leet court.*

Name		Year of appearance
John	Aillesham	Record of 1401 although he died in 1399
Adam	Alot	1407
Robert	atte Brigge	1400, 1409
John	Atte Hill	1401, 1411
Nicholas	atte Hyll	1401
John	Ayllewyn	1404
John	Baret	1401
Joanna (widow of Robert)	Barrow	1417
John	Barwe (a Chaplain)	1409
Robert	Barwe (Brother of John)	1409
John	Benet	1411, 1417
Hugo	Berker	1409
George Hervy	Bocher	1417
John	Bocher	1401
Thomas	Bosoun (a Chaplain)	1400
Radulph	Calvesbane	1405, 1415
Simon	Calvesbane	1405, 1413, 1417
John	Chapman	1413
Richard	Chapman Barkere	1400
John	Clerk (alias Blaunteyn)	1417
William	Crabbe	1417
John	Derye	1405
John	Dyry	1409
William	Ermyn	1415
John	Fabbe	1407
Richard	Fabbe	1407
John	Frache	1405
Thomas	Gardener	1411
Richard	Garyner	1411
William	Gell	1413
Elena	Helewys	1409
Thomas	Higenye	1405
William	Howghton	1400, 1410, 1418
William	Ideyne	1400, 1415

Table 19. Tenants of the Ramsey Abbey Manor appearing before the leet court. (Continued)

Thomas	Ideyngne	1405
William	Jay	1413, 1418
John	Jemes	1400, 1417
John	Kent	1410, 1413
Alicia	Kirkeby	1407
Constancia	Kyng	1401
John	Kyng	1401
John	Kyng Jr	1401
Radulf	Lane (a Freeman)	1400
Alexander	Lyne	1410
Radulph	Lyne	1415
Thomas	Lyne	1415
Andrew	Morice	1409
Thomas	Paxman	1409
John	Payntor or Peytour	1400, 1418
Joanna	Perye	1404
John	Plumbe	1413
Thomas	Plumbe	1400, 1409
John	Poket	1413
Henry	Pomeray	1404
Thomas	Poul or Poule	1410, 1411
Edmund	Poul	1401
John	Prikke	1411
John	Pryk Jr.	1418
John	Purt	1418
Thomas	Pury	1418
Robert	Rede	1400
John	Rolf	1400, 1418
John	Rolf Jr	1417
Thomas	Rolf Jr	1415
John	Roolee Jr	1405
Radulph	Rower	1418
Thomas	Rower	1400, 1413
John	Sadde	1410, 1417
Thomas	Schipwreyght	1400
Laurence	Skenale	1413
John	Smart	1404
Richard	Sowtheman	1411
John	Sparwe	1400, 1410, 1417
Thomas	Sparwe	1400
Alexander	Sparwe	1400
Richard	Spencer	1418
Thomas	Stroppe or Stop	1405, 1411
Simon	Styward	1400, 1415
Thomas	Swasham	1400
William	Swyn	1400
Thomas	Swyne	1400
William	Swynedd	1413

Table 19 *Tenants of the Ramsey Abbey Manor appearing before the leet court. (Continued)*

William	Taillor or Taylor (alias Poket)	1409, 1413, 1415, 1418
Thomas	Webstere	1417
Richard	Wilkyn	1407
Robert	Wilkyn	1407, 1415
Richard	Wrighte	1418
John	Wryght	1405
Cecilia	Wyat (widow of Nicholas Rolf)	1405
Robert	Wyot	1400
John	Wyot (Wyett)	1417
William	Ydeigne	1411

The County Court

Serious crimes were often dealt with at the County Court. The judges heard a variety of cases on behalf of the king. They then reported to the King's Commissioners, recording the events in the Patent Rolls. The commissioners themselves moved around the country and would hear complaints where necessary of instances such as riotous behaviour. The commission hearing such cases was referred to as the Commission of Oyer and Terminer. In 1279[3] a priest from Burwell, William Kennett, was recorded as the secretary to the Cambridge Court while another, Bartholomew, son of Bartholomew, was recorded as a juror.

Throughout the early to mid fourteenth century there exist a number of surviving records in the Patent Rolls of Burwellians who, due to criminal activities or riotous behaviour, found themselves before senior courts and who therefore came to the notice of the King's Commissioners.

Examples of Burwell people being named at the Commission of Oyer and Terminer, include:

- 28 May 1322 – a number of people including Henry De Gernova of Burwell entered the Manor of Soham and committed 'divers trespass'.

- 15 August 1327 – John Peivre of Burwell was among a multitude of people who tried to stop the Abbot of Ely from holding his manorial court. They assaulted the abbot's men and broke the doors of the dwelling, and of the bishop's house and stole timber and other goods.

- 24 February 1349 – The Countess of Pembroke (who lived at the Abbey of Denny which she had founded) claimed that two bondmen who had escaped from her service and had been captured in Norfolk, were set free by the people of Burwell as they passed through the town en route to Denny. 'Some evil-doers took them by force from these (her men) on the way at Borewell, in the County of Cambridge and maintained them against her so that she cannot do justice to them (the prisoners) as she ought'. In the process the people of Burwell assaulted the countess's men 'whereby she lost their service for a great deal of time' and carried away her goods.

- 20 February 1358 – Thomas Taillour and John de Swafham, both of Burwell, and other unnamed individuals broke into the closes of Thomas de Eltesle, Henry Tangemere, William de Horewode, John Raison and John de Role, burnt their houses and carried away their goods and assaulted their servants.

The most interesting case to be heard by the Commission of Oyer and Terminer is that involving John Crauden, Prior of Ely, whose family owned much land in Swaffham Prior. There appears to have been some rivalry between the Abbey of Ramsey and its larger sister foundation at Ely. The Abbey of Ely had interests in Swaffham Prior and in particular at Reach. In 1337 the rivalry spilt over as Prior Crauden was returning to Ely through Burwell.

The Commission of Oyer & Terminer, meeting on 4 March 1337, recorded the following case:

'To John De Shardlow, Ralph De Bockyng, Geoffrey Seman and John De Bridgeham (commissioners), pursuant to the statute of Northampton that none should go or ride armed or lead an armed force, to break the peace. On complaint of John Crauden, Prior of Ely, that John Hankyn of Borewell, Chaplain, William Malverne, Edmund Hubbard, John son of William Malverne, John son of John Legis, Andrew Poul, Alexander Godefrey, Robert Taillour, Robert Karlewyne, Thoms De Holme, Richard Grater, Ivo Grater, Gilbert Catelyn, Thomas Stryke, John son of Nicholas, Nicholas Elycok, Henry Fallenwolle, Geoffrey Oky, Richard ate Barre, Thomas Bonifant, John Heyne, Henry Swon, Richard Swon, John Swon, Thomas Lyne, Robert Frende, Peter Frays, John Wylkyn, Ralph Scroppe, Thomas Scroppe, Gilbert Role, John le Smyth, Thomas le Smyth, John Hildeyne, Thomas Fedde, John Bere, Henry Driver, John Lacy, John son of Ralph, John son of Thomas son of Ralph, John Morse, Thomas Helewys, John Stiward, John De Reche, Robert Hidayne or Borewell and a great multitude of others bringing an armed force and ringing the bells of the town of Borewell, for this assaulted him at Borewell, in the County of Cambridge and followed him with like insults to Landewade, there imprisoned him and assaulted his men and servants in both towns.'

Prior John Crauden was an important figure at Ely and it is known that he had relatives who owned land in Swaffham Prior and at Reach Among these was Hugh Crauden who held the Advowson of St Mary's church, Swaffham Prior. He had a property of his own in Swaffham for which, in 1332–1333, a payment was made to a local builder to 'construct a certain chamber there' (Ely Treasurers Roll 1332–33). It is probable that he used this as a retreat and on at least one occasion abbey officials visited the prior at Swaffham on official business. For example in 1337 Alan of Walsingham made a charge against expenses for visiting the prior at Swaffham.

Disputes relating to land, the detention of deeds and the alienation of land was dealt with by the Court of Chancery. There are seventeen such documents remaining from the medieval period, which either directly relate to property in Burwell or to Burwell residents and properties elsewhere. Whilst most of the surviving documents relate to disputes, as the following examples show the Court of Chancery dealt with a range of land issues.

1298	Grant of Settlement	'Payn Tibetot to settle the manor Nettlestead and the advowsons of the churches of Nettlestead and Blakenham (Suffolk) on himself for life, with remainder to William his son and his heirs.' (He retained a number of manors including Burwell).

Location	Reference	Year	Record Office Description
Bodelian Library Oxford	Bodl.11653,f113 (Rawl.3.319)	1242	Court Roll Extracts – Tiptofts Manor
British Library	Add.Roll. 34332– 34766, 39594 39720	1243–1666	Court Rolls, accompts of various officers
P.R.O.	SC 2/179/10	1299–1300	Court Rolls – Burwell Court: 28 Edw I
P.R.O.	SC 2/179/11	1301–1302	Court Rolls – Burwell Court: 29, 30 Edw I
P.R.O.	SC 2/179/15	1307–1308	Court Rolls – Burwell Court: 1–2 Edw II
P.R.O.	SC 2/179/16	1312	Court Rolls – Burwell Court: 5 Edw II
P.R.O.	SC 2/179/20	1322–1323	Court Rolls – Burwell Court: 15–16 Edw II
P.R.O.	SC 2/179/21	1323	Court Rolls – Burwell Court: 16 Edw II
P.R.O.	SC 2/179/22	1325–1327	Court Rolls – Burwell Court: 18–20 Edw II
P.R.O.	SC 2/155/71	1335	Court Rolls – various manors including Burwell,
P.R.O.	SC 2/179/32	1348	Court Rolls – Burwell Court: 21 Edw III
P.R.O.	SC 2/179/33	1350	Court Rolls – Burwell Court: 23 Edw III
P.R.O.	SC 2/179/34	1351	Court Rolls – Burwell Court: 24 Edw III
P.R.O.	SC 2/179/39	1373–1374	Court Rolls – Burwell Court: 46–47 Edw III
P.R.O.	SC 2/179/45	1399–1400	Court Rolls – Burwell Court: 1–2 Hen IV
P.R.O.	SC 2/179/51	1408	Court Rolls – Burwell Court: 9 Hen IV
P.R.O.	SC 2/179/52	1410	Court Rolls – Burwell Court: 11 Hen IV
P.R.O.	SC 2/179/53	1411–1412	Court Rolls – Burwell Court: 12,13 Hen IV
P.R.O.	SC 2/179/56	1420	Court Rolls – Burwell Court: 7 Hen V
P.R.O.	SC 2/179/63	1438–1440	Court Rolls – Burwell Court: 16–18 Hen VI
P.R.O.	SC 2/179/66	1452–1454	Court Rolls – Burwell Court: 29–32 Hen VI
P.R.O.	SC 2/179/67	1454–1455	Court Rolls – Burwell Court: 34–35 Hen VI
P.R.O.	SC 2/179/41	1483	Court Rolls – Burwell Court: 1 Rich III
P.R.O.	SC 2/179/73	1487–1488	Court Rolls – Burwell Court: 2–3 Hen VII
P.R.O.	SC 2/179/74	1490–1492, 1493	Court Rolls – Burwell Court:5–7,9 Hen VII
P.R.O.	SC 2/179/86	1526–1529	Court Rolls – Burwell Court: 17–20 Hen VIII
P.R.O.	R55/7/81	1580–1586	Court Rolls for Tiptofts Manor
P.R.O.	R56/6/1-10	1643–1694	Court Rolls for Tiptofts Manor
British Library	Add.Roll. 58885	1650–1656	Court Rolls of Burwell Tiptofts Manor 1650–1656
British Library	Add. 45880. f. 34	1699	Court Roll, Manor of Burwell Ramseys

Table 20 *Surviving medieval and immediate post-medieval Court Rolls for Burwell Manors.*

This particular record relates to an inquisition taken as a result of an application to the Crown for a licence to alienate land.

1313	Grant of Land	'Edmund son of Alexander de Herdwyck, to grant land in Burwell to the abbot and convent of Ramsey, in exchange for land by the churchyard of the church of St Mary, there to be granted to Gregory the Parson, the grantor retaining land in Burwell.'

This reference relates to the grant and exchange of land by Alexander allowing for the expansion of St Mary's churchyard. Such a grant was not legal without it being passed by the Chancery. A similar example relates to the grant of land in Burwell to found a Chantry in Burrough Green.

1406	Endowment	'Katherine late wife of John De Burgh, knight, Henry Brodyng, Chaplain, William Aleyn, William Chevele, and John Rougham to found a chantry at the altar of the Blessed Virgin in the church of Burrough Green and to endow it with a messuage and land in Burrough Green and rent from 'Seint-Omerys Maner' and 'le Peend' in Burwell.'

Medieval Economy

Burwell has always been a hive of industry and in documents throughout the medieval period references can be found to a variety of trades and trades-folk.

Milling

At the time of the compilation of the Domesday Book in 1086, Burwell was recorded as having four mills. Two belonged to Count Alan and two to Ramsey Abbey. Their location is not described in the Domesday Book. However from later documents the location of two mills is known. One of the Ramsey Abbey mills was near the Exning parish boundary close to Haycross way. This mill had ceased working by 1150 due to a lack of water[7]. The water supplying it would have been that from Warbraham Water, which in this and the last century only flows at times of very heavy rainfall. This therefore suggests that this stream was in continuous flow up to the early 1100s and probably explains the route of the parish boundary to the east.

The other Ramsey Abbey mill was situated at the Ness. The Ness family held the freehold of this mill and ground the abbey's corn free of toll. In 1259 Fabian de Ness sold the freehold to the abbey along with its millstream, ponds and 26 acres of land[31]. The purchase by Abbot Hugh de Sulgrave took place on 7 November 1259, his anniversary as abbot. He then ordained that the income from the mill was to provide for a mass and other religious celebrations on the day of his anniversary in perpetuity. While sold to the abbey the Ness family continued to live by and run the mill on a rental basis as is recorded in an extent,

> 'Henry de Nesse holds twenty four acres, and a certain mill for twenty shillings. And he ought to grind the whole farm of Burwelle without toll.'

From 1300 the abbey was letting the mill. The miller paid the abbey rent in corn (tollcorn), usually 25 quarts or more. This arrangement certainly continued until 1320 and the mill is recorded as still grinding in 1340. The lease agreements included fishing rights over the millpond and this was still being let in the fifteenth century. An example of the lease is given in the *Liber Gersumarum* for 1399. It reads:

> 'William Taylor, alias Poket and John Toys: The fishpond of La Nesse, with adjoining meadows and ponds and the mill dam, previously held by Richard Fraunceys, from the previous Michaelmas for 10 years, rendering this year 10s, and each year thereafter 11s 4d at the customary times. Further they will maintain the properties both regarding ditches and all other necessities, at their own expense, with the exception that the bailiff will assign 20 opera of the customaries of the lord in assistance, and the customaries will be suitably rewarded by the firmarii when they come. Further the Lord will be kept free of damage regarding anyone by them during the aforesaid time. G: excused because of a rent increase of 40d.'

This mill is thought to have been abandoned around the year 1500 as no records exist after that time.

Map 8 *Portion of 1768 Map of Newmarket Heath showing High Town, with the Tiptofts Manor windmill and Milne Lane.*

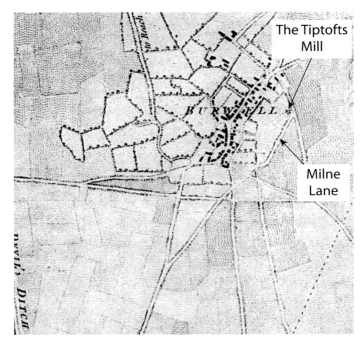

The location of the Tiptofts watermill is not known. A watermill on the manor was recorded as still operating in 1314 and was still being leased from the manor in 1627[12]. It is also known that by 1298 the Tiptofts Manor had a windmill[13]. This mill with a lane leading to it (Milnway)[14] was sited in East Field and was probably the reason that East Field was later renamed Mill Field. A mill was still held as a copyhold of the Tiptofts Manor in 1580[15] and 1640[16]. The mill is clearly shown on a map of Newmarket Heath, which shows High Town in 1768.

Brewing

While a brewer named Harold and a victualler named Osborn are recorded in jurors lists in the 1100s[7] in medieval England brewing was a trade generally carried out by women. Known as 'ale wives', these women did this as part of their year's work. Dedicated breweries were unknown. Burwell appears to have had between ten and 15 such ale wives at any time[4]. From a document of the year 1400, 13 are recorded[5] who vary in the frequency of producing brews, from six to 20 times per year. Some of these brewed annually, selling their wares at Reach Fair. No alehouses are recorded for Burwell in the medieval period. Ale production was strictly monitored and regulated and the manorial court employed ale-tasters for both Burwell and East Reach. Two or three such ale-tasters were employed by the Ramsey Abbey court to serve Burwell and Reach from at least 1312, records existing from that year and 1429[27].

Ale was particularly important in the demesne economy because in many cases ale was given, along with bread, to those undertaking customary works on the lord's land. The following extract from the 1216 extent shows this:

'And he (Walter) will mow an acre and a half and he will receive therefore loaves and companage.'

As well as the production of ale, the Burwell Manor contributed in the early medieval period to the production of the abbey's wine. A vineyard was associated with the manor house and initially tenants were required to maintain the hedge surrounding it. However, by the thirteenth century this was replaced by a tax (winesilver) for its upkeep and 36 men were required to harvest the grapes when they were ripe. It is not clear for how long the vineyard remained in existence but by 1297[29] there was a meadow by that name suggesting that the former vineyard had been turned over to meadow.

Butchers and Bakers

As Table 17 shows, the village had a *pistor* (baker), Richard[7], who was also a juror at sometime in the period 1114–1160. In a number of Court Rolls[6] of the fourteenth century butchers and bakers are referred to, but no detail can be ascertained from these records to calculate the number of such trades operating in the village.

Builders, Masons and Quarrying

As is the case for the bakers, the earliest reference to builders or masons in Burwell is to be found in the Ramsey Abbey Cartularies[7] where, in a list of jurors (Table 17) from Burwell, we have four names; two *fabri* (builders or workmen) called Thomas and Godric and two *Cementarii* (stone masons) called Robert and Richard. Given the dates of the two sections of the Cartularii where they are mentioned, it is likely that these men may have been among those responsible for the building of the lower sections of St Mary's church tower.

Other builders and masons from Burwell were involved in building projects well away from the village. Such Burwell men are named in the lists of builders working on Ely Cathedral in 1350 and at Windsor Castle[8]. This is not surprising because stone from Burwell quarries had been used from at least 1295[31] when it was used in the building of Cambridge Castle. It is known that by 1399 Ramsey Abbey[32] owned one of the quarries in Burwell. The earliest reference we have to a named quarryman is to be found in a chancery court dispute of about 1400[28].

| 1400 | Detention of Deeds | 'Nicholas, son and heir of Thomas Waleys, of Burwell, quarrier, and of Agnes, his wife. v. William Heche, late the husband of the said Agnes.: Detention of deeds relating to a messuage and land in Burwell' |

Thomas Waleys appears in the Poll Tax records of the reign of King Edward III (1327 – 1399). Prior to this reference it is recorded in 1279 that a certain Peter Afkil, freeman, was providing stone for Ramsey Abbey as part of the terms of his rental of land. It is likely that Peter was a quarryman, although this is not stated in the document.

The fact that some of the earlier quarries were worked out by the end of the medieval period and filled in is indicated by a seventeenth century sale document which states that, in 1628, a Burwell Bricklayer purchased a ¾ acre meadow known as 'the quarry'.

Carpenters and Smiths

From a late thirteenth century extent of the abbey we have a record of a carpenter. *Willelmus Carpentarius* (William the Carpenter) was, at that time, renting a toft from the abbey.

Smiths appear in the Hundred Roll, which records William de Swafham as providing a shoeing and iron production service as part of his rental agreement. In addition a thirteenth century extent records a certain Walter as providing a smithying service as part of his rental agreement.

Shipwrights, Sailors and Boatmen

Boat building has probably been a feature of Burwell life since man first settled here. As a trade shipwrighting is first recorded in 1332. Records noting a person's occupation as a shipwright, sailor or boatmen are scarce and in the case of Burwell there only appear to be five[9] in the medieval period.

The earliest of these is for boatmen and is found in the Hundred Rolls[3] where two boatmen are recorded. These were Alan Evilchild and Elyas Affaryefen.

In the year 1400 there exists a record in the *Liber Gersumarum* of the Abbey[9] for a family of shipwrights renting a property. The entry reads:

'Thomas the Schipwreyght; one tenement with one building and 15 acres previously held by Alexander Sparwe in arentatio from the previous michaelmas for 10 years, rendering annually 20s., with 4d for capitagium, at the customary times. G.: two capons.'

Another reference of 1444 records a villager as a sailor[10].

Records of ships taking goods from Burwell to Ramsey are more common in the Ramsey documents. For example:

'And he shall take corn to the mill, and flour to the ship, with the villate.'[7]

Fishing and Fishermen

From the earliest times the fens and the lodes were fished for fish and Eels. In addition there were a number of fisheries, often a collection of fishponds, associated with manorial sites or mills such as that at The Ness. Areas such as the weirs were used to catch eels that would swim in the faster flowing waters. Fishing nets were controlled in size from the fourteenth century[33], in order not to deplete stocks of fish. Fishing was clearly important to the manorial economy because in the records of Ramsey Abbey there is a reference to land being set aside to provide food for the fishermen.

Original Latin Text	Translation
Clariz et Robertus de Clervaus et Waterus de Bamvile et Radulphus de Osdene tenent unam piscaturam pro duodecim solidis.	'Clariz and Robert de Clervaus and Walter de Bamwile and Ralph Osdene hold one fishery for twelve shillings.
Et quinque acras terrae arabilis ad cibum piscatoris.	And five acres of arable land for the food of the fishermen.'

Only one fisherman, Thomas the Fisherman, is recorded in a thirteenth century extent of the manor.

Most manorial documents give an indication of the presence of stockmen of the manorial farms but do not give a name. For example, in the thirteenth century extent of the Ramsey manor we have reference to '*The shepherd of the sheep has in like manner fifteen acres of the demesne by the same service, but he has that now for his service and food by the year.*' Such references give an indication of the importance of the shepherd in that, for keeping the abbot's sheep, he has 15 acres of rent-free land for his food. However, in another thirteenth century extent there is a record of '*Johannes Pastor*' (John the Shepherd) and a document of 1335 records the trade of John Wylkins as husbandman. Other husbandmen are named in fifteenth century documents, including:

- John Wyett   - 1417
- John ate Hill   - 1418
- John Sparwe   - 1427

As much of the land in Burwell up to the fifteenth century was given over to arable production, the livestock population in and around the village for any animal other than sheep was probably quite small. This being the case it is unlikely that the Ramsey manor employed any other staff to manage its livestock other than the shepherd and possibly a husbandman. This might explain the scant references to such trades.

Other Trades

In keeping with any thriving community medieval Burwell had thatchers, wheelwrights, carpenters, smiths, harness makers, shoemakers and tailors. An early example of a reference to people in such trades is that referred to above from the Ramsey Abbey Cartularies[7] in which, in the charter of Reginald Abbot of Ramsey (1114–1130), we find a list of jurors from Burwell including the following people (not already listed) and their trades:

Richard et Imecanus *coci*, (cook)

Herbert, a Farrier

From the extent of the mid 1200's we find:

Simon the Thresher

Ivo the clerk

Elias the clerk

John the clerk

Alfric the merchant

Bernard (Carter)

Alan Rufus (Carter)

Richard the servant (described as the 'faithful servant')

It is also possible to identify further indications of trades from placenames in documents. For example, a document of the seventeenth century records a fire in which a cottage in 'Shoe Makers Row' was burned down. There are also fifteenth century references to 'Fysshestrete' (1423) and 'Fyssher street' (1440), perhaps indicating where the fishermen lived.

Markets and Fairs

Markets and fairs in medieval England were important as a source of income both for those trading goods and for the lord of the manor. Within the parish there were three such events; Reach Fair, Burwell Market and Burwell Whitsun Fair. Fairs and markets were licensed by the Crown and, in the case of Reach Fair, held at Rogation Monday. A charter was granted to the Burgesses of Cambridge in 1201[20] to hold a fair on that day.

From about 1280 they sought and gained control of Reach Fair despite the fact that a fair at Reach was never mentioned by name in the original charter. Tolls were levied on the fair and, by the fourteenth century, the Borough of Cambridge took two thirds of these while the abbey of Ely took one third because the prior claimed to have a royal grant allowing the priory to do this.

Today we think of fairs as places of enjoyment but to the medieval peasant they were another form of market. Reach Fair was one of the biggest in the region. Held on the fair green created by the levelling of the Devil's dyke, a variety of wares were on sale from the stallholders who rented their pitches from either Ramsey Abbey or the Monks of Ely.

In 1300 the bailiff of Ramsey Abbey was at the fair purchasing iron to make ploughshares and nails, the latter specifically for cartwheels.[21] The Sacristan's rolls of Ely tell us that at about the same time the Abbey of Ely was also purchasing iron and steel at the fair[22]. Similar records for the early fourteenth century tell us that the Sacrist of Ely also purchased timber, nails and pegs at the fair in the years up to 1360[22].

In its first one hundred years, Reach Fair appears to have been a busy market but by 1400 it appears to have been in decline. In that year Ramsey Abbey found itself unable to hire out pitches for stalls[23]. A similar story is shown in the records for the monastery in Ely which show that, in 1420[24,] it had unlet plots for the fair of that year. Alongside this decline in the traditional fair, a new horse fair emerged. Exactly when this first appeared is not certain but it is known to have existed by 1361. In that year the priory of Ely records show that there were plots to let next to a horse market[25] and the fair. By 1432 it was known as 'the horse fair'[26] and it remained a feature of Rogation Monday in Reach until the nineteenth century.

The two Burwell events were granted by licence to Robert Tibetot (Tiptoft) on 28 November 1277[30]. Robert's grant was to hold an annual fair at Whitsun and a weekly, Wednesday market at his manor of Burwell. Other than the grant itself little is known

Figure 15 *69 North Street, a medieval house of about 1450.*

about the market and its life may have been quite short. The market and the fair are likely to have been held on the former green next to pound hill. The Whitsun fair continued there until the nineteenth century only moving, to the opposite side of Parsonage Lane, after the loss of the green.

Housing

Just as land was rented, most people rented their homes from the manors. Evidence contained in documents such as the *Liber Geresumarium* of Ramsey Abbey shows that those renting houses and land were held responsible for their upkeep including, if necessary, their rebuilding. An example of this is to be found in a record of 1405:

> 'Same Radulph Cavesbane: eight acres of servile land once held by Thomas Ideyngne, in bondage for 30 years, rendering annually in all things as did Thomas and suit to court, with the condition that Radulph will build two houses on the property at his own expense and with his own lumber within the next two years. G:. 2s 4d and no more because of extensive repairs.'

Few complete medieval dwellings exist in the village today. One of the few that has survived is 69 North Street. With the exception of a seventeenth century gable end, a twentieth century extension and sixteenth century upper floor, this house retains an almost complete medieval timber frame.

References

1. CHRONICON ABBATIAE RAMESEIENSIS, 1886 *Chronicles and Memorials of Great Britain and Ireland during the Middle Ages (Rerum Britannicarum Medii Aevi Scriptores): The Rolls Series*, London.
2. Dewindt, E B, 1976 *The Liber Gersumarum of Ramsey Abbey: a calendar and index of B.L. harley MS.445*, Pontifical Institute of Medieval Studies, Toronto.
3. Illingworth, W, and Caley, J, *Rotuli Hundredorum temp Henry III & Edward I*, Record Commission, 1812 – 1818.
4. P.R.O., SC 2/179/11, m. 7d.; SC 2/179/16, m. 9.; SC 2/179/22, m. 7.; SC 2/179/34, m.3. (Court Rolls, 1&2 Henry IV)
5. P.R.O., SC 2/179/45, m. 6. (Court Rolls, 1&2 Henry IV)
6. P.R.O., SC 2/179/20, m. 2d; SC 2/179/52, m. 2; SC 2/179/63, m. 7d. (Court Rolls, 1&2 Henry IV)
7. CARTULARIUM MONASTERII DE RAMESEIA, 1884 *Chronicles and Memorials of Great Britain and Ireland during the Middle Ages (Rerum Britannicarum Medii Aevi Scriptores): The Rolls Series*, London.
8. Harvey, J, 1984, *Medieval Architects*, London, 47.
9. P.R.O., JUST 2/18, rot. 58 (County roll of Edmund de Oving. 14-39 Edw III); SC 2/179/45, m. 6.
10. Dewindt, E B, 1976 *The Liber Gersumarum of Ramsey Abbey: a calendar and index of B.L. harley MS.445*, Subsidia Medievalia 7. Pontifical Institute of Medieval Studies, Toronto, 36 and 300.
11. P.R.O., SC 2/179/53, m. 8 (Court Rolls, 1&2 Henry IV)
12. P.R.O., C 134/.37, No 2. (Inquisitions 8 & 9 Edward II)
13. P.R.O., C 133/85, No 3. (6) (Inquisitions 21 & 22 Edward I)
14. P.R.O., SC 2/179/15, m. 9
15. C.R.O., R 55/7/81: (Court Rolls for Tiptofts Manor, 26 Elizabeth I)
16. C.R.O. R 56/6/1: (Court Rolls for Tiptofts Manor,19 & 20 Carles I)
17. Dewindt, E B, 1976 *The Liber Gersumarum of Ramsey Abbey: a calendar and index of B.L. harley MS.445*, Subsidia Medievalia 7. Pontifical Institute of Medieval Studies, Toronto,
18. Rotulii Hundredorum, Records Commission, i. 54; ii. 498.
19. P.R.O., SC 6/765/6, m; SC 6/765/7, m. 4.; SC 6/765/9; SC 6/765/11, m 4. (Court Rolls, Records of the Reeve, 35 Edw I to 1 Edw II – Relating to Fees paid)

20. P.R.O., MAF 68/5161
21. P.R.O., SC 6/765/6
22. Sacrist Rolls of Ely, ed. F.R. Chapman, ii. 8.
23. P.R.O., SC 6/765/10
24. Cambridge University Library, Reference: E.D.C., 7/12/6. I Henry VI.
25. Cambridge University Library, Reference: E.D.C., 7/12/5: 33,37,46, 46 Edward III.
26. Cambridge University Library, Reference: E.D.C., 7/12/6. II Henry VI.
27. P.R.O., SC 2/179/10: 5 Edward II ; SC2/179/56: 7 Henry VI
28. P.R.O., C 1/111/34
29. Neilson, N., (1910) Customary Rents, p178 – 9.
30. H.M.S.O., (1903 – 27), Calendar of Charter Rolls (1257-1300), p206.
31. *Proceedings of the Cambridge Antiquarian Society*, **26**, 85.
32. P.R.O., SC 6/765/10.
33. P.R.O., SC 2/179/10. Manuscript I and SC 6/765/11. Manuscript 7d

Chapter 6

Churches and Chapels

The formation of the parish system, whereby a church served an area of land coterminous with a manor (usually a village and its fields), gradually evolved during the late Saxon period. Frequently churches were sited on land given by the pious lord close to his manor house.

The parish system was largely completed by the mid twelfth century by which time the existence of most village churches is indicated by documentary evidence. The archaeology of many churches where no evidence of early work exists above ground has demonstrated the existence of earlier structures and while this has never been undertaken in Burwell's surviving medieval church, St Mary's, there is little doubt that at church least one and probably two churches existed here before the Norman conquest.

Priests were originally all rectors, being supported by produce from their own land (the glebe) and from offerings and tithes (one tenth of the produce of other landholders). The advowson – the right of presenting a cleric with a living – generally belonged to the Crown or a powerful lord. With the growth of medieval monasticism many advowsons and rectories, and part of their glebe and tithes, were given to religious houses as endowments. This process was known as appropriation. Appropriation rectories were called vicarages because new patrons were obliged to appoint a deputy (vicar) to manage parish affairs. The bishop was responsible for the institution and induction of a cleric to a living, but monasteries were required to assign sufficient maintenance for vicars, who were not to be removed at the whim of the appropriators. Usually the appointment of a vicar, especially a pluralist one, also had to receive royal approval. The vicar received the small tithes (all tithes except grain and hay), a house and gifts to the parish church and its subsidiary chapels.

Within the parish of Burwell there were originally two churches and two chapels, these being:

- St Andrew's church.
- St Mary's church.
- The chapel of St John at Reach.
- The private chapel of the abbot of Ramsey, dedication unknown.

The church of St Andrew also supplied a priest to the chapel of St Nicholas at Landwade.

St Andrew's Church and the Chapel of St Nicholas, Landwade

Today nothing remains of the parish church of St Andrew. The earliest written record to survive is a reference to the church of St Andrew in Burwell in cartularies of the alien priory of Stoke by Clare. Up to about 1170 the advowson of St Andrew's had belonged to Robert, son of Humphrey, who probably gave it by exchange to the priory of Stoke by Clare[1]. The priory of Stoke by Clare was a cell of the priory of Bec in France and thereby considered in later years as an alien priory. Successive bishops of Norwich confirmed the advowson until the early 1200s[2].

The Priory of St Peter and St Mary Magdelen, Fordham, was a small foundation established in about 1200 by Henry, the rural dean of Fordham. It was originally endowed as a hospital but shortly after its foundation it was given over to the order of St Gilbert of Semperingham (the Gilbertines). This was the only truly British religious order. Henry III confirmed this gift in March 1227. Robert, the first prior of the foundation (1205–1227), agreed to pay the priory of Stoke by Clare the £3 due for the rector of St Andrew's. The prior also agreed to lease the advowson and lands in Burwell and Landwade from Stoke for 40s per year, an arrangement that continued up to the dissolution of the monasteries.

By 1279[3] the holdings of the Gilbertine priory included the church of St Andrew, Burwell, with 36 acres of land and the chapel of St Nicholas at Landwade, with 50 acres given by the younger Robert Hastings. From what date the parish of Landwade served as a chapel of Burwell is not recorded. It is however recorded that the parish church of St Andrew, Burwell and its chapel at Landwade had been given in 1246 to the priory of Stoke by Clare by Herluin le Franceys and his wife Avice[4]. Herluin and Avice's gift ensured the full income from the advowson could be received by the priory, and probably ensured that a mass would be said in perpetuity for their souls. In 1254, St Andrew's and the chapel of St Nicholas were valued at 12 marks and in 1291, £12[3].

There are few records surviving from the priory of Fordham and none from the period between 1291 and 1535 when the estates of the priory were valued. The record of 1535 gives a value of £40 14s 4½d to the estates of the priory but does not assign any value to the rectory in Burwell or its chapel at Landwade. On 4 November 1535 Edward Bestney, visiting Fordham Priory, wrote to Cromwell saying that 'the little religious house' in Fordham had a prior, one canon and a yearly income of £26. Fordham Priory was dissolved on 1 September 1538[5].

St Andrew's appears to have been served by canons from Fordham in its early years as no vicarage was ordained. By the sixteenth century the church had its own priest who lodged with the lessee of the priory's farm in Burwell. The lessee had to provide the priest with a chamber at the farmhouse and to allow him 53s 4d per year and two cartloads of barley and hay[6].

Following the dissolution of the priory in 1539, the lessee of the church land was required to provide the priest's pension. The church was in use and well equipped for services in 1552[8] when an inventory of the goods of churches was undertaken. For Burwell St Andrew's the inventory reads:

'taken vi day of August Anno RR. E. VI Sexto by us Richard Wylks clerke, Henry Gooderyke, Thomas Bowles, Thomas Rudston, Esquires Comyssions amongst others assigned for the

surveys and view of all manner of goodes, plate, Jewelis, bells & Orniami (ornaments) as yet be remayninge forthcominge & belonginge to ye poche (parish) churche there.'

The inventory records:

Plate

1 Chalice and Patent of silver and gilt weighing 13 ounces

1 Chalice and Patent of silver and gilt weighing 14 ounces

Ornaments

One Cope of red satin

Another Cope, old, of Silk

One vestment of red velvet

One Cope of green silk

One vestment of blue silk with borders

Two white vestments

One red vestment

One blue vestment with border

2 Latten (a form of brass) candlesticks

Bells

In the steeple, four bells and one hand bell

With the exception of some of the vestments and a chalice left for the maintenance of the church, the commissioners removed all of the other goods.

Unlike the Abbey of Ramsey, Fordham Priory was a poor foundation and St Andrew's was therefore always the lesser of Burwell's two churches. Much of the income for St Andrew's was derived from income from land in Burwell and Reach. Thirty-six acres of this land were originally endowed to the priory of Stoke by Clare. Other lands however were given to the church and these appear to have been managed through a guild. The income from the lands of the guild was given to the church either for the upkeep of the church itself or for particular chapels in the church. In the case of St Andrew's a record from 1542 says that, for the maintenance of the lamp before the Rood, John Roger had given one acre of land in tenure. In addition William Goodwyn gave the church six acres of land for an anniversary. At that time it was in the possession of widow Awdrey Barton. It was usual in such benefactions that the money from the land would have been used to offer a mass in remembrance and on the day of the anniversary.

In 1561[9] the rectory of St Andrews church was leased out to Bartholomew Kempe for 21 years. The details of the lease from the Calendar of Patent Rolls, signed at Redgrave on 13 April 1561 reads:

'Lease for 21 years, by advice of the treasurer etc, for a fine of £40 paid at exchequer, to Batholomew Kempe of the rectory of St Andrew in Burwell in the County of Cambridge, late of Bygginge Priory of the County of Cambridge; with reservations; from Lady Day last; yearly 10l; the lessee to pay yearly to the priest or vicar serving in the church of St Andrew there a pension of 53s 4d and a cartload of hay and a cartload of straw as accustomed.'

By Warranty of the Commissioners

Clearly at this time the church was still being served by a priest or vicar. It is not certain whether one priest was serving both St Andrew's and St Mary's, or if St Andrew's had an incumbent living in the rectory. The only priest of St Andrew's that is known about during this period was John Faunte who had moved from Ramsey Abbey with Abbot John Lawrence to Burwell and who, at John Lawrence's death in 1541, appears to have been living at the Hall. He was certainly rector of St Andrew's in 1551[10, 11] but had moved on a couple of years later.

As with many leases of this period, Bartholomew Kempe did not lease the rectory for the 21 years. In fact he leased it for less than three years because on 14 July 1564 it was leased out to Thomas Reve, William Revet and William Hechins. St Andrew's rectory was but one of a large number of estates across the country that were leased to the three. Whereas these documents refer to 'the Rectory of Burwell St Andrew', it is not the physical building that is being referred to but the lands belonging to the rectory, all of which had sitting tenants. The conditions of the lease being that the priest should be paid from the rental income.

During the reign of King Edward VI, much of the property from church guilds was sold off with the money going to the Crown. In the case of St Andrew's a Patent Roll record details the sale for £1,111 17s 7d of a great deal of former guild-owned land to William Ward, gentleman of London and Richard Venebles, esquire and Sergeant at Arms. Included in this sale were two acres of arable land in the tenure of Thomas Burrowes 'in the common fields of Burwell, Andrews', which had been given for the upkeep of a lamp in the church there[12].

Between 1566 and 1567 Queen Elizabeth I stripped from the guilds what little wealth they had remaining. Once again, a record of the particulars of the sale, dated 10 May 1566, exists. It tells us the details of the land then held by the St Andrew's church guild, for the upkeep of the church and its chapels. This included a messuage (dwelling with the adjoining lands appropriated to the household) in Burwell that had been given to St Andrew's by Richard Parson, one acre and three roods abutting on Hathedd Acre, which were escheats (properties that fell to the feudal lord or to the state for lack of an heir or by forfeiture), two acres of land, of which one lay in 'Dychfield, abutting the Great Dyche', the other in North Field, given by Richard Hancock of Burwell for an Obit (obituary) in the church and half an acre given by Richard Hancock for maintaining the sepulchre light. These lands belonging to St Andrews were granted in 'fee simple' to William Grice, the Queens servant and Charles Newcommen.

In 1571 these lands were once again granted in 'fee simple', this time to Willam James of London and John Grey of Nettlestead in Suffolk. The roll reads:

'In Burwell in the county of Cambridge, given by Richard Parsonne to St Andrews Church there (4d.)in Rechecroftes and abutting on 'Halfheddam', escheated (2d) in Burwell, given by Richard Hancocke of Burwell for an anniversary in Burwell church (2d.) in Burwell by Halfheddam aforesaid, given by said Hancocke for 'a taper light', before the sepulchre in Burwell church (1d.).'

Such was the ruthlessness of the exchequer of Queen Elizabeth I in leasing out church lands that even a graveyard in Reach was leased in 1571. In both the court rolls of Burwell Tiptofts for 1578[13] and a probate record of 1575[14] it is recorded that the churchyard was unfenced and cattle were grazing there. The probate record for a villager records that he doubted if it would be possible for him to be buried there as he had wished.

At sometime between 1600 and his death in 1613, Lee Cotton[15] offered to endow £100 to endow a godly man to take a service in St Andrew's each week, preach monthly and keep a free school in the then disused St Andrew's church. His only stipulation was that the parishioners should repair the church within three years so that it would be fit for worship. Cotton believed that the tenants of Burwell Tiptofts manor, with which the church had been associated over many years, were primarily responsible for its upkeep[15]. The manor of Burwell Tiptofts had certainly believed that it owned the advowson of St Andrew.s in 1569[16].

Lee Cotton's wish did not come true and in 1646 the University of Cambridge purchased the impropriated rectory of St Andrew's and, in the same year, the two parishes were incorporated. This incorporation was drawn up earlier but permission to incorporate took longer. By this time St Andrew's was probably already in a poor state of repair. In the incorporation document, dated 1629, the lessee of the manor of Burwell Rectory, Sir W Russell, was to give up his existing lease and take on a new lease for both St Mary's and St Andrew's. As part of the lease he was charged with repairing and re-edifying the church and repairing the chancel within two years of his re-leasing the manor. This also suggests that the church may have been in a poor state. This document[17] suggests that the purchase of St Andrew's and its rectory by the University may have occurred in or prior to 1629 and the 1646 document was the formal legal approval of the purchase.

Additional stipulations put of Sir William Russell in respect of St Andrews included:

'Once every seven years, he bestows £5 at least for ye beautifying of ye chancel.'

These works were to be at the direction of the vicar. He was also required to provide the stipend of the vicar of St Andrew's and give £13 0s 6d to the poor each year. In addition the two vicars were allowed to have titheable lands for their own use at a rent of £20 per annum. '

'That ye vicars of Burwell shall have a lease of ye small tithes for £20 rent, as they are now.'

Although the stipulation was that the lessee should pay the vicar a stipend, no vicars are recorded as being in post and the church fabric appears to have been largely neglected. It may well have been that a vicar was difficult to recruit to St Andrew's as no vicarage had ever been ordained and the vicar was to lodge with the lessee of the church's lands – a less that satisfactory arrangement.

At the time of incorporation, St Andrew's rectorial glebe and rights to tithe amounted to about 41 acres of arable land. In addition there were six and a half acres of closes and a large barn that had been part of the Fordham Priory farm or homestead. The barn was still standing in 1710 and the closes were still known in 1850 as the Priory Closes[18].

In 1652, the 'slates' were removed from the roof of St Andrew's for use on the new vicarage roof. However there was a protest by the parishioners and the slates were said to have been replaced[19]. The new vicarage for the combined parish was the first on the site of the present vicarage. The former vicarage for St Mary's was the parsonage.

The loss of its lands and the income from them and its subsequent incorporation with St May's eventually led to St Andrew's church being made redundant. By the early 1700s the fabric of the church had become ruinous.

On May 30 1727, at a court session in Newmarket, the *ffeoffees* (trustees) of Burwell church were empowered to take down its remains. A witnessed transcription of the instructions of the court survives in the memorandum and accounts book of the *ffeoffees* for the years 1726 – 30[20]. It reads:

> 'It is ordered by the Reverend Minister and worshipful Michael Hagett official of the Archdeanery of Sudbury that the church wardens of the parish of Burwell in the County of Cambridge be empowered to take down the remains of St Andrews Church in Burwell aforesaid and that the great stones and pillars be laid by and (used?) in some convenient place and that the rubbish shall be used in mending the church ways as they shall be more convenient.'

It is probable that the work was started but not completed because, on 19 September 1743, the antiquarian Cole[21] visited Burwell and gave a good account of what he saw at that time, including the ruins of St Andrew's church which he drew.

Coles account reads:

> 'The part that still remains of ye other church of Burwell shows that in its prosperity it was no inconsiderable church; for by ye ruins of ye grownd that you may easily discover that it consisted of a rown tower, after ye Danish manner of building of churches, at ye west end, a nave, 2 side isles, ye chancel, with a south porch; which with part of the bottom ye said tower & part of ye S. side isle wall are ye chief remains of this church, which was dedicated to St Andrew, & was a vicarage valued in ye Kings Books at £20:00:00.'

Cole goes on to say:

> 'It is but a small distance from its sister church of St Mary, on ye other side of ye road, & stands on a Hill.'

From Cole's drawing and description we can deduce a number of things about the church. Firstly, while smaller than St Mary's, it was quite substantial in size, having a nave, chancel, aisles, tower and porch. It was probably about the same size as either of Swaffham Prior's two churches.

Secondly Cole describes the church as having a round tower. Two round tower churches, Snailwell and Bartlow, remain in Cambridgeshire, both of which are thought to be of eleventh century construction. Such round towers are a peculiarity of East Anglia and a number of them, in both Suffolk and Norfolk, are of the late Saxon or early Norman period. It is therefore quite probable that St Andrew's was a late Saxon or early Norman church.

It is also possible that this church lay within the early Saxon settlement and may have been the church associated with the Anglo-Saxon burial site excavated in the 1930s.

Figure 16 *Drawing of St Andrew's Church, by Cole 1743 showing the South Porch*

S. of ye dilapidated Church of St. Andrew at Burwell.

Figure 17. *The School House built in 1863 on the site of St Andrews Church.*

This contained a number of Christian burials and was located about three or four hundred yards away.

The final destruction of St Andrew's church appears to have occurred in 1772[21] when the new incumbent of St Mary's, a Mr Turner of St John's College, wrote to Cole reporting that he had 'totally pulled down these ruins, in order to make the Church yard more agreeable for his horse'. He also reported finding two bodies in a stone coffin, which he claimed lay in a north to south direction. These he found while 'digging up the foundations'. However it appears that the foundations were not completely dug up because in the notes of Canon A.G. Walpole Sayer it is recorded that when the girls school was built in 1859 on the St Andrew's site, the foundations of the church were clearly visible and a number of carved stones were found. Some of these were moved to the vicarage garden and incorporated into the new church of St Andrew when it was built in North Street in 1863.

Chapel of St Nicholas Landwade

As noted above, the chapel of St Nicholas, Ladwade was served from the mid 1200s by St Andrew's rectory, Burwell. Before 1445, the date when Landwade was accepted as a parish within its own right, it was probably part of Exning Parish. It was only after the chapel there had been rebuilt by the Lord of the Manor, William Cotton, who wanted a larger church that could serve as both church and burial place for his family that it became a separate parish. Despite this, in 1535 it was still attached to Burwell rectory (St Andrew's), which presumably supplied a priest for masses there. A portion of the tithes, however, were due to Exning parish church and remained so even after the parish was formed. It was not until 1763 that the parish was formerly annexed to Exning, although from at least 1548 the church had its own curate who was entitled to all tithes except those due to Exning.

St Mary's Church and its Chapel at Reach

St Mary's, the last parish church to consider, may always have been the larger of Burwell's two churches. It has clear evidence of good quality Norman construction, such as the lower half of the tower, and clearly shows the results of its ownership by the Abbey of

Ramsey from the thirteenth century, although it probably had a number of wealthy benefactors prior to that time. Like St Andrew's, St Mary's probably existed in Saxon times. As a royal manor and later a manor of a powerful abbey like Ramsey, Burwell could have been expected to have had a church by at least the tenth century, although no records mentioning such a building exist from this period.

Everard, the priest of Burwell in 1115, gave the church its lands and eight tithable fields to Ramsey Abbey. However, this gift was not formerly recognised until 1225. On 12 April 1225 Pope Honorius III confirmed the ownership of the church by Ramsey Abbey in a papal bull[22]. This was in response to a request by the abbey to officially hold the church (and another at Depedale) and to receive into the abbey certain pensions associated with the living of the rector of the church. Thus Ramsey Abbey became responsible for the church, its upkeep and the appointment of priests. A copy of the papal bull is contained in the Cartularies of the Abbey. Its translation reads:

'Honorius, Bishop, servant of the servants of God, to his sons the Abbey and Convent of Ramsey, health and apostolic benediction.

It is indeed meet that we should yield a ready assent to the just desires of suppliants, and to fulfil by due performance those desires which are not discordant with the path of reason.

Wherefore, beloved sons in the Lord, concurring with an agreeable assent in your just petitions, the annual rents which ye do ?? to have obtained in Burewelle and Depdale churches, Norwich diocese, ye do obtain them justly, canonically and peaceably, to you, and by you, to your monastery, by apostolic authority, we do confirm, and by the proctection of this present writing do secure.

To no man then shall it be lawful to infringe this writing of our confirmation, or by such daring to withstand it. And if any one shall presume to attempt this, let him know he will incur the indignation of Almighty God, and the blessed Peter and Paul his apostles.

Given at the Lateran, the second ides of April in the ninth year of our Pontificate.'

From 1115 onwards the abbey, as patron, became the rector and thereafter appointed vicars to St Mary's. This was not, however, without problems for the abbey. Between 1160 and 1180 a former vicar who had left the parish 20 years earlier claimed his right to return and take up his former post, which was held by the abbey through it's appointed vicar. In response the abbey complained to the diocese. In 1185 the abbey had to accept a judgement whereby the abbey, as farmer or rector, should give to that clerk the tithes of the Burwell demesne in return for a pension of £2.

How large the church was at that time is not known, although if the tower is any indication it was already quite a sizeable building. It is recorded that in 1254 the church was assessed for taxation at 40 marks and was therefore worth considerably more that St Andrew's. In 1279[3], the *Rotulii Hundredorum* (Hundred rolls) records Fulco Lovel as the rector of the church and states that he had 24 acres of land. This land would have been made up of the glebe (church land), which was separate from the manorial land and, possibly, other pieces of land that had been donated on the condition that prayers or services were given at specified times. The income from such land would have been used to provide for the priest and for the chancel of the church. It was usual for the parishioners to be collectively responsible for all of the other parts of the church fabric.

From the late twelfth century many of the priests, supposedly vicars of Burwell, were pluralists. These were priests who were held in high regard by Ramsey Abbey and who were granted St Mary's along with other churches but who were never resident. In such arrangements the priest took the pension, paid a curate to do his duties and became a benefactor of the abbey or the church. Examples include:

- William Bodeksham, (1225) Archdeacon of Nottingham
- Fulco Lovell (1279) Archdeacon of Colchester
- John le Chaumber (1325), the Queen's Clerk
- Henry de Burwell (1349) the King's Clerk

From about 1390, Ramsey Abbey only accepted pluralist graduates from Cambridge, most of whom were Theologians. Most eminent of these was Thomas Wolsey, vicar from 1513–1514.

In 1288 Pope Nicholas IV granted Edward I one tenth of the ecclesiastical income of England and Wales to pay for a crusade. Between 1288 and 1292 a survey was made for this tax, which lists benefices worth more than six marks (£4) for most of the country. This document, the *Taxatio Ecclesiastica*[4], records the value for St Mary's as £53 6s 8d, £2 of which was recorded as the abbot's portion, namely the pension referred to above.

The churchyard around the fabric of St Mary's was quite small up to 1315 and probably covered a similar area to that of St Andrew's. In 1315, a licence was given for an exchange of land to take place between Edmund, son of Alexander de Herdwyck, and the Abbot of Ramsey that would allowing the extension of the churchyard. Such exchanges of land required royal approval and the application was confirmed by the King's Commissioners on 7 June 1315 and recorded in the Patent Rolls[9]. The entry reads:

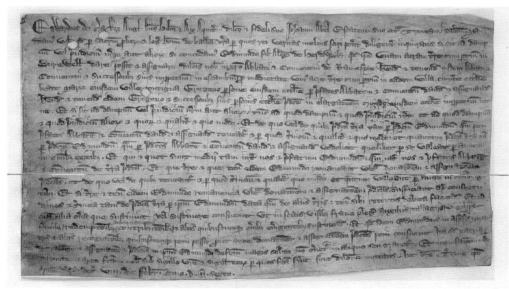

Figure 18 *Part of the patent roll licence to alienate land for incorporation into St Mary's churchyard in 1315. (Public Record Office)*

'Licence for the alienation in mortmain to the Abbot and Convent of Ramesey, by Edmund son of Alexander de Herdwyck of an acre of land adjacent to the cemetery of the church of St Mary, Burewelle, to be assigned by the Abbot and Convent to Gregory de Basyng parson of that Church and his successors, in enlargement of that cemetery.'

The acre of land was probably a piece of land from what is now Spring Close to the church tower, with the existing church land to the north, south and east.

Few documents exist which give more than a cursory mention to St Mary's between 1315 and the mid 1500s. Where such references do exist they refer to the protection of incumbents. For example the Patent Roll entry for 15 May 1337 reads:

'Protection with clause 'nomulus' for one year to John de la Chaumbre, parson of the church of Burwell.'

Other references include presentations such as that of Henry de Burwell recorded on June 6 1349, which reads:

'Presentation of Henry de Burwell to the church of Burwell, in the diocese of Norwich, in the kings gift, by voidance of Ramsey Abbey.'

Such references where incumbents are named are useful and give some indication of the number of clergy at St Mary's. If we take 1337 as an example, we have a rector (the abbot's representative), a parson (John de la Chaumbre) and a chaplain (John Hankyn). In addition to these there would be the church's clerks. The chaplain would have said masses at the chapel of St John at Reach as well as performed some services at St Mary's. This was probably the case from the thirteenth century when a chapel was to be built there. The *Liber Gersumarum*[13] of the abbey records a Thomas Bosoun as chaplain in 1400.

The tenure of the parson of St Mary's seems to have been quite short. Throughout the fourteenth centuries, the parson seems to have been in post for little more than two years. Records exist for exchanges, such as a parson moving to another area in exchange for someone else moving in. For example, on 23 July 1395, Walter Brugge, parson of Burwell, was presented to the Archdeaconry of Meath in exchange for Thomas Sprot.

'Presentation of Walter Brugge, Parson of St Mary's Burwell in the diocese of Norwich, to the archdeaconry of Meath with the parish church of Kealys annexed on an exchange with Thomas Sprotte.'

Thomas Sprotte was well connected as his father, Hugh Sprotte, had been a collector of petty customs for the Crown in the port of London. Hugh appears to have become in debt to King Richard II and Thomas became liable for this and had to pay to the king £23 6s 8d per year at Easter for life.

However, during his tenure at Burwell, Thomas seems to have failed to make his payment in the year 1413 and two records exist which refer to this failure. The second indicates the involvement of the Sheriff of Cambridge in recovering the money owed to the king.

Unlike St Andrew's, which had no vicarage, St Mary's had a house for the rector (Parsonage farm) from the early 1300s. Records clearly show land associated with a parson in 1305 and a house in existence by 1320. The road leading to it was known as Parsonage Lane from about 1351.

During the twelfth, thirteenth and fourteenth centuries, despite the apparently frequent changes of clergy, St Mary's appears to have been well supported by both

Figure 19 *Parsonage Farm. (Cambridgeshire Collection)*

Ramsey Abbey and local benefactors such as John Piers, son of Haukyn of Burwell. John gave 60 acres of freehold land to St Mary's in 1350 to support a chantry at the altar of St Mary in the church. However this land was subsequently forfeit to the Crown in 1361 after the chaplain transferred the land without licence to the Cambridge Corpus Christi Guild. It was then returned to the church in 1372[25, 26].

Another benefactor was William Sygar who, in 1470[27], left money for the making of the bell tower. This money was either not used or it was used to pay for new bells because the bell tower that we see today pre-dates the rebuilding of the nave and chancel. It is in the rebuilding of the church that the true power and wealth of St Mary's benefactors was truly seen. It is apparent that the rebuilding of the nave, chancel and aisles was executed to a very high standard.

This work was probably based on plans drawn up by Reginald Ely, the king's mason and builder of Kings College Chapel in Cambridge. This rebuilding is believed to have taken place between 1439 and 1467, during which John Heigham was the incumbent. We know the name of at least one of the main benefactors, John Benet, the lessee of the Ramsey Abbey manor, who paid for the chancel arch and wall above to be constructed along with the carpentry in the church. An inscription above the chancel arch records his benefaction and tells us that the nave was completed in 1464 The inscription reads:

> Orate pro animabus Johis. Benet Johane et Alicie uxoris eius parentum que suorum qui fieri decerunthunc parietem ac carpeteriam navis ecclesie
>
> Pray for the souls of John Benet and Joanna and Alice his wives and his parents who caused to be made this wall and the carpentry work of this Church AD 1464

It is not clear when all the rebuilding was complete but it is likely to have been sometime after the completion of the nave in 1464 because in 1465 John Andrew, chaplain, made a bequest of 40 shillings for 'the new building of the church'. This bequest may have been made towards the chancel. The clergy were generally responsible for the upkeep of the chancel while the parishioners were responsible for the upkeep of the remainder of the fabric. John Heigham, in keeping with this tradition, made a bequest of funds to complete the chancel. His coat of arms can be seen there.

At the dissolution of the abbey the advowson of St Mary's came into the possession of Sir Edward North, along with the Ramsey Abbey manor. Before Sir Edward gave back the manor to the Crown he agreed to sell the advowson of the church to the University of Cambridge for £600 and arranged its appropriation. The patronage of the newly established vicarage was assigned to Sir Edward's heirs who were to appoint one of two students of the university to the church. Accordingly Sir Edward's heirs, the Lords North of Kirtling and then the Earls of Guildford continued to present the university's nominations until the mid 1800s. From 1884, however, Lord North, who was the heir at the time and a convert to Roman Catholicism, claimed to present on his own authority.

For its part, and according to the terms of appropriation, the university was to provide an annual sermon at Burwell. By 1598 this was occurring during lent. In that year William Pamplyn, having provided a sermon, gave £10 for a distribution to the poor. The practice seems to have continued from then onwards because in the 1830s the vice-chancellor of the university gave 13s 4d for this purpose.

With the advowson the University of Cambridge gained Parsonage Farm, with 42 acres of land attached to St Mary's parsonage, a rectorial glebe comprising 17 acres of closes and a further 41 acres of arable land. As noted above, Parsonage Farm had been

Figure 20. The Rose window and carvings above the chancel arch showing the Benet inscription.

Figure 21 *The North side of St Mary's church as drawn by Cole in 1743.*

in existence since the early 1300s and while some of its fabric is medieval in date, most of the house was rebuilt in 1600 during the university's occupation. The university sold the farm in 1922 to Cambridgeshire County Council.

While the University owned the parsonage, the vicar was only entitled to a room in the house, which at that time was known as the University Mansion House. It was not until 1629 that a vicarage was provided. Occupying the site of the present vicarage, the building erected in 1629 used considerable amounts of reused materials, probably including stone from Reach chapel and, as noted earlier, tiles were stripped from St Andrew's church for its roof before villagers intervened. This first vicarage is recorded as having four hearths in 1674. In 1826 the university rebuilt the house and carried out improvements in 1841, by which time it was recorded as having seven bedrooms. It was ceded to the living in 1922 and remains in use as the vicarage to this day.

From 1544 the vicar of St Mary's received a stipend of £20 from the university. This initially decreased in value to such an amount that by 1600 it was only worth £14 until restored by augmentation. By 1650 it had increased in value to £35 and continued to rise, so that by 1770 it was worth £80 and then, by 1816, £300. It then remained at £300 until 1921.

Burwell appears to have had a number of interesting vicars since 1539. One such man, resident in 1560, was described as being unable to preach. Another, Robert Metcalf, Regius Professor of Hebrew, appears also to have had difficulties in preaching. During his sermons in 1614, sleeping and playing games were occasionally reported[28]. In 1647 puritanical members of his congregation accused one vicar of preaching that work rather than Christ would bring salvation. They also accused him of being inaudible in their complaint to the university and petitioned for a 'Godly Minister'. In opposition to this 130 members of the congregation defended the man as 'painful in his calling'. However, he resigned in 1650[29].

Also during this period it is recorded that on 3 January 1644 William Dowsing visited St Mary's. Dowsing was a puritan from Suffolk who visited and defaced over 100

Table 19 *Incumbents of St Mary's church.*

Period	Priests/Rectors/Vicars	Chaplains
1114–1130	Everard	
1225	William Bodeksham	
1226–1279	Fulco Lovel (Rector) William Kennett (priest)	Simon
1298	John Langton	
1305	Henry Cosyn	
1312	Gregory de Basyng	
1325	John le Chaumbre (alias Camera)	John Hankyn (1337)
1349	Henry de Burwell	
1392	Richard Petir	
1393	Edmund Caldicote	
1394	Walter Brugge	
1395–1413	Thomas Sprotte	Thomas Bosoun (1400–1409) John Barwe (1409)
1436	Clement Denston	
1439	John Heigham	John Andrew (1465)
1467	Roger Keye	
1492	John Raven	
1506	John Hall	
1507	Richard Dudley	
1508	Simon Stalworthy	
1511	William Preston	
1513	Thomas Wolsey	
1514	Thomas Scarisbret, B.D.	
1531	John Reynes, LL.D	
1539	John Laurence de Warboys	
1544	William Devenish	
1545	William Catterick	
1549	William Parkyn	
1554	John Elwood	
1565	Owen Duckett	
1577	Thomas Banier	
1618	Robert Metcalfe, D.D.	
1652	John Cole	
1655	William Spencer	
1656	Thomas Wilson	
1658	Joshua Wilson	
1665	Thomas Huxley	
1681	Anthony Lyster	
1705	John Badcock	
1725	Alexander Edmundson, B.D.	
1733	John Gee	
1772	Henry Turner, B.D.	
1808–1854	James Johnson Baines	
1854	Charles Thornhill	
1858	John William Cockshott	
1885	Nevill Arthur Blackley Burton	
1921	Alfred George Walpole Sayer B.D.	
1944	Richard Seymour Cripps B.D.	
1954	Thomas Geoffrey Stuart Smith B.D.	
1961	Kenneth Gordon Haynes	
1970	David Nigel De Lorentz Young M.A.	
1975	Ian Russel Secrett M.A.	
1996	Stephen Geoffrey Franklin Earl B.A.	

churches in East Anglia. In the churches he visited he, with help from the local puritan community, frequently defaced inscriptions, removed paintings and smashed stained glass which contained what he considered to be 'superstitious imagery'. Dowsing kept a journal of his visits and for his visit to Burwell he wrote, '*We brake down a great many superstitious pictures*'. In Burwell much escaped Dowsing's attention, in particular the Benet inscription above the chancel arch, which begins with the Latin words *Orate Pro Anima* (pray for the soul of). In most churches he visited, *Orate* inscriptions were defaced. It is likely that the Latin inscription around the Warboys brass was removed at this time.

During the next decade St Mary's saw three vicars, two of whom left after very short periods. This was followed by a period in which vicars stayed for considerable periods. In the period from 1660 to about 1680, these vicars were supported by Bachelors of Divinity sent from the university to preach up to ten times per year. It was not until 1734 that Burwell had an absent vicar who employed curates and who preferred his Suffolk living to Burwell. One Henry Turner who succeeded to the living in 1772 was rarely away, despite the fact that from 1782 he was also rector of Newmarket.

In this period the size of the congregation varied. In 1603 one vicar claimed 600 communicants and another in 1676 claimed 500 potential communicants, 120 of whom had attended that Easter. During his tenure in the 1770s, Henry Turner recorded 30–40 communicants at his quarterly sacramental services.

Turner's successor was James Johnson Baines. A formal, high and dry churchman who Charles Lucas[30] informs us was from a Cornish family and had many friends amongst the leading families in the county and elsewhere. He personally catechised the parish youth every Sunday using printed matter. He was very hostile to the dissenting churches in the village and caused considerable controversy in 1837 for his misuse of charitable moneys for the poor. He took £20, which he gave to Addenbrookes Hospital who made him a governor for life. He was reported to the Charity Commissioners who held a public inquiry in Cambridge where it was found that he had put charity money into his own bank account where it had accrued interest. He took none of the interest gained on the money and thus claimed he had not benefited from the practice. The Commissioner ruled he should repay the money, but Parson Baines refused and the case was taken to the chancery court where the case languished for sometime. It is not clear whether Baines repaid the money in his lifetime. He died in 1854. One year later, the charity was reformed so that such poor practices could not occur again.

Parson Baines was followed by a man of a different character altogether. J W Cockshott was appointed vicar of St Mary's in 1857 and quickly set about organising the parish so that by 1885 he had restored St Mary's church and established three church schools. In addition, he acquired a curate to serve the people of North Street who, by 1863, were holding services in a public house in the street. In 1863 he raised £1050 to erect a new church dedicated to St Andrew. The new church was built in brick and could seat 300 people. At about the same time he set about organising the church choir, ensuring that each of the members had a surplus and participated in local choral festivals. In 1873 he re-organised the seating in St Mary's so that seats for 700 were provided. He reported 700 churchgoers and 148 communicants, which amounted to almost two fifths of the population of Burwell in 1873.

Reverend Cockshott was succeeded by the Reverend N A B. Borton. It was during Rev Borton's time that attendances started to decline. In 1897, shortly after his arrival, he reported 150 communicants. By 1920, however, the churchgoing population attending St Andrew's was greatly reduced to such an extent that communion services were only held once a month. After 1920 the vicar had to perform services at both churches because no curate was provided. By 1987, only two services each month were held at St Andrew's which finally closed in 1990. In this year St Mary's reported 80 communicants.

St Mary's Church – the Building

Much has been written in the past century and a half about the church building dedicated to St Mary since at least the thirteenth century, and much of that by eminent persons such as Sir Nicklaus Pevsner who described the church as 'the most perfect example in the county of the perp(endicular) ideal of the glasshouse'.

As seen today, the building consists of a west tower, nave, north and south aisles and a chancel with crypt.

Figure 22 *Showing the lower stages of St Mary's church tower with its blocked Norman windows and a Norman buttress.*

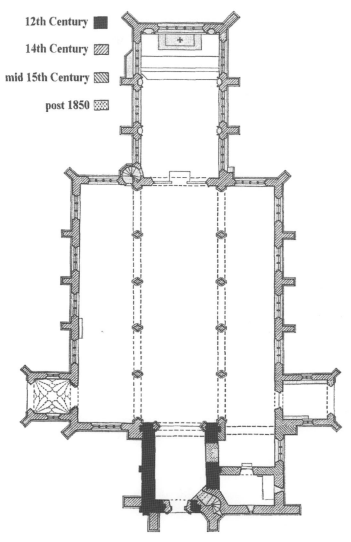

12th Century ■

14th Century ▨

mid 15th Century ▧

post 1850 ▦

Figure 23 *Plan of St Mary's church.*

The Tower

The tower is the earliest part of the present fabric and dates from the twelfth century. Of five external stages, the lower two date from this period and the construction suggests a building of considerable size and are built from field stones and dressed at the corners, buttresses and window surrounds etc with Barnack Stone. This is an oolitic limestone of a type found in a band from Dorset to North Yorkshire, known locally as Barnack Stone after the quarries at Barnack near Peterborough where this stone was extensively quarried from Saxon times onwards. In its second stage the tower originally had a pair of double-light, round-headed windows on its north and south faces and similar but single-light windows on the east and west faces. Those on the north, west and south sides have been blocked but one set on the north face is still clearly visible.

The tower, which probably originally comprised three storeys, was heightened in the fifteenth century. At this time a new stair was added to the south-west angle, new buttresses added to the north-west angle and the twelfth-century windows were blocked in. Also a new doorway with window above was inserted into the west wall of the tower. The fifteenth-century addition to the tower comprises two stages; the first is a square stage surmounted by a second, octagonal stage with diagonal buttresses. This is finished off with battlements and pinnacles.

The lead spirelet on the top of the tower is marked with the date of 1799 upon it. The tower contains eight bells, four of which are dated 1705, one is dated 1725 and contains the names of two churchwardens of that time, Robert Bridgeman and William Peachey. The remaining three bells were donated in 1955 by Arthur Mason in memory of his parents. An additional bell, originally a sanctus bell, is housed in the spirelet. Records show that money was spent on the bells in 1637-8 and it is likely that the older bells were recast in 1705 and 1725.

The tower also houses a clock with dials on the north and south faces.

North porch

The north porch is the present entrance into the church. Externally the porch has an embattled parapet and diagonal buttresses at its corners. At the top of these diagonal buttresses are finiales; the western one terminates with a carved figure thought to be a wild man of the woods, or *Woodwose*. At the apex of the gable of the porch is the very worn remains of the figure of St George. Below the parapet are carved heads and foliate bosses and then, between these and the arch of the door, are five symmetrically placed niches with miniature vaults and statue bases.

Internally the porch has a fan-vaulted ceiling and is lit by windows in its east and west sides. As is the case for many other parts of the church, the porch was heavily restored in the nineteenth century.

South porch

By comparison with the rest of the church, the south porch is a plain structure with little of architectural note. It was heavily restored in the nineteenth century and more recently converted into a vestry for female staff. It does, however, retain its medieval roof with angel corbels and cornice panels (see below). Like the north porch it has windows to the east and west.

Nave and aisles

The nave is very spacious, rising to a height of some 60 feet, with a length of approximately 70 feet and a breadth of 22 feet. It is made up of five bays with arches, to the north and south, each being supported on tall slim piers with continuous, hollow-chamfered mouldings. Above the arches are carved tracery panels and then large clerestory windows. Between the windows slim pillars rise from the point of the arches to form the platforms for the roof.

To the eastern end of the nave is the chancel arch, which, much like the nave arches, has arcaded panels above it with niches and three shields. The two outer shields are blank while the centre one contains the Royal Coat of Arms for the years 1816–37. Above the shields is an inscription to the Benets, the principle benefactors of the church, and above the inscription is a rose window surrounded to left and right by more carved tracery work.

The east and south windows of the two aisles are uniform and the north and south doors are approximately opposite one another. At the western end of the south aisle is the vestry. Thought to have originally been a treasury, this particular building, which abuts onto the tower, is believed to date from the fourteenth century. In the mid 1880s, after the gallery had been inserted, panelling was installed and an arch in the south side of the tower was blocked to form two vestries out of the western end of the south aisle and the former treasury. The new arrangement formed a choir vestry in the former aisle and the priest's vestry in the former treasury.

Chancel

The chancel is approximately 41 feet long and 22 feet wide, and is dominated by seven very large windows, three to the north, three to the south and the great east window. The north and south windows are all uniform with one another and parallel in their setting in the walls. The east window is flanked by two large niches. The window on the north side is larger than that on the south.

Below the south window at the eastern end of the chancel is a *sedilia*, a stone seating for clergy. Next to this is a *piscine*, a stone basin and drain in a niche south of an altar into which water used in washing the sacred vessels was emptied. The chancel floor, below which is the crypt, is raised at the eastern end. The tie beams of the roof are carried on corbels; the intermediate ones are carved as demi-angels. Each demi-angel holds an object; those on the north side have a heart, a mitre and a small organ while those on the south hold a book, a shield with the arms of John Higham and a musical instrument called a *cithern*.

Crypt

The crypt is reached via a set of steps from the north side of the chancel. It measures 21ft by 8½ft in size and is entered through a doorway at the base of the stairs. The present floor level is lower than when it was first built.

The roof has a four-centred barrel vault of clunch and is lit by a small window in the east wall. In the south wall is a fireplace with a hood built at the same time as the crypt while on the east wall, within a recess, is set an altar stone. Various suggestions have been given for the unusual layout of the crypt, there being a window, altar and fireplace, including its use by an anchorite or as a vestry.

Roofs

The wooden roof timbers are beautifully carved. Where the main timbers meet there are carved bosses which depict either heads or foliage. In addition, along the upper courses of the walls where they join the roof, there are carved cornices depicting a variety of subjects (figure). In total there are some 76 cornice panels throughout the church.

The subjects depicted are shown overleaf:

Chancel – North side

1	Squirrel between crocodile and chained lion	4	Crown between lion and hyena?
2	Censing angel and the hand of God	5	Nest of fledglings between birds
3	Hare between hounds	6	Crown between leopard and lion

Chancel – South side

7	Crown between hounds	10	Hare between lion and stag
8	Phoenix between angels	11	Hare between hounds
9	Crown between lions	12	Mirror between tigers

Nave – North Side

13	Assumption between censing angels	18	Hare between hounds
14	Chalice with host between emblems of St Matthew and St Mark (figure)	19	Lopped tree between dragons
15	Vine between tigers with mirrors	20	Lopped tree between chained bears
16	Mitre between chained antelopes	21	Blank shield between stag and hind
17	Castle between elephants with castles (figure)	22	Crowned head between lions

Nave – South Side

23	Pot with lilies between the Virgin and Gabriel	28	Flowering bush between yales
24	Chalice with host between emblems of St John and St Luke	29	Tree between foxes carrying geese
25	Blank shield between griffins	30	Flower between unicorn
26	Flower between cows	31	Tree between ram and goat
27	Crown between camels	32	Blank shield between ram and goat

North aisle – North side

33	Castle between elephants with castles	38	Patera between unicorns
34	Patera between unicorns	39	Monkey with urine flask between mermaid and fox carrying cock
35	Tree between griffins	40	Mitre between dragons
36	Crown between angels	41	Castle between elephants with castles
37	Vine between griffins	42	Crown between chained antelopes

North aisle – South side

43	Plain panel	48	Flora sprig between tigers with mirrors
44	Plain panel	49	Floral sprig between eagles
45	Oak sprig between chained antelope	50	Sprig with bird between yales
46	Crown between angels	51	Foliated sprig with squirrel between goats
47	Floral sprig between hind and hound	52	Human head between wyverns

South aisle – North side

53	Plain panel	58	Head of woodwose between unicorns
54	Plain panel	59	Floral sprig between eagles
55	Oak sprig between chained antelope	60	Sprig with bird between yales
56	Foliated sprig between leopards?	61	Foliated sprig with squirrel between goats
57	Tree between eagles	62	Human head between wyverns

South aisle – South side

63	Mirror between tigers	68	Sunflower between griffins
64	Mitre between chained antelope	69	Foliated sprig between yales
65	Crown supported by lion	70	Blank shield between animals
66	Woodwose or monkey holding antelope by rope	71	Unidentified shield between angels (this is thought to be a nineteenth century panel)
67	Crown between lions (this is thought to be a nineteenth century panel)	72	Hare between Hounds

South Porch – East side

73	Mirror between two tigers	74	Foliate tree between chained antelope and yale

South Porch – West side

75	Floral bush between lions	76	Crowned and bearded head between dogs

Figure 24 *Cornice panel 17 from the north side of the nave, showing a castle between elephants with castles on their backs.*

Figure 25 *Cornice panel 14 from the north side of the nave showing a chalice with host between the emblems of St Matthew and St Mark.*

Furnishings

Rood Screen – The present screen under the chancel arch comprises a modern top and fifteenth century lower half. The modern upper half was a replacement for the original made by A W Blomfield in 1877[51]. He also heavily restored the fifteenth century lower section, which has traceried and embattled panels.

Pews – The seating in the nave and aisle are box pews without doors and were installed in 1816.

Pulpit – The present pulpit dates from the nineteenth century. Earlier pulpits are recorded for the church including one for 1734, which was at that time against the second pillar of the south arcade.

Gallery – The gallery at the western end of the nave was installed in 1824. Today it is occupied by the organ, which was moved to this location in 1967.

Panelling – In the chancel, this incorporates a number of fifteenth century panels and stiles with miniature buttresses, end posts and tracery with birds. The modern sections were probably incorporated as part of Blomfield's restoration work in 1877.

Stalls – The present choir stalls, while relatively modern, also incorporate fifteenth century panels and may also owe their present form to the restoration of the mid nineteenth century. It is known that the original choir stalls were removed in 1860.

Monuments

The North aisle contains a large wall monument to Thomas Gerard and his wife. Originally this monument was in the chancel. In 1743 it was described there by Cole on his visit to Burwell. He drew the monument (Figure 26) and wrote,

Figure 26 *The Gerard Monument as drawn by Cole in 1743. (Cambridge Record Office)*

'Fine old mural monument wch quite fills up ye nich & reaches almost to ye top of ye chancel. It consists of a man & woman kneeling wth their Hands up-lifted under a canopy supported by Corinthian pillars: Ye whole gilt & carved over ye Pillar nearest ye woman & on ye dexter side are these arms: (he then goes on to describe the arms of Gerard and Elliot in heraldic terms which will not be described here).'

Alicia Gerard died in 1608 and it is this date that is given on the tomb. Thomas died in 1613. His date of death is not recorded on the tomb but it does appear in church records.

A brass on the floor of the chancel is thought to be that of John Laurence de Warboys, the last abbot of Ramsey Abbey, who retired to Burwell after the dissolution of Ramsey Abbey. The brass was ordered in his lifetime and altered after his death to show him as a priest in cassock, surplice and amice with his head on a cushion. Protruding above the latter is a lozenge shaped indent in the stone which, had the dissolution not occurred, was probably cut out to receive the mitre on the abbot's head, A canopy originally surrounded the brass, of which only fragments survive including the image of Christ

Figure 27 *Monumental brass to John Laurence de Warboys, 1542, last Abbot of Ramsey.*

rising from the tomb. Much of the material of this brass is re-used. The brass itself is a palimpsest; a reused brass with the reverse showing parts of an earlier brass. The lower part is of a figure in either the robes of an abbot or some other ecclesiastical person in episcopal vestments. The crozier is clearly present, and this lower section of the figure may be the lower half of the abbot's original brass.

The centre part of the reverse of the canopy has been ascribed as part of the brass for a deacon of the fourteenth century, while the upper part of the reverse of the canopy has part of the head of a priest wearing an amice. This part is thought to be of foreign, possible Flemish, workmanship.

In the vestry is the tomb of Lee Cotton who died in 1613. This, like the Gerard memorial, formerly stood in the chancel. This is a canopied tomb that shows Lee lying in armour of the period. The chest below his effigy has panelled sides with mouldings on both its top and sides. It is painted although much of the paint has worn away. Columns arising from the tomb chest support the canopy. The inscription on the monument is very much obliterated but it was recorded by Cole in 1743. It records Lee's death on 16 December 1613 and describes him as 'Generous'. Another inscription also recorded by Cole, tells us:

> 'Lee testifies what Cotton is content
> To be intered under this monument:
> The poor he first doth feed, next by his will
> With other food ye little ones doth fill:
> Since piety cannot within them flow
> Till witt with learning and good manner grow.'

This is a reference to the will of Lee Cotton to found a school in Burwell. The inscription continues:

> 'Lee Cotton lived in ye honour of his name,
> Who dying showed he did diserve ye same
> Heaven first contains his soul that never died
> And next his body when tis purified.
> Though combat was by death long time intended,
> By death his soul and bodies strife is ended.'

The church contains a number of tablet monuments including those to, Sir William Russell 1663, the Reverend James Johnson Baines 1854, and Eliza his wife 1842, the Reverend Henry Turner 1808 and Elizabeth his wife 1820, John Isaacson 1830, Elizabeth Isaacson 1825) and her husband Wooton Isaacson 1840, to list but a few.

Wall Painting

The north aisle contains the remains of a wall painting depicting St Christopher carrying the Christ child. In the south-east corner of the north aisle is the entrance to the stairs of the former rood loft.

Restoration

In the eighteenth and nineteenth centuries St Mary's was extensively repaired. Major restorations to the fabric appear to have been undertaken in 1725–1731[53] and 1899[54], when the tower and clerestory were restored. The church clock was cleaned and restored in 1766 and then restored and a new clock case provided in 1787. The tower was restored at the same time. The bell frames were repaired and altered between 1791 and 1794.

Churchyard

Before 1315, the date when Edmund son of Alexander de Herdwyck gave in exchange land to expand it, the churchyard must have been of a similar size to that of St Andrew's. The land received from Edmund probably extended from somewhere in front of the tower to Spring Close. In 1859, after the demolition of the Guildhall, the churchyard was again extended to give it its present shape and size. The trees to the north of the church now stand in approximately the place where the boundary of the pre-1859 churchyard once stood. The present Guildhall was built to replace the former Guildhall.

The graveyard contains a few interesting memorials including the flaming heart tombstone in memory of those who died in a tragic fire on 8 September 1727. Seventy-eight bodies were buried in a mass grave here. Near the door to the tower is the Palmer family vault that includes within it the bodies of two Palmer children who died in the 1727 fire. The Royal Commission for Historic Monuments[52] reports 22 headstones of the seventeenth or early eighteenth centuries in the churchyard.

The Chapel of St John, Reach

When a chapel in East Reach was first built is not known. However it is clear that by the reign of Abbot Hugh Foliot (1216–1231) a chapel was in existence. The Cartularium of

Figures 28 & 29 *The flaming heart gravestone in Burwell churchyard.*

the Abbey[31] records the confirmation of William de Bodeksham of the Archdeacon of Nottingham to the chapel. The record of confirmation does not give the dedication of the chapel but states that it is sited in Reach, that it is within the parish of Saint Mary, Burwell and that a chaplain supplied by the rector will say mass there three times each day. It is clear from this document that this is a confirmation of an earlier agreement and that William, or his chaplain, was to say mass in the chapel and was to honour an obligation to read scriptures and say mass for Alan de Reche of the parish. It is likely that Alan donated land, the income from which was to pay for prayers or a mass to be said for him and his successors. The income to the chaplain from the men of Reach at that time was one mark and this income was reserved for the rector. While undated, it is known that William de Bodeksham held office as rector (in absentia) of St Mary's in 1224.

As was the case with St Mary's and St Andrew's, the chapel of St John in Reach was endowed with money and various pieces of land for its upkeep and for the saying of masses there[32]. A guild of St John is known to have existed between 1490 and 1525 and, as for the other church lands, those of St John's were confiscated and leased out by the Crown in 1547. In 1550 these endowments comprised 45 acres with a value of 23s 4d. In 1552, these lands were sold by the Crown and, as recorded in the Calendar of Patent Rolls of Elizabeth I, dated 1571, the chapel was also sold to John Mershe and Francis Grene both of London along with other lands in Cambridgeshire and other counties. John and Francis were granted:

> 'A grave yard in Reche in the county of Cambridge in which late stood St Andrews chapel (parish of Swaffham Prior) ; St John's chapel in le Reche in Burwell, with all lands belonging thereto in Burwell and Shopham (Swaffham?)in the county of Cambridge.'

Though sold, the chapel remained standing and was possibly in use in 1650 when, due to its poor state, repairs were recommended[33]. Whether the chapel was repaired or not is unknown but less than 100 years later the chapel was ruinous. Cole visited the ruin on Rogation Monday 1768 and drew the ruins (Figure 30). He not only gives a description of the ruins in 1768 but also states:

> 'So that great part of what was standing when I was here in 1743, is now pulled down.'

This suggests that some of the destruction of the church may have been deliberate. Unlike St Andrews church in Burwell, no records giving authorisation to pull down the chapel remains survive.

Cole's description of the remains of St John's reads:

> 'I observed that only the east wall of the chancel was standing, with a small part of the chancel north and south walls by it: so that great part of what was standing when I was here in 1743is now pulled down'.

He also states:

> 'but its church also, also ye poor remains of which stand on the east side of ye great ditch which divides ye whole town. How ye revenues of this church are vested, or whether a rectory or vicarage, or to whom dedicated, is more than I am at present to determin.'

From Cole's description and his drawing of the remains in 1768, the chapel probably comprised a nave with aisles and a chancel, thus making it a good-sized building for a

Figure 30 *Cole's drawing of the ruins of the Chapel at Reach (1768).*

chapel. Today only the east end of this building survives. The lower section of this wall is thought to be from the original thirteenth-century building while the upper courses, which have larger squared stones, are thought be from a fifteenth-century rebuilding. By the early nineteenth century the chapel yard was being treated as part of Burwell Town lands

In the mid nineteenth century, the incumbents of both Burwell and Swaffham Prior saw Reach as a hotbed of dissent. Therefore, in 1857, in order to deal with this, open-air services were held at the chapel ruins[34] and in 1858 a curate was found who then held services in one of the public houses[35]. Two years later, in 1860, St Mary's church sold the chapel remains and its ground to the vicar and churchwardens of Swaffham Prior, who then raised £750 to build a new chapel south-west of the ruin.

Nonconformist Churches

Dissent amongst the people of Burwell and East Reach commenced in the fifteenth century when it is recorded that a lollard, with thirteen followers, was operating in Reach. The lollard was abjured by the Bishop of Ely in 1457[36, 37]. No further activity is then recorded until 1650 when dissenting baptisms were reported[38]. In 1676 the vicar of St Mary's reported 33 dissenters. Subsequently in 1687 the vicar recorded that five husbandmen had received indulgences as dissenters and in 1690 a Scots Presbyterian left Burwell, having been discouraged by the 'odd opinions' of those listening to his sermons[39].

Burwell Independent Church

Burwell's first nonconformist congregation was that of the Independent Church, whose house was licensed for worship in 1672[40]. By 1692, 15 people were covenanting to the Burwell Independent church, which was being led by one George Doughty who had, for some time, been actively preaching in the locality. George was ordained as the pastor of the church in 1693–4.

The Independence movement grew quickly in the area, initially recruiting from Burwell and Reach, but people regularly came from as far away as Isleham before a church was founded there. In 1707 the terms for covenanting to the Independence church were tightened and on renewal it was recorded that there were 36 full members (equal numbers of men and women) and 135 'hearers'. From about 1690, member's children were regularly baptised as infants. This caused some disquiet both in the church's membership and amongst the local Anglican community and, consequently, it was not until 1707 that this practice was formally accepted[41].

Burwell Independent church regularly excommunicated members in its early years. Such excommunication was usually due to absence from regular attendance at its weekly gatherings for the breaking of bread. However, they also occurred for other misdemeanours such as drunkenness, swearing, fighting and 'vain singing'.

By 1712 George Doughty had based himself in Soham and the Burwell congregation separated from him, registering three houses successively for worship; two in 1711, registered by a Tailor and, in 1718, one was registered by a Tanner from Bury St Edmunds. In the 1740s the congregation was using local barns as places of worship, registering one such barn in North Street in 1746[42]. Also in 1741 they registered a house in Reach for worship. The following year, 1747, the Burwell Independent meeting house was built on ¼ acre of land in the High Street[43]. In 1798 this was further added to with the installation of a gallery.

However the congregation then seems to have started to decline and in 1800 the vicar of Burwell reported that the congregation attending the independent meeting-house was diminishing. This, however, was soon to change due to the support of the local merchant family, the Balls. With the support of Edward Ball, the congregation once again started to increase in number and by 1850 a Sunday school was open[44].

In 1820 Edward Ball became concerned at the neglect of Reach by the vicars of Burwell and Swaffham Prior and the regular 'Sabbath breaking' by the population of Reach, who were regularly to be found gambling, cock fighting and prize fighting on Sundays. He therefore began to preach there regularly himself on Sundays in a hut and continued to do so until a meeting-house was constructed in 1830[45], after which he preached only occasionally. The meeting-house in Reach had been rebuilt by 1847, after which it could accommodate 260 people sitting. Two afternoon and evening services were held each Sunday and 190 people were said to regularly attend. In addition Sunday morning Sunday school attendance averaged 95 children per week..

In 1860 a young revivalist preacher frequently preached at the Reach meeting house and attendances increased rapidly so that by the end of that year a gallery was installed. Numbers remained high and Ball gathered funds to rebuild the chapel at the north-west end of The Green. The resulting building could, by 1863, seat 350 people. From about this time the Reach Chapel was linked to the Burwell Congregationalist Chapel and it remained in use until its closure in 1963, at which time the congregation stood at just six persons.

In Burwell the history of the Church did not run so smoothly, for in 1862 a minister refused to resign even though three-quarters of the congregation demanded it. The result was that 80 members of the congregation left. The Ball family gave them assistance and allowed them to move and worship from the British School (see *p.* 151). The congregation swelled after Ball brought in the revivalist preacher who had done so much for increasing the congregation at Reach. They remained at the British School for one year. By 1865 the preacher, whose refusal to leave had caused the split, left and the church once again re-united. The increased number of the congregation required a larger building and the chapel was rebuilt on the same site. The work was completed by 1866 and the new chapel seated 420 persons.

A resident minister held three Sunday services at the new chapel. A residence was acquired for the minister in 1881, which was across the High Street from the chapel. This was retained as a manse until the 1960s.

In the twentieth century the numbers attending declined from 121 in 1905 to about 90 in 1915 and then to 70 by 1920. It remained between 60 to 70 from 1920 to the 1960s. In 1972 the church was linked to the United Reform Church and a minister was provided from Newmarket. In 1976 services moved to the Sunday school building across the road and then, in 1988, the church merged with the Burwell Methodist Church to form the Burwell Trinity Church. The former chapel was sold in about 1990.

Methodism

It is not clear when Methodism first came to Burwell. However, a barn was registered for worship by 1816. The applicant was a methodist minister from Bury St Edmunds and a congregation grew to such an extent that by 1830 worship was being held regularly in the village. Between 1834 and 1835 the Wesleyans built a chapel on the eastern side of The Causeway. From 1839 this chapel was incorporated into the Mildenhall circuit. This early chapel could seat 140 persons. However, by the 1880s this was to small and in 1884 it was enlarged. It was again enlarged in 1913. In 1851 the average attendance was 55 and Sunday school regularly attracted 45 children.

At about the same time as the building of the Wesleyan chapel in The Causeway in 1836, a Primitive Methodist chapel was being built in North Street. This chapel was part of the Primitive Methodist Soham circuit, except from 1857 to 1885 when it formed part of the Ely circuit. This was always the smaller of the two Methodist congregations, and merged with the Wesleyan congregation in 1939. In 1940 the Primitive Methodist chapel was sold.

In 1976 the Methodist church in Burwell had 48 members and the membership was in decline to such a level that by 1988 there were only 12 members. In that year they joined with the Congregational Church and the United Reform Church to form Burwell Trinity Church. The chapel in The Causeway had been sold for conversion into dwellings the previous year.

Baptist Church

Burwell Baptist church commenced in 1790 when four members of the Soham Baptist Church began baptising people in Burwell. In 1815 they broke away from the Soham church to form a church in Burwell and, by 1818, they had leased a house which stood on the site of the present Baptist church in North Street and registered it for worship.

The house burnt down in 1835 and the church purchased the site. By 1846 a Particular Baptist chapel had been constructed. This building could seat a congregation of 250 and in 1851 the average attendance was 130 adults and 50 children. At this time the minister travelled in from Fordham.

Baptisms were held in public in local streams until the early 1900s, many being sponsored by the revivalist minister from Reach. From the 1860s the congregation had a resident minister whose manse was in Toyse Lane. A Sunday school building was built at the rear of the chapel in 1882 to take account of the increasing numbers of children attending the church. There were over 100 in that year.

As with the other churches in Burwell, numbers declined throughout the twentieth century from an average attendance of over 100 in 1900 to about 45 in the 1940s. Numbers rose again to 93 in 1985.

Other Religious

Burwell is known to have had an Anchoress, a female religious hermit resident in about 1230[47]. Little is known about her and it may be that she was in some way allied to the nuns of Chatteris who held a small amount of land in the parish.

It is also thought that a similar hermit or recluse may have been resident in the late fifteenth century in the crypt at St Mary's. The crypt was blocked off until 1861 when the stair was re-opened and was known as the monk's hole. It contains both a fireplace and an altar. A crypt chapel would contain an altar but would not generally contain a fireplace, suggesting its intention as a residence for a recluse or a religious person.

Guilds and Chantries

A Guild, or Gild, was a medieval association, particularly of artisans or merchants, formed for mutual aid and protection, for masses for the dead and the pursuit of a common purpose, religious or economic. Guilds became politically powerful throughout Europe but after the sixteenth century their position was undermined by the growth of capitalism.

Burwell is known to have had at least five guilds operating in the late medieval period, these were :

- Guild of the Holy Trinity (St Mary's church)
- Guild of Corpus Christi (St Mary's church)
- Guild of St John the Baptist (St Mary's church)
- Guild of St Andrew? (St Andrews church
- Guild of St John (St John's chapel at Reach)

All of these were religious guilds and provided a service to the sick and provided a burial service as required.

The Guild of the Holy Trinity

The largest of these was the Guild of the Holy Trinity, which was also the only guild known to have a guildhall in the village. The Holy Trinity Guild was founded at some time before 1492 when it was given 5 marks as a bequest from a rector[48] for the building of a guildhall. This was probably the same guildhall demolished in the mid nineteenth century and described by Charles Lucas.

Other donations to this guild included 12 acres given for obituaries and the provision of lights in St Mary's church, including the sepulchre light and a bequest made in 1496 by Thomas Forster for a light before the crucifix. The guildhall and the land and possessions associated with it were confiscated in 1553 by the Crown and sold in the same year. It was subsequently resold in 1566 and 1571. It was then sold again to Sir Robert Chester, from whom the parish bought it back.

The Guild of Corpus Christi

This was Burwell's oldest guild, founded before 1361. In that year the chaplain of St Mary's transferred without licence 60 acres of land to the guild. The land had been given by John Piers[25, 26] to support a chantry at the altar of St Mary. The guild does not appear to have ever had a guildhall associated with it and, other than the donations made to it in its early years, no other references appear to survive.

Guild of St John the Baptist

A guild associated with St Mary's church, this guild was a late foundation, with only one record associated with it. This is a Lay Subsidy record of 1542[49].

Guild of St Andrew

When the guild of St Andrew was founded is not clear. Sale records of 1569 in the Patent Rolls describe the property of the guild which was sold at that time. This included:

'that messuage in Burwell given to Burwell St Andrew by Richard Parsonne and that one acre and three roods of land in Reach Crofts and one and a half roods abutting on Hallthed acre, which were escheats, and two acres of lands, of which one lies in Dytchfield, abutting on the great dyche, the other in North felde, given by Richard Hancock of Burwell for an obit in Burwell Church and half an acre given by the same for maintaining the sepulchre light......and an acre of land in tenure of John Roger, given in maintenance of a lamp before the rood in the church of Burwell St Andrews, and six acres in the occupation of Awdrey Barton, given by William Goodwyn for an anniversary in Burwell Church.'

Guild of St John, Reach

As with the guild of St John the Baptist, little is known about the Guild of St John at Reach. It is known to have existed between 1490 and 1525[50], but nothing else is known.

References

1. Suffolk Record Society. Stoke by Clare Cartularies, iii pp. 292 – 3.
2. Suffolk Record Society. Stoke by Clare Cartularies, i pp. 59, 63, 76 – 79.
3. Illingworth, W, and Caley, J, *Rotuli Hundredorum temp Henry III & Edward I.* Record Commission, 1812 – 1818.
4. P.R.O., CP 25/1/24/22, No. 5.
5. B.L, Record Commission, 1802 *Taxatio Ecclesiastica Angliae et Walliae auctoritate P. Nicholai IV*, Additional MSS 24060.
6. P.R.O., SC 6/HENVIII/7258.
7. Victoria County Histories, *A History of Cambridgeshire, Volume II*, 256 – 257.
8. Muskett, J J, (ed), *Inventories of Cambridgeshire Church Goods, temp Edward VI,* (reprinted from East Anglian, N.S. Vols vi-x, 1895 – 1904) 27.
9. H.M.S.O. Calendar of Patent Rolls preserved in the public record office (1891 – 1986), 1560 – 1563, 168.
10. Baskerville, G. *Married Clergy*, 222.

11. Norfolk Record Office, REG/31, P.1260.
12. B.L., Add Ms. 5813, folio 98v.
13. C.R.O., R 55/7/81.
14. P.R.O., PROB 11/57, folio 402.
15. P.R.O., PROB 11/123, folios 30v. – 31.
16. P.R.O., CP 25/2/259/1, East. No. 3..
17. C.U.L., Add 23.f.24.
18. C.U.A., D. XVI. 46, 119. Also Cambridge University Library, G. Tithe Award and Map 1841.
19. C.U.L., University Register (1693), Reference: 32/1
20. C.R.O., P18/26/98
21. C.R.O., Fiche copy of Cole Manuscript 1743.
22. Hart, W.H., Lyons, P A, Ed, 1884 *Cartularium Monasterii De Rameseia, Longman & Co, London. Vol II*, 160.
23. De Windt, E B, (ed), 1976 *The 'Liber Gersumarum' of Ramsey Abbey: A Calendar and Index of B.L. Harley Ms. 445.* Subsidia Medievalia 7. Toronto: Pontifical Institute of Medieval Studies.
24. P.R.O., SC 2/179/20, m. 2.
25. Norfolk Record Office, Norwich Diocesan Documents. Reference: REG 31, p. 1260.
26. H.M.S.O. Calendar of Patent Rolls preserved in the public record office (1891 – 1986), 1370 – 1374, 188; 1374 – 1377, 99.
27. West Suffolk Record Office, Reference 500/1/R 2/11, folio 80.
28. Norfolk Record Office. Reference:VIS/5/2, folio 22; VIS6/1, folio 5.; VIS6/4, folio 90v.
29. C.U.A., CUR32/1, no. 15.
30. Lucas, C, 1936 *The Fenman's World*
31. Hart, W.H., Lyons, P A, (ed), 1884 *Cartularium Monasterii De Rameseia, Longman & Co, London. Vol I*, 190 – 191.
32. P.R.O., PROB 11/14, folio. 325v,; PROB 11/17, folio. 18v,; PROB 11/20, folio. 77,: PROB 11/24, folio. 23.
33. Lambeth Palace Library. Ecclesiastical records of the Commonwealth. Reference: MS. COMM. XIIa/3, folio. 256.
34. Cambridge Chronicle, 23 June 1857, p. 4.
35. C.U.A., CUR32/1, nos. 103 – 104.
36. Victoria County Histories, *A History of Cambridgeshire, Volume II*, pp. 163 – 164.
37. C.U.L., Ely Diocesan Records, 42 – 44;
38. *Proceedings of the Cambridgeshire Antiquarian Society*, **61**, 78.
39. Gordon, A, (ed) *Freedom after Ejection*, 14, 26.
40. Turner, G.L. (ed), 1911 – 1914 *Original Records of Early Nonconformity*, **1**, 571; **2**, 870.
41. *Transactions of the Congregational History Society*. **6**, 413 – 28; **7**, 3 – 15.
42. P.R.O. Ely Diocese, Court of Archdeacon of Sudbury – Registration of places of worship. Reference RG 31/2, nos. 165 – 6.
43. C.U.L., Ely Diocesan Records, G, Tithe Award 1841, 6, 33.
44. Cambridge Chronicle, 14 October 1854, p. 5.
45. Cambridge Chronicle, 4 March 1854, P. 8.
46. P.R.O., RG 31/2, no. 470.
47. Curia Regis Rolls preserved in the Public Record Office (H.M.S.O 1922 – 79).
48. P.R.O., PROB 11/9, folio. 148.
49. Lay Subsidy 82/192
50. P.R.O., PROB 11/9, folio. 168.
51. Cambridge University Library, Ely Faculty Register.
52. Royal Commission for historic Monuments (1972), An Inventory of Historical Monuments in the County of Cambridge, Volume II, North East Cambridgeshire, P25. HMSO, London.
53. C.R.O., P18/25/98
54. C.R.O., P18/25/104

Chapter 7

Open Fields

There has been much debate in recent years about the increasing enlargement of fields and the removal of hedgerows. The pattern of small fields enclosed by hedgerows, which we consider as the traditional British countryside, developed following the enclosure of lands that occurred by acts of parliament from the mid 1700s onwards. This enclosure marked a complete change from the medieval landscape, which in this area was for the most part open with occasional clusters of trees.

By the late medieval period, most of the land in the parish of Burwell was in cultivation. There were, however, some notable exceptions including:

- Much of the fenland,
- The heath land now known as Newmarket Heath,
- An area of common land and enclosures near to Breach Farm
- The area immediately surrounding the village, which comprised enclosures or closes.

The cultivated land was mostly arable, although some land was set aside as meadow as part of the three-year cycle. This arable land was subdivided into narrow strips.

The strip was the smallest unit of cultivation and was in many cases referred to as a 'land'. Often these 'lands' had names. For example, fourteenth- and fifteenth-century records refer to 'Larklond' (near the present Larkhall Farm) and 'Ayllyhanedlond' in the East Field. Research into field systems suggests the average size was 8 by 200 yards or a third of an acre. From Cambridgeshire to the Welsh borders[1] these strips were usually ploughed in an anticlockwise manner, which caused the soil to be ridged up about one foot in the centre, leaving two flat sides sloping from ridge to furrow. Lands were usually raised up to assist the natural drainage with furrows aligned down the steepest gradient. In Burwell that never seems to have been the case, probably because the drainage here is good. There are no ridge and furrow fields remaining in the parish, although there is some evidence of this type of field system in the form of furlongs, which survive as low ridges in the fields.

As the rearing of sheep became popular some land was allowed to grass over. Such pieces of land were called 'Leys' a term that means pasture. Here in Burwell, the area of former fields between The Causeway and Low Road was known as the Leys, although today that name only survives in the footpath which runs from Newnham to Parsonage Lane. This area was probably turned over to pasture in the fourteenth century when sheep rearing became important.

Furlongs

Groups of lands with furrows running parallel were called 'furlongs'. In the fields adjoining the Devil's Dyke a number of furlongs can be seen as low ridges in the fields and medieval and later documentary evidence exists for the presence of furlongs in other fields. This term furlong should not be confused with the modern term as it referred to an area, not a length. Each furlong had a name and these are of historical importance.

Where two furlongs had furrows at right angles to one another, the first land of one furlong, which was made up of the heads of all the lands in the other furlong, was known as the *'headland'*. The Causeway is the best example of a raised headland in Burwell. Furlong boundaries with lands running at right angles to them on either side were made up of double rows of heads, and were called 'joints'.

Sometimes a furlong was turned over to arable or other use. Where this occurs we get references to 'curtilages'. For example, in 1404 we have the following record[2]:

'John Ayllewyn, one curtilage recently made of a furlong of the lord, at the eastern end'

For this he was charged 10d rent per year. The same record also refers to John being allowed to rent *'Two Butts alongside an old furlong'*. A butt in this case being where the furrows joined the furlong.

Balks and Roads

Often in the Middle Ages narrow lands were allowed to grass over and became used as permanent rights of way called 'balks'. Nineteenth-century documentation and maps show a number of such balks in existence. Like furlongs they all had names, such as 'Mile Balk'. The best example remaining today can be seen in the track from North Street to Ness Road near Judy's Hole, which is still known as 'Howland Balk'. Bunting's Path, part of which is now a metalled road, probably started out as such a balk. As late as 1806 it extended from Silver Street to Ness Road as now, but carried on over the fields to the parish boundary with Exning. Other balks in the parish included, Dale Balk and Mile Balk both in the South Field and Hillamore Balk in the East (Mill) Field. These balks and the roads that went behind the gardens of the houses, such as 'Dark Lane' and 'Spring Close', allowed access to the fields. In the case of the lanes at the ends of the gardens or enclosed areas adjoining gardens of houses, known as 'closes', they also provided a means to move animals from the protective enclosure of the garden with its hedge or fence to the meadows or into the open fields after the harvest had been gathered in. At the time of enclosure most of these roads and paths disappeared into the new fields.

These paths and roads were essential to the survival of the open-field village and the community was constantly concerned to maintain these rights of way, free from obstruction and in serviceable repair. Usually this required each tenant to be responsible for the maintenance of the roads alongside his property. In Wistow, another Ramsey Abbey manor, this had to be carried out with stone by 20 September on pain of a fine of 12d. Furthermore, the villagers were constrained to use the accustomed ways and not create new paths by taking short cuts. The penalties for taking short cuts and damaging, or potentially damaging, crops were usually severe. A similarly serious view was also taken if anyone blocked a footpath as a record of 1320 from another Ramsey Abbey manor, Broughton, shows:

'the jury said that Richard de Long had closed a certain way next to his house,which ought to be common the whole time between the Gules of August (1 August) and the Feast of St Martin (11 November) so that all may drive their wagons over it for the reaping and carting of grain.'

In Burwell, no records appear to exist regarding such bye-laws or breaches of bye-laws relating to roads. However, records show that one quarry was used to provide stone specifically for the purpose of road repair and that this quarry remained open until at least the early 1900s.

Closes

As noted above, each dwelling had with it one or more enclosed areas including what we would today consider as the garden. These areas, known as 'closes', were used to keep livestock that were only allowed out into the common fields at certain times of the year. As with roads and balks, closes also had names associated with them and a

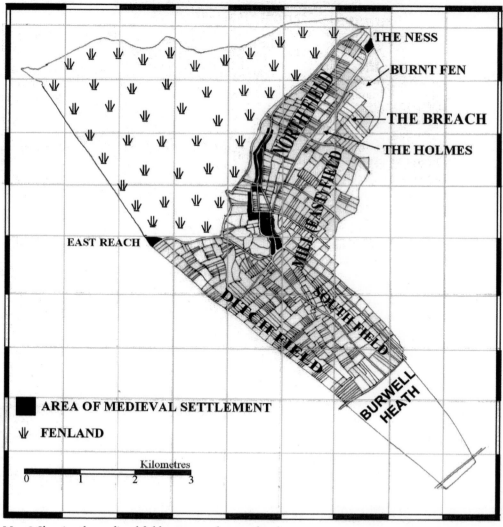

Map 9 *Showing the medieval field pattern and areas of settlement.*

few of these survive in records. Amongst these are 'Stone Close', which was an enclosed area between Tan House and the cricket ground, 'Tenters Close', 'Scotred Close' and 'Crownall Close'.

Fields

For the purpose of crop rotation and communal grazing furlongs were grouped together into areas known as 'fields'. Burwell like most villages started with a three-field (*triennial*) system. These three fields were known as North Field, Ditch Field and East Field. By the nineteenth century, East Field was known as Mill Field. In about 1232 a further field was added as more land was brought into cultivation. This smaller field was called South Field.

A typical peasant holding during the medieval period consisted of about 20-40 acres scattered throughout the parish in about 60-80 strips. Few of these strips of land lay next to one another. In this way all parts of the parish, good soil and bad alike, were shared out amongst the village community. These strips of land tend in most places to be referred to as 'small virgates' or, later, 'cotlands'. However in the documents of Ramsey Abbey the land being referred to is usually given in acreage, although a 'croftland' is commonly referred to in respect of Reach. Each strip was clearly marked out either with poles or stones and it was the tenant's responsibility to maintain these markers and not encroach on the neighbouring strips. Failure to do this and/or encroachment usually resulted in a fine and the awarding of damages.

The meadows (permanent pastures) were also divided into strips. These were called by various names such as, Rood, Rod, Dole, or Pole.

Today, due to modern farming techniques, we have to rely on archaeological techniques and historical records to determine the location of the furlong boundaries, balks and tracks. Some furlongs still survive as long banks of soil, while most former tracks and balks are only visible on aerial photographs.

Dating the field system

There are a number of theories about when the pre-enclosure field systems were created and recent archaeological evidence has shown that many field systems probably originated in the Neolithic period, some in the Roman period and a few later.

In Burwell much of the alignment of field boundaries seems to relate to the alignment of the Devil's Dyke and this is especially true of land to the south of the village, in Ditch Field, suggesting a field system that was created by the Anglo-Saxons by about the eighth century.

Burwell Fields

The layout of the medieval fields for Burwell covered almost all of the land above the ordnance datum and some areas of fen adjoining the fen edge (Map 10). The whole pattern is of small strips with varying sized enclosures or closes immediately surrounding the houses in the village. The various manors, initially Ramsey, together with that of the Tiptofts and the smaller manors, all have their lands interspersed in these strips.

As noted earlier, Burwell had a three-field system from an early date. In this pre thirteenth-century field system, the three fields covered the following areas:

1. North Field originally extended northwards from Parsonage Lane to The Ness and from the fen edge in the west to the Ness Road in the east. From the present Ness Road to the parish boundary the area of the North Field was separated out into smaller areas; 'The Breach', 'The Holmes', 'Burnt Fen' and 'Hay Croft'.

2. The Ditch Field (first recorded in 1232) extended from the ditch at Reach Corner in the west to somewhere close to where Ditch Farm now stands in the east, and for the most part stretched between the ditch and the village, or to the fen in the western half.

3. East field (later known as Mill Field) was brought into agricultural production. This field stretched from Ness Road in the west to the parish boundary with Exning in the east and from Haycross lane in the north to Sandpit lane in the south.

The thirteenth and fourteenth centuries saw a number of major changes in this field system. There may have been changes occurring earlier but records are not available for these periods. The first major change was the abandonment of much of the North Field to agricultural use, the village being allowed to extend over the former fields. In the case of The Leys, former plough lands were turned over to pasture

The loss of this agricultural land appears to have been compensated for in a number of ways. Firstly a fourth field, The South Field (first recorded in 1232) extended roughly from the present Ditch Farm in the west to Warbraham Farm in the east, and from the Devil's Dyke to Sand Pit Lane (a former lane roughly halfway between Heath Road and Newmarket Road), which ran parallel to Heath Road.

Secondly sections of the fen were being drained, most notably:

- an area between the present Anchor Bridge and Hythe Lane Bridges
- an area south of that close to the present junction between the present Weirs Drove and the Reach Road
- the Broads.

Thirdly additional areas of former heathland were brought into production. Up to the 1840s, that around Warbraham Farm and extending to the present Heath, were referred to as an extension of the North Field. The area from Haycross Lane to Burnt Fen (adjoining The Ness), appears to have been separated out into three small fields; Hay Croft, which may have been a number of small meadows, The Holme, which by 1308[3] was recorded as the common meadow and The Breach, so named because it was an area brought late into production. At the time of enclosure these were referred to as areas comprising '*old enclosures*'.

From records that survive it is possible to determine that each of these new areas were in use before the year 1400. Table 19 shows pre-enclosure names associated with the open fields (fields, balk, road and fen names).

At what time The Ness itself came into use is not clear. The first record relating to The Ness is not until 1267 when a mill is described there. However that mill was probably one of those referred to in the Domesday Book and therefore it is likely that some settlement activity was taking place here before 1066. Subsequent references regarding The Ness refer to cottages and may further indicate a longstanding settlement around a watermill.

In addition to these areas there was The Heath. Little is recorded about The Heath prior to the sixteenth century when it was split into five sheepwalks held by the larger estates. It is likely that this was a continuation of the medieval practice. In 1650, the largest of these was owned by the Ramsey Manor, which had the grazing right for 480 sheep. The manor of Burwell Tiptofts had, until it sold its sheepwalk in 1681, the right to graze 300 sheep on the Heath. The manors of Burwell Dullinghams and St Omers each also held the right to graze 300 sheep each on the Heath.

Table 20 *Pre-enclosure field, balk, close, road and track names in Burwell.*

Name	Date	Description	Source Document
Ayllyhanedlond	1400	Reference to a piece of land in East Field.	Liber Gersumarum
Birds Acre	1678	An acre of land owned by Queens College.	Queens College Terrier
Le Blake	1608	A piece of land, probably fen (The Black).	Town Lands Charity Papers
Bottom Way	1451	A road leading to a piece of land called the bottom or bottom piece in ditch field.	Queens College Muniments
Le Breche La Brach La Brach Le Breche Le Brache Le Braach	1232 1294 1322 1357 1378 1398,1400	Field name. The word 'Breach', means newly cultivated land, and is to the east of the Ness Road.	Feet of Fines Court Rolls Court Rolls Feet of Fines Feet of Fines Ministers Accounts
Braddeye Bradweye	1400 1423	The Broad Way, the trackway at the far end of North Street.	Liber Gersumarum
Le Broud	1398	The Broads, an area of fen to the north of the village at its boundary with Fordham Parish.	Ministers Accounts
Buntynges Paath	1399	A Path across the East Field, probably associated with Thomas Bunting.	Liber Gersumarum
Burnt Yard	1817	An enclosure which was recorded as being very old by 1817.	Inclosure Act Award
Bynnges	1400	A piece of land. No indication of its location is given.	Liber Gersumarum
Le Causie	1604	The Causeway.	Ramsey Manor Court Rolls
Cheselenspightill Chestevynespightill Chastelyn's Pithel	1415 1447 1455	The name of a Pightle (*a pightle is a small enclosure, often associated with a croft*).	Liber Gersumarum
Cromwell Crompwell Crownall Ground	1307 1307 1798	The name of an old enclosure, presently known as Crownall, off the Swaffham Road. By 1817 it was known as Crown Well.	Ramsey Manor Court Rolls Queens College Terrier
Dale Balk	1806	A balk in the South Field.	Map of Manor 1806
Dichefeld Dychefeld	1232 1399	Field name – Ditch Field is the field abutting the Devil's Dyke.	Feet of Fines Liber Gersumarum
Estfeld	1399	Field name – the East Field.	Liber Gersumarum
Foxhole Way	15th cent 1798	A balk in Mill Field.	Queens College Terriers
Fysshestrete Fyssher street	1423 1440	The name of a road, either Fish Street or Fisher Street. Possibly the street where the Ramsey Manor fishermen lived.	Liber Gersumarum
Galewhyll	1399	Reference to a piece of land adjoining the Devil's Dyke to the eastern side of the Swaffham Road.	Liber Gersumarum
Gilbertescroft	1409	A croft, (house and land), either at Reach or The Ness.	Liber Gersumarum

Table 20 *Pre-enclosure field, balk, close, road and track names in Burwell. (Continued)*

Name	Date	Description	Source Document
Gyllescroft	1400	A croft, (house and land), either at Reach or The Ness.	Liber Gersumarum
Grizzel Hill	1798	An area in Southfield.	Queens College Terrier
Halfheddam	1571	A piece of land.	Patent Rolls Series
Hallode in maresco Hallhed Fen Halled Fen	1419 1563– 1587	Hallards Fen.	Ramsey Manor Court Rolls Ramsey Manor Court Rolls
Howland Balk Harleys Lane Harlond Way	1760 1793 1817	A balk in North Field, off North Street. The name seems to suggest a path or lane leading to the Hoo Land or meeting place. That it intersects with another lane known as Staploe Balk suggests the presence of the meeting place for the Hundred near where they meet.	Terrier of Church Lands Queens College
Hathedd Acre	1506	A piece of land, possibly part of Hallard Fen.	Patent Rolls Series
Havelode Causeway Heavlode Causeway	1420	A Causeway, possibly the bank at the side of a lode.	Ramsey Manor Court Rolls
Hedges (The)	1793	A path or an enclosure near to Buntings path.	Queens College Terrier
Heystrete Le Highstrete	1347 1452	The High Street.	Queens College Muniments Ramsey Manor Court Rolls
Hillamore balk	1730	A Balk on the Ladwade (Eastern side) of East/Mill Field.	Terrier of Church Lands
Hinlandes	1216– 1272	Refers to Higher Ground (High Lands) in the North Field.	Ramsey Abbey Cartularies
Holmes	1308	An area of former permanent meadow of the village, situated to the east of Ness Road, between Ness Road and the parish boundary with Exning. The road leading to it was known as Holme way in 1793.	Ramsey Manor Court Rolls
Knaves Acre	1793	An acre of land on either side of Holme Way.	Queens College
Lammas Ground Lammas Meadow	1806 1817	Described as a meadow in 1817, on the 1806 map of the Manor of Burwell Ramseys it is shown as a large field with eight sub divisions, its south-eastern boundary being next to the spring emanating from Spring Close. The name suggests a close association with Lammas (Loaf Mass), either the celebration (1 August) of, or the use of the meadow for livestock from Lammas Day.	Map of Manor of Burwell Ramseys 1806 Survey of Lands to be Enclosed
Larklond Larkdene	1398 1460	A piece of land, 'Lark Land', presently the area around Lark Hall Farm.	Ministers Accounts Pembroke College
Le Layes	1439	The Leys, an area of land removed from arable use and made into pasture. The Leys covered the area between The Causeway and Low Road.	Ramsey Manor Court Rolls
Le Peend	1406	A piece of land. No indication of its location is given. It was part of the lands of the Manor of St Omers.	Pro Chancery Records
Longcroft	1415	A house and land at The Ness.	Liber Gersumarum
Littleholm way	15th century	A road probably to the north-east of the village.	
Mile Balk	1806	A balk in South Field.	Map of Manor 1806
Del Nees Nesmelne Le Nesse La Nesse	1267 1273 1307 1398	The Ness.	Ramsey Abbey Cartularies Rotuli Hundredorum Ministers Accounts Liber Gersumarum

Table 20 *Pre-enclosure field, balk, close, road and track names in Burwell. (Continued)*

Name	Date	Description	Source Document
New Piece New Piece Balk	1793	A piece of land and the path leading to it, probably formed out of a larger piece of land, hence 'new' piece.	
Newnham	1446	Newnham.	Ministers Accounts
Northfeld le Nethfeld	1400 1411	Field name – The North Field.	Liber Gersumarum
Northstrete Northstrete	1351 1401	North Street.	Queens College Muniments Liber Gersumarum
Le Personslane	1351	Parsons Lane – lane going to the Parsonage, the present day Parsonage Lane.	Rentals
Terram Persone	1307	The Land of the Parson. Reference to a piece of land.	Ministers Accounts
Pellams	1418	A house and land, location uncertain.	Liber Gersumarum
Pymys or Prymys	1442	Name of a piece of land.	Liber Gersumarum
Puttokys	1447	A piece of land. No indication of its location is given. It was part of the lands of the Manor of St Omers.	Liber Gersumarum
Randsom Balk	1793	A balk in Ditch Field near Reach Road.	Queens College
Reach Croft Rechecroftes	1493 1567	An area of East Reach, comprising of crofts (cottages), the rental of which included land in the fields of Burwell.	Ramsey Manor Court Rolls Patent Rolls Series
Reach Way	1678	The road to Reach – prior to it being renamed to Scotred Lane.	Queens College Terrier
Rebynes Hanedlond	1400	A piece of land.	Liber Gersumarum
Sand Pit Way	1793 1806	A Balk in East (Mill) Field leading towards the Heath.	Queens College 1806 Map of Burwell Ramseys
Scotridge Close	1840	A Close off Scotred lane (Reach Road).	Tithe award
Southfeld le Sowthfeld	1232 1405	Field name – The South Field.	Feet of Fines Liber Gersumarum
Viam de Stapilhoue Stapilhamweye Stapilhoway Staploe way Staploe Balk	1198 1451 1678 1730 1806	A trackway in East/Mill Field heading in a northerly direction towards Landwade. This still survives as a lane in the parish of Exning.	Feet of Fines Queens College Muniments Terrier of Church Lands 1806 Map of Burwell Ramseys
Swaffham Way	1678	Swaffham Road.	Queens College Terrier
Tinkers Piece	1793	A piece of land in Ditch Field.	Queens College
Wakeleysmegate Wakelynsgate	1409 1442	A piece of land, probably that recorded in the early 1400s as being formerly in the possession of Wakelin comprised at that time of 15 acres. No indication of its location is given in the medieval documents. However, documents of the early 1700s refer to a piece of enclosed land off Scotred Lane (Reach Road) called Wakelands which is probably the same piece, which, by that time, had been split up. Part of this is referred to as a meadow called Wakelices. In which case it was situated between Stone close and Lammas Ground.	Liber Gersumarum
Walbrom Walbron	1398 1504,1507	A piece of Land. The Present day Warbraham Farm occupies this area.	Ministers Accounts Queens College Muniments
Wodelane Woodland Roadway	1425 1730	The name of a road (Wood Lane), probably that known as Woodland Roadway in 1730 and Timber Hill in the early 1800s, now Isaacsons Road.	Liber Gersumarum Terrier of Church Lands

Open field regulations

The land in the village was worked as one or possibly two communal farms overseen by a *firmarius*. We only have records relating to the Ramsey manor so it is not clear whether each manor had its own *firmarius*. The *firmarius* ensured that the regulations governing the management of the land were adhered to. The reeve and the beadle took up breaches of regulations on his behalf. In a largely open landscape with cultivated land scattered in strips and animals being allowed to graze on the meadows, on the fens in the summer months and on heaths, the potential for trespass and crop damage was great. Where such trespass occurred the animals were impounded and the owners had to pay a fine before they were released. The pound was situated next to the former green on Pound Hill and was still in existence as late as 1806 but it is not shown on maps later than that date.

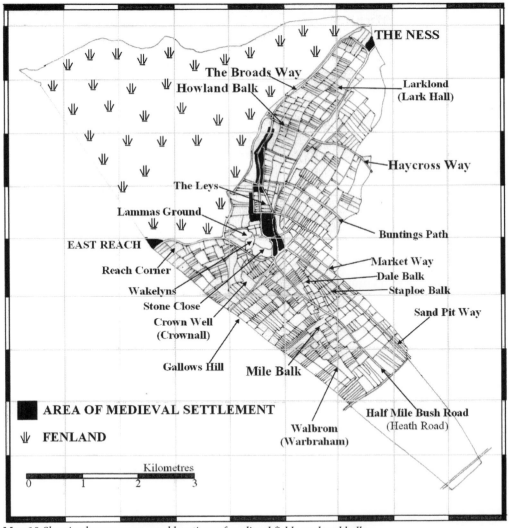

Map 10 *Showing known names and locations of medieval field, road and balks.*

There were a number of offences that could be committed in the open fields, such as failing to carry out a customary service such as mowing, overstocking a pasture or ploughing your neighbour's land. All of these offences were dealt with by the reeve through the manorial court as the example below shows[4].

> 1312 'Adam Idayne overstocked a pasture by 50 sheep. Therefore he is (in mercy) to six pence with pledge John Idayne.'

Distribution of estates and peasant holdings

The land in the parish in the medieval period comprised the demesne and the common fields. The demesne was that belonging to the manor, in other words the land reserved for the support of the lord's household, and cultivated by his bond tenants who were referred as naifs or natives on the Ramsey Manorial estate.

In the case of the Ramsey Manor in the mid twelfth and early thirteenth centuries, the abbot appropriated much of this demesne land for his personal income while the convent received the rental of the common fields and the tithes.

It is clear from documentation that some of the demesne was being leased out for much of the twelfth century and onwards. Accordingly, the labour services of some of the peasantry were commuted or sold introducing a distinction between tenant's works (*ad opera*) and their rent (*ad censum, censarii, molmen*).

The demesne is referred to in all rentals throughout the period to distinguish it from other land being rented. From these rentals we can see that, in the case of the Ramsey Manor, the demesne was not land confined to an area around the manor house as is the case in some places. A good example of this is the leet record, recording the rental of land in 1400, to Thomas Bosoun the Chaplain, which reads:

> 'Thomas Bosoun, Chaplain: eight acres of demesne land lying at Le Nesse, four acres of demesne land at 'Bynnges' and 'Rebynes Hanedlond', four acres of demesne land at Estfeld previously held by John Walden, two acres of demesne at Ayllyhanedlond recently held by John Walden, two acres of demesne in Dychfeld at Galowhyll and one rod of demesne in Northfeld at Braddeye touching upon Gyllescroft, and three acres of demesne in Le Braach.'

From this and other rental records we can see that the demesne land was spread out across the parish and comprised of at least the following,

Table 21 *Demesne lands in common fields, identified from records.*

Area	Location	Present day name/location
8 acres	La Ness	The Ness
1 Rood	Northfeld at Braddeye	Off North Street near to the Broads
4 acres	Estfeld	Somewhere between Slade farm and Newmarket Road
3 acres	Le Braach	Near Breach Farm
5 acres	Dychfeld at Galowhyll	Near Ditch Farm
2 acres	Ayllyhenedlond	Reach
2 acres	Estfeld at Buntynges Paath	Buntings Path

In such documents land not held in demesne is rarely referred to by name. Rentals indicate the name of the person to whom the rental is granted and its location is given as being next to the land of another tenant. For example;

> 1411 'Richard Sowtheman: one tenement of 15 acres and two crofts with one piece of meadow, once held by Richard himself, with a half acre of land in le Nethfeld next to the land of John Prikke.'

It is also frequently the case that the previous owner, or owners, is referred to rather than a location, as in the following example,

1409   'John Barwe: Chaplain, and Robert his brother: one tenement of 15 acres of land once held by Thomas Swyn at Wakeleysmegate and once held by John Barwe, their father, for 24 years, rendering annually 17s at the customary times and all other services and customs rendered by their father; another tenement of 15 acres once held by Robert atte Brigge and once held by their father, for life, rendering 17s annually at the customary times; one croft once held by John Sadde and adjoining Gilbertescroft, for life, rendering annually 12d four acres of demesne in Estfeld in one piece once held by Hugo Berker, for life, rendering 4s annually; two crofts once held by Thomas Plumbe against the land of the rector, for life, rendering 4s annually. They will build a new house on the cote once held by Sawyer and also once held by Elena Helewys.'

In addition to the demesne lands in the fields, we also know that adjoining the manor house there were orchards and fishponds and that the mill and ponds at the Ness were considered to be within the demesne following their purchase by the abbey from Robert de Ness.

The remaining land of the manor, known as the common fields, was broken up into plots, known as furlongs, for ploughing. These were sub-divided into strips, which were delimited by a piece of unploughed land one or two furrows in width. The holding of every tenant, irrespective of extent, comprised a number of these strips scattered across the furlongs of the common fields. The demesne lands were interspersed with the common lands in each of the furlongs, rather than being compressed into a compact block.

Cropping and cultivation

Records pertaining to individual peasant farmers working the land do not exist, however the records of Ramsey Abbey give a good indication of the overall production of the land.

Arable crops

Arable crops provided the majority income from Burwell fields, with corn (wheat) being the principle crop. The Ramsey Abbey accounts give some idea of what was grown and how much, and from 1324 a *responsio* or yield ratio was included. From these documents Dr J Raftis[3] has estimated the average arable land usage for each crop. Table 22 shows these as percentages:

Table 22 *Estimates of crop yields for Burwell in the fourteenth century.*

Crop	%
Wheat	23.4
Barley	19.6
Rye	6.3
Dredge (Drage)	9.3
Maslin (Mixed Corn)	10.6
Oats	16.2
Peas	14.3

Land rental records from the early 1400s include references to customary services on the lord's land including reaping of wheat and barley. For example[2].

'John Poket................ the reaping of one acre of wheat and one acre of Barley, and the carrying of grain.'

'Nicholas, son of John atte Hyll......... and reaping, binding and tribute of two acres of grain in the demesne land.'

By 1314 the Burwell farm was producing 45 quarters per year of malted barley and dredge and 80 quarters of wheat, which amounted to half of the available crop for that year. By 1447 approximately 185 quarters of wheat was sent to the abbey via Reach despite the demesne being rented out.

Harvesting

The time of the harvest depended upon the ripening of the crop and the weather. Grain crops were cut by hand and put into a sheaf bound together with a twist of spears. The sheaf was small and it took 20 sheaves of oats to fill a one-bushel basket. It appears that there was great temptation for some in the community to steal the odd sheaf by tucking it under his arm and creeping away. In Burwell the fine for anyone caught doing this was 40d per sheaf. Similarly no one was allowed to pay another in sheaves on the field.

Pasture

Burwell had only one area of permanent meadow for pasture, The Holme (meaning 'a Marsh-Meadow'). This was a common pasture and those with livestock paid a tax, a *'holmsilver'* for its maintenance and permission to pasture their animals. Rules strictly controlled the number of animals allowed in pasture and fines were levied on anyone found guilty of overstocking a pasture.

The five larger estates all had strips of pasture on the heath, which were used mainly for sheep. In addition, sections of fen were used in the summer months, for grazing, mainly by cattle. As for the remaining land, the common fields were generally used for arable crops. However, after the time of harvest they became of prime value to the peasant community as additional pasture. To ensure that animals were not put out too early, bye-laws were introduced that regulated when animals could be placed in harvested fields. This ensured that the animals did not eat any of the valuable grain. One such bye-law is that from a court roll of 1411[4] which states:

'It is ordered by the lord and by the whole homage that no one henceforth shall have or pasture any foals in the grain or grass of the community whether of the lord or of his tenants under pain for each one of 2s.

And that no one henceforth shall pasture sheep or pigs in the meadows within the grain of the community as above under pain of each one of 40d.

And that no one shall pasture with sheep or pigs through the whole of the autumn or until the grain shall have been removed and raked by the space of one land under the aforesaid pain. And that no one shall glean through the whole of autumn who is able to earn 1d. a day and food under the aforesaid pain.

And that no one shall leave town in time of autumn who is able to earn 1d. a day as above.

And no one shall pasture or trample any stubble with any animals during autumn before the Feast of the Nativity of the Blessed Virgin Mary next to come, under pain of 40d.

Again it is agreed and ordered as appears in the preceding court more fully that no one henceforth through the whole autumn shall cart any grain away from the field by night nor shall he transport it any other way neither in the evening nor in the morning while it is still night under pain each one paying the lord 40d. without mitigation.'

In many villages fields were declared open to pasture at Lammas (1 August) one month after hay-making had ended. However, as the text above shows, in Burwell the fields were not to be opened to pasture until the Feast of the Nativity of the Blessed Virgin Mary, on 8 September. The reason for this is unclear, however it may have been to allow for the harvesting of a second crop of hay in exceptional years. One area (see Table 19) was still referred to as Lammas Ground up to the enclosure of Burwell's fields and this name may suggest that this area was open to pasture from 1 August (after the cutting of hay), while the rest of the fields remained closed until after 8 September.

It was usual in the period for the announcement declaring the rights of pasture and the opening of the fields to be given from the pulpit on the preceding Sunday.

In Burwell other bye-laws dictated that:

- Sheep were to be put out to pasture only after Holy Cross Day (14 September) and that between 8 September and 14 September, cattle could be put out to graze on the barley stubble before the sheep were released. This was probably introduced to ease the concern felt throughout the Ramsey manors about the over-pasturing of the fen by cattle.

- Fen straw could only be mown after Easter and any villager employing a man to mow with a scythe could only employ one man and no more.

- The sedge fen was closed to communing beasts between mid summer and Michaelmass.

- The sale of turf and sedge outside the village was strictly forbidden.

The bye-law regulating the sale of sedge outside of the village, while in force from the fourteenth century had ceased to exist by 1604 when it was recorded as being common practice. The regulation regarding turf, however, was still in place in 1612 and appears by that year to have been extended to cover the removal of turves by people leaving the village. The records of Land Revenues for the manor of Burwell Ramseys for that year states that residents who leave the village should only remove 5000 of the turves stacked at their farmsteads.

The fen areas of the village, while valuable pasture areas in the drier summer months, were not considered in the economic evaluation of the manor as pasture except, up to the end of the twelfth century, as a source of fish. In the thirteenth and fourteenth centuries, when some areas of the fen, such as the broads, were reclaimed, it is likely that the rules applying to other pastures were applied. However all rights of common in Burwell's fens and any rules applying to them came to an end in the seventeenth century.

Sheep

Up to the end of the thirteenth century the numbers of sheep were small, largely because most land was used for the production of arable crops and also because sheep were not often used for food. Sheep were valued for their wool and areas such as Newmarket

Heath and Devil's Dyke would have been used to graze them. As noted above, in the summer months the drier areas of the fen were also used for grazing.

By the fourteenth century things had changed and sheep farming had become popular across much of England including East Anglia. Many monasteries such as those in Yorkshire became very wealthy at this time as a result of income from sheep and while sheep farming did not seem to achieve the same popularity in the Ramsey Manors, land, such as The Leys, was clearly being set aside as pasture. It is likely that the area of Newmarket Heath that was within the parish continued to be used for this purpose and was not brought into use for arable crops. In addition, by the early fourteenth century, a number of enclosures had created around what is now Breach Farm and in part of the East Field near Slade Farm. Up to the nineteenth century the latter area, near Slade Farm, was referred to as the Sheep Walks. As noted previously, before to this time but after *circa* 1100, much of the fenland was used for pasture. However this would only have been used in the dryer summer months and with an increase in the sizes of flocks the need for pasture grew. This increase in livestock can be identified by the increase in pasture and enclosures in the thirteenth and fourteenth centuries.

From a surviving extent during the reign of King Henry III[5], we know that the manor employed a shepherd who was paid in kind. He was allowed to farm 15 acres of the demesne for his service and his food.

The manorial accounts for the numbers of sheep in the Ramsey manors is poor. It is evident that in the thirteenth and first half of the fourteenth century the reeve was concerned only with ensuring that enough sheep, usually 6 to 8 carcasses, were available for sustenance and livery by the manor. The remaining carcasses and hides were sold direct from the manor and so generally not recorded. Records usually only show the number of fleeces sent to the abbey and up to the early fourteenth century these are both unweighed and unvalued. The first good record we have regarding fleeces occurs in 1361 when 274 fleeces, weighing 1 woolpack and 5 stones was sent to the abbey.

There are two exceptions, in 1325 and 1399, which indicate the of the size of the sheep flock on the Ramsey manorial farm. In 1325 the shepherd employed on the farm was caring for 170 wethers and by 1399 this had increased to 500.

Sheep seem to have suffered more than other animals from disease in medieval times and murrain was the chief illness that decimated the lamb population. There are no figures relating to such diseases in Burwell, however there are records for other Ramsey manors, for example Houghton where 53 out of 59 lambs born in 1393 died of murrain.

Cattle

On most of the Ramsey manors records were made of all cattle. These records included the age and sex of the animals and formed part of the annual account of the holdings. The surviving records of the abbey deal mostly with the Huntingdonshire manors. It is known however that by 1325 a cowman was employed on the Burwell farm and that in that year he cared for approximately 25 cattle. Milk from the herd, averaging between 15 and 25 cows in the fourteenth century, was used mostly for making cheese, which was consumed by the abbey or within its manor. What is clear from the records that survive from these manors is that the cattle population was often hit by disease and that stocks often took a long while to build up, suggesting that new stock was not purchased to replace cattle that had died.

The small number of cattle was probably due to the lack of winter food and the need to keep the cows and calves in close, controllable proximity for milking. By the fifteenth century this changed. Cheese was no longer as important to the abbey as it was not accepted as a food rent and cattle were therefore allowed to roam in the fen meadows more freely, although the principle use of the fen was to become pasture for sheep. Some cattle were grazed on the Devil's Dyke, a practice that continued until at least the Elizabethan period when a dispute occurred over the right to graze cattle on the dyke.

Pigs

In the medieval economy pigs were important from the earliest times. Bacon was used both as a food rent and as an important source of food, supplying much of the fat that was a scarce item in the medieval diet. Pigs had two litters of half dozen or more each year and were usually eaten in the second year of age. Unlike today when pigs are mostly grain fed, the medieval pig had to forage for its food. Foraging pigs will go anywhere in search of food and are difficult to stop. They frequently gain access through hedges that will bar other animals and were therefore usually left in the care of a swineherd when out of their sty.

Most manors supplied the abbey with up to 30 flitches of bacon each year. After the Black Death, with the commutation of food rents, Burwell and all the other Ramsey Manors continued to supply the cellarer of the abbey with three or four flitches of bacon each year.

Besides the supplying of pigs to the abbey for food, 15 or 20 pigs were sold each year from the manor. The amount of pigs sold usually depended upon the effects of disease in any year and the maintenance of the manorial flock.

Ploughing and other work

The basic pattern of work undertaken by the villeins (peasants) was determined by the nature of the demesne production and involved routine weekly work throughout the year (customs and services), as well as concentrations in certain periods for seasonal needs. The most regular obligation was that of ploughing, which, using an eight or ten stock team, must have been a slow process. This would have been a constant need and was very much dependent on the availability of plough animals. In the autumn some land was ploughed for winter seed, while in the spring other land was ploughed for Lenten sowing. Land that had been fallow was ploughed twice. The first ploughing turned under the previous crop residue, weeds and grasses. This had to be done after the spring ploughing and before summer to allow for the decomposition of the organic material. The second ploughing, less deep, aerated the soil and was in preparation for sowing.

Those who had ploughs, which cannot have been many (in 1086 there were seven ploughs in Burwell for at least 58 people including slaves) had an obligation to plough on the demesne for one day per week throughout the period from Michaelmas to the following August. This is very clear from all the manorial extents of the Abbey in the twelfth and thirteenth centuries. Friday was usually the day when the obligation for this ploughing was undertaken. Those providing this service were exempted the obligation on the Holy days of Christmas, Easter and Pentecost as the following example relating to Alan Rufus shows.

> 'to plough one rood and a half, except twelve days at Christmas and in the Easter week, and in Whitsun week.'

Important servants of the manor (referred to as *famulii*), while exempt from most obligations, were not exempt from ploughing on the demesne land. Similarly, if a villein were sick and confined to his bed he would be excused from all duties except ploughing. If he died, the surviving family members were expected to carry out his duty.

Strips of plough land varied in length and width and may have originated as the distance a plough team of oxen could pull without having to stop to catch their breath. The furrows also needed to be long enough to compensate for the inconvenience of having to turn the plough team about. That the strips in Burwell vary in length can be seen from the 1806 pre-enclosure map of the manor in the Public Records Office. It has been established from careful study that a day's work for the average medieval plough team was from one-third to two-thirds of a statutory acre.

For works other than ploughing there was considerably more flexibility in how they were carried out and the extents describe a general formula for how the other services could be performed. For example, '*he works two or three days a week*'. Again we can see this from an extent entry for Alan Rufus[5],

> 'Alan Rufus holds twenty four acres with his croft. And he ought to work from the feast of St Michael until Pentecost for one day each week.'

The work done on these days was usually at the discretion of the reeve or the farmer and varied according to the season. For example in the winter a villein might be employed for one or two days a week in cleaning or extending ditches, repairing fences or hedges, or at threshing.

The medieval requirement to plough continued right up to enclosure. A seventeenth century bye-law records that all those with a plough must provide no more than six horses for ploughing.

In Burwell like most of the fen-edge manors, the mowing, gathering and carrying of fen grass and meadow hay was major annual work. From the Burwell extent we can see that while only a couple of people are charged with gathering in they were expected to find others to assist.

> 'Maurice...... And after reaping he will afford help in collecting the Lords hay. And with others he will bring it home.'

At harvest time everyone became involved in bringing in the lord's harvest. This was known as boon works and varied in length. The first day of the boon usually involved the whole family. A number of references to 'love boon' are given in the *Liber Gersumarum* of the abbey as the following example of a rental 1418 shows:

> 'Richard Spencer Sr. and his wife, Alicia: one tenement of 12 acres with a cotland and one and a half acres in a croft and three acres in the fields recently held by Radulf Calvesbane, for 20 years, rendering annually in all things as did Radulf, common fine, suit to court and leet and one love boon. Gersumarum: 6s. and two capons.'

As well as harvesting, the records also make reference to the digging of ditches and the maintenance of hedges. For example in the thirteenth-century extent of the manor we have a variety of references to payments to the lord, usually of between one half penny and one penny, for the vineyard hedge. Similarly many tenants were also required to make a payment towards the upkeep of the *fulstyngpounde*.

A reference to the upkeep of ditches is to be found in the *Liber Gersumarum* when on 2 August 1398:

> 'William Taylor, alias Poket and John Toys: The fishpond of La Nesse, with adjoining meadows and ponds and the mill dam, previously held by Richard Fraunceys, from the previous Michaelmas for 10 years, rendering this year 10s, and each year thereafter 11s 4d at the customary times. Further they will maintain the properties both regarding ditches and all other necessities, at their own expense, with the exception that the bailiff will assign 20 opera of the customaries of the lord in assistance, and the customaries will be suitably rewarded by the firmarii when they come. Further the Lord will be kept free of damage regarding anyone by them during the aforesaid time. Gersumarum: excused because of a rent increase of 40d.'

In this instance it is in relation to the property, including the mill, being rented at The Ness.

The medieval system of providing customary works continued well into the seventeenth century as the parliamentary survey of 1649 shows (Appendix 2). This document demonstrates that all of the copyholders were expected to continue to provide customary services, as the example below shows, and all were hereditary copyholds held, presumably, since before the dissolution of the monasteries.

> 'Phillip Fyson vidua oweth as before, and is to reape one acre and one roode of wheate worth per annum
>
> The same is to mowe and make ready for the carte one acre and one rood of barley worth per annum
>
> The same is to plowe 5 roods of the lordes land worth per annum
>
> The same is to worke one day in making hay for the lord worth per annum'

The big difference between the medieval surveys, which describe such works and the post-medieval surveys is that, in the latter period, the cost of everything is itemised so that the post-medieval lord always knew the worth of the work provided in financial cost and thereby the cost of replacing customary works.

Fish and other fen produce

To the medieval community, the fen was a valuable source of food and livelihood. Medieval lords valued fish highly as part of their staple diet and monastic lords valued fish even more, especially in the early medieval period. During this period, strict adherence to the rule of St Benedict meant that monks did not eat meat, preferring large quantities of fish and eels instead. By the fourteenth century this had been relaxed but fish was still eaten on Fridays.

The Records of abbeys such as Ramsey and Ely shows that vast quantities of herrings and eels were required. For example, the fishery at Stuntney provided 24,000 eels per year to the abbey of Ely. No such records exist regarding quantities of fish and eels from Burwell's fenland, but as a fen edge village there is little doubt that such production did occur. This is seen in records relating to land being used specifically to provide food for the fishermen and in the numerous rental documents relating to fishponds and fisheries.

One such fishery was The Weirs, known as *Wydeswereswater* by 1353[6]. This was situated between the present day Anchor public house and the electricity substation. Looking at this stretch of water today it is hard to see why it should be called 'The Weirs'. In the medieval period it would have had stakes in the water along its length from which eel traps and nets were placed. In addition documents of the medieval and early post-medieval periods refer to fisheries and piscaries. These suggest not only areas such as The Weirs were used for fishing, but fishponds within the manorial demesne, such as those referred to at The Ness, and at The Hall in the twelfth to seventeenth centuries.

Fowl from the fen was probably a staple in the diet of those better off in the period and the range of fowl collected would have been considerable.

In the summer months the fen was a good source of pasture for cattle and sheep. In addition reeds and the sedge grass that grew in the fens was used for roofing. Most houses in Burwell in the medieval period would have had a thatched roof, either of reed, sedge or straw. Much of the fuel used to warm houses and cook with, would have been turves cut from the fen. From the early medieval times sedge, known locally as 'Hall Straw' was collected from the fens as part of customary works. This practice continued well into the seventeenth century, when tenants were expected to provide either 'whole (or full)' or 'half' Hall straw. 'Whole' Hall Straw was 40 sheaves of sedge and a 'load' of Hall Straw comprised of 120 sheaves. In 1649 the total amount of Hall Straw due to the manor of Burwell Ramseys was 1200 sheaves with a value of 30 shillings.

References

1. Hall, D N, 1982, *Medieval Fields*, Aylesbury.
2. De Windt E B, (ed), 1976 *The 'Liber Gersumarum' of Ramsey Abbey: A Calendar and Index of B.L. Harley Ms. 445*. Subsidia Medievalia **7**. Toronto: Pontifical Institute of Medieval Studies.
3. Raftis, J A, 1957, *The Estates of Ramsey Abbey: A Study in Economic Growth and Organisation*, Pontifical Institute of Medieval Studies. Toronto.
4. P.R.O., SC 2/179/16
5. P.R.O., SC 2/179/53
6. P.R.O., C 133/85/3
7. C.U.L. Queens College Muniments. Reference QC 35: 39/3

Chapter 8

The Post-Medieval Burwell

In Burwell as in many places across England the pace of change in the post-medieval period was slow. For the majority, life was hard and they were tied to the land and, instead of the monks of Ramsey as their principal landlord, they now had the lessee of the king. Most lessees were absentees and many of these sublet the land, as had been the case before the reformation. The manorial courts continued to operate and in many cases they began to tighten regulations concerning the use of land.

Those letting property of the lord of the manor still had to continue, as in medieval times, to give service on the manorial demesne and this persisted even during the Commonwealth period as is shown in the Parliamentary Survey of 1649 (Appendix 3). Thus those who had always been poor and tied to the land remained so, with most people renting both house and land from the manors.

The Poor

The numbers of poor, partly due to population growth within the village and the immigration of persons from outside the parish, continued to increase throughout the seventeenth to the nineteenth centuries. This caused concern to the lessees of the manors and the church, both of which had a duty to give alms to the poor. Early measures that were imposed to deal with this increased burden on the resources available for the poor included a law forbidding existing residents from letting or subletting their houses to newcomers not already resident in the parish, unless they could pay a surety to the churchwardens to discharge the parish of responsibility for any costs.

Houses were often crowded as the admissions and surrenders to a cottage in Shoemaker Row in High Town reveals. In 1558 the property was referred to as a messuage and was rented out to the Baldwyn family. However by 1634 the house had been split into a number of tenements of which two tenants are known, John Bavine and Henry and Susan Hitch. The house was then subdivided further, as the records show that Henry and Susan surrendered part of their tenement to a Robert Parnes in 1640. Despite at least part of the building being damaged by fire in 1671, it was recorded that a John Babing was admitted as renting a *moiety* or share of a tenement there. These records[54] appear to show that most of the new admissions were probably to people lodging in the property prior to the landlord realising they were present, and were then admitted as tenants in their own right. The landlord then received the income. Other such tenements are known to have existed, such as that in North Street, sold by John Casburn to John Bulger in 1677[55].

The onus of enforcement of measures to keep the laws such as those relating to lodgers etc. shifted from the beadle and the reeve, who in medieval times had upheld the law to new appointments, to the parish and the individual manors. By the 1720s[2] St Mary's vestry had its own constables besides the parish officers and the officers of the manorial courts. Parish officers could carry out settlement examinations and the lodgers removed and sent back to their own villages. A number of records relating to such examinations and removals exist, including 30 removals from Burwell between 1767 and 1808, and a number for Burwell people who had moved into Cambridge parishes.

Such examinations and removals, however, seem to have had little impact and by about 1736[3] the church wardens purchased a house for use as a workhouse where paupers might spend their day spinning in return for food. By 1776 this house held 20 inmates and by the early 1800s a married couple was being sought to manage the poor in the workhouse, which was now (and may have been from the outset) in the old guildhall. From the mid 1780s[4] it had been leased from the church lands trustees as a workhouse to accommodate paupers and lunatics.

At this time, the 'inmates' were given alms in the workhouse, but they were not necessarily resident there and many did not work on the premises. In 1818 while 20 people were in the workhouse, 175 others were in receipt of support outside the workhouse and a great many more were helped on an occasional basis. The cost of sustaining the poor was increasing throughout the period. One additional cost to that of feeding the poor was incurred in 1797 when the parish entered an agreement with a surgeon from Newmarket to tend to the poor[5]. Another was the cost of employing 'overseers' to assist able-bodied labourers and a couple to run the workhouse. By 1803 the cost of this was £877, almost double what it had been 20 years earlier.

The destitute were not the only people to receive help from the parish in the late eighteenth and early nineteenth centuries. Approximately 900 people were being assisted from the rates at a cost to the parish of £1500 and those with large families received parish allowances.

In the two decades prior to 1835, when Burwell joined the Newmarket Union, the expenditure on poor relief to permanent paupers had seldom fallen below £1400 and on occasions almost reached £1800[6]. In 1835, 49 permanent paupers were recorded, only 15 of these were males and nine of those were aged over 60 years[3,7]. In that year Burwell joined the Newmarket Poor Law Union.

Local Government

During the early post-medieval period, local government rested mainly with the lords of the manors who settled minor disputes through the manorial courts. The Cambridge Assizes continued to handle the more serious misdemeanours carried out by individuals. In 1586 such a case was taken by the Attorney General on behalf of Queen Elizabeth I against Andrew Pearne, Dean of Ely Cathedral, Elizabeth Edwards, William Cook, John Ruse, Francis Tuthill, John Chambers, and others[49] from Swaffham Prior who had taken out of the Manor of Burwell and were despoiling and using for their own gain the ditch and bank of the Devil's Dyke. To make matters worse, instead of beating the bounds of the parish along the ditch side of the field, as had been done for centuries at Rogationtide, the people of Swaffham Prior were processing on the bank, along the route used for the procession of the people of Burwell in their beating the bounds procession. This was obviously too much for the people of Burwell who complained. Three documents survive relating to the dispute and in one it transpires that the reeves of Burwell did at some point seize some of the animals of the people of Swaffham that were grazing on the ditch and place them in the communal pound.

The result was that the defendants wanted a commission set up to investigate whether the boundaries should be changed. The defendants wanted to participate in the commission requesting,

'a commission to be awarded wherein the parties maye joyne for the examinacion of wyttmesses'

Whether such a commission was formed is not clear because the document is blank at the place where the decision should be recorded. However there are no other records of further charges being levied or any similar actions after that.

From the seventeenth to the nineteenth centuries, the parish was not only responsible for the poor but for a range of other local government issues. Despite joining the Newmarket Poor Law Union, it continued to elect parish constables to keep order[8] and from about 1848 had an association for the prosecution of felons[9,10]. This association continued to meet well into the 1870s, despite employment of a resident policeman from that time[11,12]. The village had a small two cell lock-up in The Causeway from the early nineteenth century that still survives to this day. This probably succeeded an earlier structure in the village. Animals, impounded as a result of their wandering into the arable fields or taken in fine, were placed in the village pound on Pound Hill. This had been in existence at least since the middle ages and was most likely the pound used when the cattle of the people of Swaffham Prior were impounded for grazing on the Devil's Dyke. The 1806 map[13] shows a square pound next to the former village green at the top of Parsonage Lane.

Crime in Burwell throughout the period appears to have been particularly prevalent on the fen, especially with smugglers operating in the area around Pout Hall. Charles Lucas[14] writes that Pout Hall was built as an inn but was never granted a licence and due to its isolation it became a rendezvous for thieves and scoundrels. Other prevalent crimes in the nineteenth century included poaching and sheep stealing. Intimidation of witnesses also appears to have been rife, as reported to the press by 229 people in 1892[15].

Burwell gained its first recorded fire engine in 1744[16]. This engine was initially kept in the sacristy of the church and was maintained by the Burwell Town Lands Charity. From 1860 the fire engine was kept in the village lock-up in The Causeway. It appears to have been regularly used throughout the nineteenth century and up to about 1920, by which time it was obsolete.

Charities

In the post-medieval period, Burwell's principal charity that supported local people was the Town Lands Charity. A number of other charities rented land in Burwell's fields to provide money for the poor of other parishes. An example of such a charity was the Shepherds Charity, which appears to have been set up according to the will of Samuel Shepherd of Bottisham in 1739. The trustees of the Shepherds Charity were, from as early as 1784, renting in excess of 38 acres in Burwell with appurtenances from the manor of Burwell Ramseys. These were then being sublet and the money that was raised was used for the poor of Exning and Bottisham.

Burwell Town Lands Charity

Throughout its history the St Mary's church has always benefited from generous benefactors. In the 1400s three benefactors, Thomas Catelyn (d. 1445), William Sygar (d. 1477) and Thomas Forster (d. 1496) donated land to St Mary's for the relief of the poor[17,18]. Both Catelyn and Sygar are known to have died without heir. Between the three of them, they bequeathed a total of 99 acres of land. The rentals from these lands were used to pay the tenths of the people of Burwell and given when the tenths were levied. In addition, both Catelyn and Forster had left the residue of their property for charity.

Those holding the land for the town, the *ffeoffees*, were expected to administer the money and also appear to have had a role in giving other donations, such as that given by John Ellis in 1600[19]. John left £10 for stock for the poor in that year. By 1595, these charitable lands, which had been known as St Mary's Land, were referred to as Burwell Town Lands[20].

In 1613 the first of the parish almshouses was bequeathed. In his will proved in 1613, Lee Cotton[21] left 'a little mansion' and a yard with a barn for the *ffeoffees* to be used as almshouses for four men to occupy, rent free, for life[22]. The residents were also entitled to half a stone of sedge annually and to keep two bullocks. These would have been pastured through the right of commons. A bequest by William Thompson in his will, proved in 1627, ordered his executors to build three almshouses for three poor widows or three other poor parishioners[23]. These were to be built within one year of his death. William also bequeathed £40 for apprenticing poor fatherless children. In the next 25 years a number of such bequests were made, including those by William Mounford, who left a house and a rood for two poor men to inhabit and that of John Wosson or Watson who, in his will of 1642, left a house to support church repairs. This house was later let as an almshouse. By about 1710 the charity had 16 almshouses in the village. These included four houses next to the churchyard occupied by widows.

Smaller donations were also made in bequests during the period, such as that by Thomas Frierston in his will of 1650. He charged the lessee of a close and dovehouse with paying £1 yearly for the poor on St. Thomas's day. Similarly in 1711 Jacob Webb gave a dovehouse yielding ten shillings a year to support apprenticeships.

In 1678–79, Burwell fen was divided. At this time the Town Lands Charity was allotted four lots each of $10^1/_2$ acres. This was for the common rights of its town houses. Three of these lots were for the residents of Thompson's bequest and the fourth for Cotton's bequest. By about 1730, in land, the *ffeoffees* held 100 acres of arable land, four fen lots and two town closes.

With the increase in land and property the uses for the income changed. Originally it had been to pay the tenths of the poor, so relieving them of that debt, but by 1720 the income was being used for a variety of charitable purposes, such as the apprenticeships previously referred to and the purchase of property as 'almshouses'.

In 1727 a problem occurred when the vicar, Alexander Edmundson B.D., with the support of the Archdeacon, asked new *ffeoffees* to agree that the income from the100 acres of arable land be solely used for the repair of St Mary's[25]. The people protested and this led to an enquiry being held in 1730. The result was that the vicar's supporters were displaced as trustees. A compromise was made that allowed money to be taken to repair the church and the remainder to be given to the poor. This was applied to the 100 acres and the four fen lots. All other possessions of the charity were returned to their original purposes. This decree had the effect of reducing the number of 'almshouses' because houses such as that given by Wosson had to be returned to their former state as bequested, that is, for rental with the income being used for church repairs. Income from property rents in 1730 amounted to £75.

By 1790 the trustees maintained ten town houses in their possession. This increased to 15 by 1805. The income from land and property was issued principally as a cash dole, which amounted to £15–£20 each year in the 1740s. However the trustees continued to fund other causes, including occasional apprenticeships, and in 1744 they funded Burwell's first fire engine and continued to maintain it throughout its life.

In 1770 the vicar regained control of the charity but things had changed little and approximately ten percent of the income was given directly to the poor and from 1788 subscriptions were given to Addenbrookes Hospital in Cambridge for the benefit of the poor[26]. In fact cash handouts appear to have continued through to, about, 1830 by which time an increase in the distribution of bread became apparent along with the sale to the poor of turf and coal at a greatly reduced rate[27].

In 1817 the fields of Burwell were enclosed and the Town Lands *ffeoffees* were allotted 56 acres for their arable lands, owning thereafter 92 acres, including 28 acres of fen.

In 1835 the three cottages given by Thompson, which adjoined the churchyard, were pulled down and the land they occupied added into the churchyard. This and a number of other decisions appear to have caused a second dispute over the charity, which was investigated. A decree resulted in 1855, which assigned half of the net income of the charity to the maintenance of the church and the rest, together with the interest on a £360 fund, was to be accumulated to cover large church repairs and to benefit the poor through education.[28] Despite this dispute, donations were still received by the charity including that from Anne Turner, daughter of Henry Turner who had been vicar from 1772, recorded in her will proved in 1844. Ann left £500 for the poor of Burwell, which, when it was invested in 1858 (the year it was received), yielded £15 a year. This interest was usually given thereafter in cash to 30, 60, or 120 people or, at times, as clothing.[29] Such donations continued well into the twentieth century; for example, Charles William Hunt in his will proved in 1927 left £500, invested to produce £18 yearly, to buy coal for the elderly poor of Burwell. The residue of his estate, worth £900, was bequeathed to the vicar and churchwardens also for good causes.[30]

By 1860, the charity's total income was approximately £165. This did not include royalties from coprolite diggings[31]. By 1900 this income had reduced by half to £80. The charity still maintained almshouses, 13 in 1865, scattered along the village streets, which were let to poor people at nominal rents. From the 1930s these cottages were either left empty and fell down or were condemned as insanitary and sold with their sites. In addition some land that was let as allotments was also sold. Two properties by the churchyard, thought to be those given by Mounford, went in 1933-4.

In the late twentieth century the charity retained approximately 91 acres of rented land and drew increasing sums from invested accumulations. Its income, still officially shared equally between church and education as ordered in 1855, grew from £250 gross in the 1960s to over £4500 of rent, besides up to £1000 from investments, by the early 1990s, when much capital was spent on restoring the Victorian Guildhall.

By about 1850 Poor Fen had been worked out and the Chancery ordered the 169 acres, to be cultivated to produce income for the poor. After their resistance had been overcome in 1851, the land was leased as Poor's Fen Farm. However, compound interest on large mortgages raised to pay for legal costs and agricultural improvements absorbed and eventually exceeded the rent, which was reduced, from 1894, by two thirds to £84. From about 1899 through to the 1960s Poor Fen produced much vexation for its trustees, but no money for distribution. From 1899 to the 1930s its tenant farmer, having acquired the mortgage cheaply, occupied it effectively rent free. Only after the whole farm had been sold in 1964-5 for £23,000 and the mortgage completely paid off, did the invested price begin to yield an income; initially £800 yearly, but by the 1990s over £3000 which was mostly distributed, as prescribed in 1883, in coal to 300 people and by the 1998 to 450 persons each year.

Education

Church schools

No school existed in Burwell prior to 1713. A proposal to establish a free school in St Andrew's church, which was probably redundant by that time, was proposed by Lee Cotton[21]. This proposal was made at some time between the year 1600 and his death in 1613. In his will, alongside the bequest to set up an almshouse previously described, Lee also left a sum of money to train apprentices.

In 1713, a school is said to have started by subscription[32]. By 1730 this school was linked to the Society for the Promotion of Christian Knowledge, which had been founded fifteen years earlier. A decree of 1730 on church lands had set out that rentals from church lands should be used to provide benefits to the poor. It was this that enabled the trustees to employ a schoolmaster from the late 1740s. The schoolmaster received £10 each year from the trustees and £1 for each child taught free. In 1756 the schoolmaster received only £6. By 1770 these payments stopped altogether[33].

By 1776 the school was known as the charity school and from 1777 the schoolmaster was licenced, following which he received £10 each year as an annual grant. From 1799 to his death in 1838, the schoolmaster was Michael Bayly. Mr Bayly was also the parish clerk at that time, and the school was in a house built on the southern end of the North Town Green, separated off from the rest of the green for that purpose, facing Cuckolds Row. From 1816 to 1825 the annual grant was shared equally between Mr Bayly and a colleague[33]. One teaching the boys, the other girls. In 1818, between the girls and boys schools, they had 220 pupils. In 1816 a church Sunday school was set up[34, 35] also using charitable funds. Like the charity schools, the Sunday school taught reading and writing. In 1840 the school moved to the Guildhall.

In 1837 the vicar, who was found with £400 of unspent parish funds in his bank account, was taken to court. In 1855 a Chancery decree was issued which devoted half the church lands income to fund what was in effect a church school. The school was to be for poor boys aged between four and 13 years of age. This appears to have ratified the existing arrangements for the school now in the Guildhall, but established a funding stream and effective financial management of the funding.

The Guildhall building was probably in a poor state of repair but despite this the school was thriving. Its masters continued to receive £1 for each child taught free, which by 1839 was £12 – £14 annually, with a further £14 annually being given to the mistresses of the girls school from 1839[36].

The unsatisfactory nature of the Guildhall was a concern and in 1859 the new vicar, the Reverend Cockshott, raised through subscription and government grants £850 to build a new girls school on the site of St Andrew's church. The northern end of the building was to incorporate the teacher's house[37]. The following year the Guildhall was demolished and a new boys school commenced on the western side of the churchyard. This was completed in 1861 and, in that year, the two schools had 320 children attending. As 170 of these came from North Street, the Reverend Cockshott set about establishing a National School. Initially this was founded in 1864 in the new church of St Andrew, in North Street, and was attended by 80 children of labourers, their desks standing in the nave of the church. In 1871, following the purchase of a piece of land adjoining St Andrew's church on its north side, a school and teacher's house was built[38]. Unlike the other two church schools, St Andrew's was always a mixed school.

In 1867 the Reverend Cockshott set up a middle school for the children of farmers in a rented house. In 1868 he brought in a headmaster from Manchester, and in that year the pupils, some of who were boarders, numbered 40[39]. Also from 1867, the Cockshott established a night school for young farmers and labourers, which, by 1873, had 70 pupils. From 1873 it waned and was revived again by 1895 when its pupil numbers reached 85[40].

Due to reducing numbers, the boys school closed in 1922 with all the boys transferring to the council school. The girls school however received a new classroom at the rear of the building and took younger boys from 1904. In 1938 it had 122 pupils and remained in operation until 1961 when, along with St Andrew's school in North Street, it closed.

The British School

In 1845, Mr Edward Ball secured government grants to cover one-quarter of the 300 pounds required to establish a British School in a building he had organised just off the southern end of North Street. The site for the school was purchased from Mr Joseph Kent of Swaffhan Prior for £5, who then redonated the money, so that in effect the land was given free of charge. The school opened on 9 April 1846. The Headmistress was a Miss Poulter who was appointed on a salary of £40 per year. Initially the mistresses carrying out the teaching were uncertificated and were mainly paid from the 'school pence' paid in by the pupils attending. The first child from each family attending paid two pence and all other children from that family paid one pence per week. In the first year there were 160 pupils on the register.

Burwell was one of four British Schools established in the locality, the others being at Barton Mills, Fordham and Newmarket and it was the only one to keep running.

That it did was largely thanks to the Ball family, who on a number of occasions made donations to keep the school going.

Following fund raising by the children and others, by October 1846 the school acquired its own library, the books being supplied at a much-reduced rate by the Religious Tract Society.

Miss Poulter left the school in 1851 and was replaced by a Miss Butcher in February of that year. However she did not stay long and by the following year a Miss Baker was headmistress. She remained in post until 1856. In that year the school agreed to participate in the new voluntary inspection scheme as part of the new Education Act.

School attendance was variable throughout this period as it was not compulsory, and the school's revenue position varied accordingly. Numerous and frequent bazaars and other fund raising initiatives were held. In 1865, with the death of Mr Kent, his will gave the school a bequest of £40, which was used to provide books, improved ventilation and a new stove.

In 1871, further improvements were made to the school. These included new desks (as the pupil numbers had risen to 210), a new gate and a new wall. However, once again by 1875 there was a £30 deficit in school funds, cleared by fundraising, and a new committee was appointed. The new committee felt that an increased teaching input was required and an assistant mistress was appointed with a salary of £30 per annum. The Headmistress was a Mrs Badcock and her assistant, a local woman, Miss Lois Peachey.

In 1877 both were given three months notice following an adverse report by Her Majesties Inspector of Schools. On 17 September 1877, Miss H Little commenced as Headmistress, with a salary of £70 per year and shortly afterwards Miss Rose Cockerton was appointed as assistant mistress at £40 per year. At the same time the fees for attendance increased by one penny to 3d for the first child and 1d for each subsequent child from a family. Poor families were excused payment. Further works were carried out on the fabric of the schoolhouse in 1878.

The succeeding reports on the school by Her Majesties Inspector in 1881 and 1882 were both satisfactory. However the school was again in debt. Miss Cockerton left in 1882 and was followed by Miss Gibson who stayed on for a very short while. Her replacement was Miss M A Jennings who was paid at a reduced salary of £20 per year. In 1882 the method of paying the headmistress also changed. She was given a guaranteed salary of £50 plus one third of the government grant, which in 1882 was just over £81.

Despite changes in teaching staff, the school progressed well until 1888 when the school again received an unfavourable HMI report. The then headmistress, a Miss Jefferson, was asked to resign and left in March 1889. A Miss Kemp of Glasgow was appointed to succeed her and later in that year the school received a satisfactory HMI report.

By 1894 the school was becoming overcrowded, but despite this it had satisfactory HMI reports for both 1894 and 1895. The HMI inspector commented that the room was inconveniently filled with desks and there was no room for marching. The infants class fared better and the teacher was noted to have two classroom monitors to assist her. Another classroom was therefore added in 1896 and in 1904 the British School was taken over as a council school.

In 1964 the school buildings were demolished to make way for the present village college on the site.

Fen Trade

The fenland water trade that had existed in the medieval period flourished in the seventeenth to nineteenth centuries, both in Burwell and Reach. Reach remained an important port with its Hythe. Once the new lode had been completed in the mid 1600s, Burwell saw a marked increase in the number of private wharves or hythes from which trade was undertaken as well as the development of the common hythe. By the nineteenth century the trade was sufficient for the establishment of a toll collector's office in the hythe, which, part of a cottage, still stands to this day. The toll collectors could demand to see the accounts of any boatman they so chose. The tolls applied were standardised and included rates such as four pence per ton of coal. Fen products were exempt from toll, but a charge was levied for landing goods on the common hythe. This probably explains the development of private wharves or hythes along the whole of North Street.

The ships plying their trade across the fens were flat-bottomed barges, which carried Coal, timber, clunch and other products. At the end of the Burwell Lode, where the lode meets The Weirs and Catchwater drains, a coal merchant's wharf existed.

Other Trades

Burwell seems to have flourished in the post-medieval period and in the eighteenth and nineteenth centuries a variety of trades-folk operated within the village, supplying the fen trade, farming or building trades. Amongst these were blacksmiths, saddlers, boat builders, a coal merchant, butchers, bakers, clothiers, shoemakers and many others. Many people plying these trades are recorded in a variety of record sources, such as probate records and records of court apprearances. Examples of such records include:

Figure 31 *The former Customs office and cottage in the Hythe. One half of the building was the office, whilst the other was the collector's residence.*

Figure 32 *Barges awaiting repair at the junction between Burwell Lode, The Weirs and the Catchwater Drain.*

Date	Record Office	Record Type	Name	Trade
1709/11	Norwich RO	Probate Record	George Robeson	Cordwainer
1723/24	Norwich RO	Probate Record	Ralph Hart	Carpenter
1723/24	Norwich RO	Probate Record	William Adams	Tailor
1758	Suffolk RO	Bastardy Bond	Henry Mills	Glover & Breeches Maker
1826	Huntingdon RO	Quarter Session Record	George Shaw	Lighterman

By the end of the nineteenth century Burwell had a wide variety of shops from which the village inhabitants could purchase just about everything they needed. In addition the village boasted a number of public houses including:

The Ship	North Street? Recorded in a sale document of 1880[51]
The Five Bells	High Street
The Crown	High Street
The Fox	Junction of The Causeway and North Street
The Bushel	Junction of The Causeway and North Street (opposite the Fox)
The Rose	North Street
The White Horse	North Street
The Anchor	North Street
The King William IV	Junction of The Causeway and Ness Road
The Maids Head	North Street
The Queens Arms	North Street
The Red Lion	North Street

Some of these were quite small pubs, for example the Bushel is referred to in one document as an ale shop and it is clear from such documents that landlords supplemented their income from land associated with the pub. For example the Bushel, when sold in 1870, included 16 acres of land[52] and in the marriage settlement of 1766, the Red Lion in North Street also included a considerable amount of land. In the case of the Bushel it was originally a butcher's shop, which subsequently sold ale before becoming a public house.

Industry

Quarrying

Before the early nineteenth century Burwell had retained very much its medieval character, with the majority of its industry being agriculture or quarrying. Clunch was still in demand for building, and throughout the early years of the nineteenth century the High Town Quarry (the clunch pits) was being worked. At that time, the quarry was owned by the Arber family, a family of bricklayers, who both extracted clunch and burned lime. In 1804 the area they occupied for the quarry and limekilns was 3½ acres[41, 42].

The clunch pits remained in operation until 1962, at which time it was owned by Carters. They were briefly reopened in 1972 to obtain stone for repairs and restoration to Anglesea Abbey and Woburn Abbey in Bedfordshire. Other quarrys in existence were to be found in North Street, past Howland Balk, which was used well into the 1900s for road repairs, and another on the south side of Toyse Lane.

From 1885 to 1905, the Victoria Lime pits were open for the production of Lime and while they ceased operation in 1905, lime burning in Burwell continued until the 1940s.

Another large quarry for cement production existed off Ness Road, near the parish boundary with Exning and close to Breach Farm. Developed in the early 1900s by a Mr Robert Stephenson, the cement works employed about 40 men and the quarry was said to have been 80 feet deep. The works was closed in 1926–27.

Fertilizer and bricks

The Ball family established Burwell's largest and most important nineteenth-century industries. These were based out on the fen. Its first beginnings were in 1806 when a business dealing in iron, timber, coal, corn and salt was established by a partnership of local men in North Street. The partnership built its own windmill, but by 1812 had gone bankrupt[43]. Edward Ball took over this business[44] and by 1830 had a large trade in Burwell. By 1837 his company was making bricks, and had bought and worked the last surviving windmill in High Town. Edward Ball retired to concentrate on his 450-acre farm and was succeeded by his sons in 1861[45]. They expanded upon their father's business, and in 1861 they employed 38 men digging turf from North Street where several small dealers sold it and transported it to customers. At the same time they also employed 28 'fossil diggers' to extract coprolites from the fen. This increased to 36 men employed in 1871[46]. In 1871 there were a total of 50 coprolite diggers employed in North Street. Salisbury Ball worked over 300 acres, the Parsonage Farm and ran the family windmill into the 1890s. His brother, Richard Ball, employed 108 men in 1861 to convert coprolites into fertilizer using locally developed practices. In 1864–5 he and his younger brother erected a chemical works on the banks of the Burwell Lode and shortly after they built a brickworks just north of the chemical works, next to the Burwell Old Lode, which became known as Factory Lode.

By 1881 following the death of Richard Ball, Mr T T Ball employed 33 men at the chemical works, most of whom lived in the village. By this time the chemical works

Figure 33 *Burwell Brickworks. (Cambridgshire Collection)*

was run in partnership with W and G H Colchester a Suffolk fertilizer company. By 1900 the works had grown considerably in size and had its own rail link to the Cambridge to Mildenhall line. The partnership continued to produce fertilizer using imported phosphates and to make the distinctive 'Burwell Whites' bricks until 1919 when Colchester retired. The business was the taken over by Prentices, another East Anglian fertilizer company. Prentices also acquired at this time the Droford Mineral water business, which was situated on the northern end of the High Street, where it had existed since its foundation in 1809. Prentices merged in 1929 with Fisons and fertilizer production continued in Burwell until the early 1960s, when less than 20 people were employed.

The brickmaking part of the business acquired by Prentices continued to run successfully and in 1926 a new and much larger factory was built. This also remained in production to the 1960s, when it employed 45 people and produced up to 10 million bricks per year.

In 1966 Fisons sold the brickworks to a Leicestershire brick manufacturer. Brick making continued until 1971, when the works closed due to the fall in demand for white bricks. The works were then demolished in 1972, with the chimneys being blown up. Today only one row of the former brick workers cottages survives.

Milling

By the early seventeenth century Burwell had one mill for grinding corn. The watermills had ceased operation at least a century before. The mill in the East Field (renamed Mill Field as a result) was owned by the Tiptoft Manor and was in operation from 1298 until at least 1640. By the early 1700s, leased to a Susannah Chappel, it was unused and ruinous as the following text from a manorial document[48] shows:

BUSY·BEE·MILL.
BURWELL.

Figure 34 *The Busy Bee Windmill. (Cambridgeshire Collection)*

'All those three roods of arable land with a windmill (the mill has been down these forty years) thereupon built. And also all that close of pasture called the Trap Close containing by estimation one rood and a half more or less.'

This mill (see Chapter 5) had existed on the south side of the Newmarket Road and, by 1806, this mill had completely gone. Two new mills were evident on the Map of the Manor of Burwell Ramseys in that year, both off the Ness Road. One was near to the junction of Toyse lane and the other a little further south near the junction of a former track that lay between Buntings Path and Toyse Lane. The first of these had been built in 1776 and was demolished in the 1930s and the second was demolished in the1950s to make way for housing.

By the mid 1800s four mills were in existence, one off Toyse Lane to the north-east of the one previously described, a second one on the northern side of Toyse Lane, the third, of which the thatched stump remains, was at Portland Farm and the fourth was that now known as Stevens Mill. Stevens Mill, which was built in about 1812, stands next to the village museum. It ended its working life in 1955, but has been restored to working condition by the Museum Trust. In 1851 three millers were reported to be working their mills in the village.

Transport

Roads

Prior to the enclosure of the common fields in 1814, Burwell had a number of roads, tracks and paths across its fields, many joining with roads and paths in neighbouring parishes. With enclosure most of these were removed and some, such as the present Heath Road, were realigned.

Mostly these were private roads created by the landowner or his predecessors where the villagers had rights of way, for example to gain access to the fields. A few were what might be considered today as public roads. These were the village streets and main roads such as Ness Road. Such main roads became known by the term 'The King's Highway' in 1835 when the Highways Act was passed by Parliament. This act defined highways as, all roads, bridges, carriageways, cartways, horseways, bridleways, footways, causeways, churchways and pavements.

Section 23 of the 1835 Act provided that no road or other way was to be deemed a highway maintainable at public expense unless notice of dedication had been given in writing to the parish surveyor. The form of such notification was printed as a schedule to the Act. This provision remained in force until repealed by the Highways Act 1959.

The following main roads were made deemed maintainable in the parish:

1. Ness Road
2. The High Street (known as Town Street)
3. North Street
4. The Exning and Newmarket Road (Newmarket Road)
5. Timber Hill (Isaacson's Road)
6. Swaffham Road.
7. The Exning and Cambridge Road (the remains of this road run parallel to the A14, behind the A14 Services)

From at least the mid 1700s Tolls existed for all roads leading into the parish. Toll gates were erected at:

1. Swaffham Gap (Devil's Dyke)
2. The Ness
3. Running Gap (Devil's Dyke)
4. Exning Gap (Devil's Dyke)
5. Cambridge Gap (Devil's Dyke)

Those using the roads were required to pay a toll or fee, which was used for the upkeep of the roads. These roads were really only trackways packed with stone and other rubble to stop cart wheels from sinking into mud or potholes. The toll also paid for the maintenance of the tollgate and the payment of its keeper and for the quarrying of stone from a public quarry off North Street.

Evasion of tolls was a problem on the roads coming from the south and the east, especially at the Running Gap on the Devil's Dyke and in the 1700s it was decided to do something about it. Therefore in 1743, Running Gap was reduced in size to a foot-way to stop its use by those wishing to evade payment of tolls.

The use of tolls on Burwell's Roads eventually ceased in 1905, the toll at The Ness closing in December of that year, by which time the fee for entry was six pence.

The railway

Parliament approved the Cambridge to Mildenhall line proposal in 1881. It was given Royal Assent on the 18 July that year. The act allowed for the building of the railway in three stages, from Barnwell to Swaffham Prior, from Swaffham Prior to Fordham and from Fordham to Mildenhall. Work commenced on the railway in 1883 and the line to Fordham was opened for passenger traffic on 2 June 1884. The railway was a single-track line and the timetable was organised with 'Down Trains' going to Cambridge and 'Up Trains' going to Fordham. The final section of the line, from Fordham to Mildenhall, opened on 1 April 1885.

At Burwell, a station was built along with a bridge to take the road across the line and a further bridge was built to carry the Exning road over the line. Steps down from the Exning Road bridge allowed access to the line for passengers wishing to get off or on at that point. As well as passengers, goods were carried on the line, which closed to passenger traffic in 1962 and goods traffic in 1965.

Farming

Farming in the post-medieval period continued largely as before, until the enclosure of Burwell's fields. The only big difference before that time being the increase in the number of sheep being pastured. By 1795 it is recorded that 1,700 sheep were kept in Burwell, most individual farmers having 100 – 200 sheep each. By 1815 the two largest flocks were kept by Salisbury Dunn who in that year claimed sheepwalks for 360 sheep and the Earl of Aylesford who claimed the right of sheepwalk for a further 180 sheep.

The 1727 Tragedy

On the 8 September 1727 a terrible tragedy struck the people of Burwell, when between 72 and 105 people died in a fire whilst watching a show. There are a number of accounts of the period, with some variation between them. All agree however that a (puppet) show was held in a barn, which had been hired for the occasion. The barn was filled and to stop others from trying to force their way in the doors were locked shut.

During the show a fire started and when 'Fire' was shouted everyone rushed to the doors. This prevented those in charge from unlocking the doors. The barn was thatched, and straw was used for seating. Consequently everyone inside perished.

The accounts vary in the number of people who died, ranging from 72 to 105. With the exception of two children from the Palmer family all of the bodies were buried together in either a single grave or two pits (depending upon the account), marked with a single headstone with a flaming heart upon it. All of the dead were said to be unrecognisable even to their families and it was said that hardly one family in Burwell was not affected.

It was believed that the fire was started from the outside by someone up near the thatch, with a candle, hoping to get a free view of the play through a hole in the barn wall. However, it was also reported that a man from Fordham, on his death bed, did confess to setting fire to the barn. He stated that at the time he had an antipathy with the showman, which in the account in the Cambridge Chronicle[50] is described as a puppet show man. Another theory was that a servant was responsible and the man, one Richard Whitaker, was tried and acquitted for lack of evidence. It appears however that Richard was probably the person who raised the alarm.

A few people are said to have survived, rescued by a Tomas Dobedee, who managed eventually to get the doors open. Sadly, however, two of these are said to have died within a few days.

Lucas[14] believed that the barn in question belonged to a man named Wosson and was situated on the *ffeoffees* allotment ground near Cockles (Cuckolds) Row.

References

1. P.R.O., LR 3/8/3.
2. C.R.O., P 18/5/1
3. Hampson, E M, 1934, *The Treatment of Poverty in Cambridgeshire, 1597 – 184?,*
4. C.R.O., P 18/25/99 (period 1785–1816).
5. C.R.O., P 18/18/2 (1797).
6. Reports from the Select Committee on Poor Rate Returns, 1816–1834.
7. C.R.O., P 18/19/1.
8. Cambridge Chronicle, 2 March 1850, P2.
9. Cambridge Chronicle, 15 December 1860, P5.
10. Cambridge Chronicle, 27 December 1873, P4.
11. P.R.O., RG 10/1597 folio 7.
12. P.R.O., RG 11/1676 folio 9v.
13. P.R.O., MR 1/509.
14. Lucas, C, 1930, *The Fenman's World, Memories of a Fenland Physician*, Norwich.
15. Cambridge Chronicle, 22 August 1892, P4.
16. C.R.O., P 18/25/99 (1794).
17. P.R.O., C 93/57/8.
18. B.L., Add. MS. 5804, Folio 115.
19. P.R.O., PROB 11/97, folio 170v
20. Cambridge University Library, Queens College Muniment – Terrier 1595. Reference QC 19.
21. P.R.O., PROB 11/123, folio 31
22. P.R.O., C 93/57/8.
23. P.R.O., PROB 11/151, folio 75.
24. P.R.O., C 229/6. (1677-1680).
25. C.R.O., P 18/25/98.
26. C.R.O., P 18/25/99.
27. Report from the Committee of the House of Lords on the State of the Poor Laws, H.C. 227 (1831), viii, 320 – 321.
28. C.R.O., P 18/25/32c.
29. C.R.O., P 18/25/88-9.
30. C.R.O., P 18/25/91.
31. C.R.O., P 18/25/130.
32. Victoria County Histories, Cambridgeshire, Volume II, p343.
33. C.R.O., P 18/25/99.
34. Norfolk Record Office, References VIS/47/10 and VIS/54/4.
35. C.R.O., P 18/25/100.
36. C.R.O., P 18/25/101.
37. C.R.O., 391/P6.
38. C.R.O., 391/P7.
39. Cambridge Chronicle, 22nd February 1868, P8. Also Cambridge Chronicle, 24th October 1868, P8.
40. C.U.L., EDR C3/24.
41. Cambridge Chronicle, 5th May 1830, P3. Also Cambridge Chronicle, 17th May 1845, P1
42. C.U.A., CUR32/3, No 77.
43. Cambridge Chronicle, 22nd March 1806, P3., 20th March 1812, P2., 17th April 1812, P2., 12th June 1812, P2.
44. Cambridge Chronicle, 23rd December 1825, P1.

45. P.R.O., RG 9/1032, folio 29v.
46. P.R.O., RG 9/1032, folios 24 – 43.and Census records 1881, RG 11/676, folios 35 – 42.
47. C.R.O., 773/B12.
48. C.R.O., R 52/25/17.
49. P.R.O., E 134/28Eliz/Hil5
50. Cambridge Chronicle, February 19th 1774.
51. Suffolk Record Office, Bury St Edmunds, Property Sales Catalogues, HE 500/1/14, sales of The Anchor and The Ship pubs in Burwell.
52. Suffolk Record Office, Bury St Edmunds, HE 500/1/14.
53. C.R.O., R52/9/5/24, 28, 29
54. C.R.O., P18/25/4 -14
55. C.R.O., R52/9/5/4

Chapter 9

The Enclosure

Prior to 1800 most of Burwell's fields were open and followed the medieval pattern of agriculture. The only enclosed areas were those immediately around the village, the closes, some enclosed fields and meadows (known as the Holme, Hay Croft, Lammas Ground and The Breach), and those Fen Edge areas such as the Broads and alongside the Weirs, which had been drained in the medieval period.

Originally, each house would have been allocated a garden or close as can be seen by the earthwork remains of the houses destroyed by the building of the castle. As time progressed, additional areas surrounding the village were enclosed as closes, some encroaching on to the open fields as can be seen at Crownall Farm, which is well within the open field system of the Ditch Field. In contrast the enclosures off the Ness Road were, from the time the land was brought into cultivation by the late 1200s, intended as enclosed pastures. Even so, in a few such places, arable strips were still in existence by the 1800s.

If Burwell had not been fortunate in having a large area of heath much of the open field might have been turned over to enclosed pastures by the sixteenth century. This happened in many Cambridgeshire and Suffolk villages.

However, as this was not the case, Burwell retained its medieval farming pattern on all its upland fields until 1817 when the Act of Enclosure was enacted. In the pre-enclosed system most of the arable upland areas were owned by a number of small landowners. Along with the manors, the church and the charity estates, only three individual landowners owned more than 100 acres. Amongst these was Mr Salisbury Dunn who then owned 414 acres.

Enclosure was first considered in 1808[1] when 160 were asked to consent to enclosure. The notice of intent was fixed to the door of St Mary's church. The majority declined and the enclosure did not proceed. By 1813, however, there had been many changes in land ownership in Burwell. John Harwood had purchased the manors of Tiptofts, Dullinghams and St Omers and wanted to revive the idea of enclosure. He along with approximately two thirds of the smallholders in the village petitioned for enclosure, although between them they owned only about one-third of the land to be enclosed.

The owners of 1047 acres of the 3570 acres to be enclosed were either not in favour of or indifferent to the idea. This included the University of Cambridge and Mr Salisbury Dunn. Despite this an act was obtained in 1814. The act deliberately excluded the heath and the fens but the arable fields and old enclosures were included. The old enclosures comprised 330 acres, of which about 200 acres were arable, and 2752 acres of open, arable lands. The division was calculated in 1815 and executed in 1817[2,3].

The Commissioners charged with carrying out the act established exactly what everyone held and identified the rights of way that were to be maintained, either as public or private roads. Petitions and claims were then received and their accuracy checked before the commissioner's surveyor commenced his work. The surveyor listed and assessed the value of every piece of land in the village and made a written record of it. Once done the commissioner's clerk calculated the size of the new holding to be allotted. In doing this the clerk had to allow for common rights and tithes. Unfortunately, the records of these calculations have not survived.

Once completed, the surveyor marked out the new allotments with pegs and the proprietors had to dig ditches and set hedges to make boundaries. This was commenced in 1814 and complete by 1817. The expense for ditching and hedging, surveying and marking out of new roads, boundaries etc. fell to the landowner or occupier with the exception, that is, of the vicar. The record, dated 1815[4], detailing the persons rated to pay for the enclosure can be found in the Cambridge Record Office.

The final document recording all that had taken place was called the award. This was then enrolled at the court in Cambridge. This document has also survived in the Cambridge Record Office along with the map made in 1817 showing the new field layout[5].

Location	Title	Year	Reference
CRO	Persons rated to pay for enclosure	1815	P18/26/3
CRO	Public roads from enclosure Award	1815	P18/26/1
CRO	Enclosure Award, enrolled copy	1817	Q/RDz 9
CRO	Enclosure Award	1817	R51/25/17 (b)
CRO	Enclosure map	1817	Q/RDc219
CRO	Enclosure Award map	Undated	Q/RDz29
CUL	Enclosure papers	1728 – 1821	Doc.625, nos 148 – 150
CUL	Plan of allotments under enclosure	1815	MS.Plans.536
House of Lords	Enclosure Act	1814	HC/PO/PB/1/1814/54G3 n 315
PRO	Enclosure	1808-1816	CRES 2/109

Table 23 *Records pertaining to enclosure of Burwell's open fields.*

Once allotted[2], the manorial estates held 794 acres, the church, colleges and charities held 265 acres and Mr Salisbury Dunn and one other farm held 510 acres. A further 40 people were allocated 750 acres between them. Thirty-one households were allotted $1/_2$ acre each as residual rights of open field common.

By the 1840's most farms were operating a four-field rotation system and the larger farms were growing mostly wheat and barley. By 1841 most farms were, as in medieval times, to be found in either High Town or North Street. In High Town there were 12 in existence, working 1150 acres of arable land. Three of these were farms of over 200 acres each. In North Street there were 18 farms working over 330 acres. However, only three of these occupied over 30 acres.

References:

1. C.U.L., D.XVI. 180.
2. C.R.O., Q/RDz 9. pp. 73 – 74
3. C.U.L., Doc 625. nos. 197 – 8.
4. C.R.O., P18/26/3.
5. C.R.O., Q/RDz29 also Q/RDc219 (undated Enclosure Map).

Chapter 10

FEN DRAINAGE

The fen has always been an important part of Burwell life. Up to the mid nineteenth century the fen was a source of food such as fish and fowl, a source of raw materials such as reed and sedge for thatching and a source of pasture for animals, mainly sheep, in the drier months.

Early settlers in the Neolithic, Bronze and Iron ages built their settlements on the fen edge and in some cases on the fen itself whereas later peoples preferred higher, drier areas for their settlements. These later people were able to till the upland soil as well as utilise the fen resources.

The earliest evidence for the use of the fen for farming comes from archaeological excavations near to The Weirs in 1969 where evidence of both Iron age and Roman ditch systems for draining fields was found. Within the fields evidence of ploughing from the Iron Age or Roman period was also found[1]. This area, which would have been dry in summer and wet in winter, would have provided highly fertile ground for the Iron age farmer.

Fen drainage appears to have commenced with the Romans who built large drainage channels across the fens to the river Cam. A number of them survive, albeit altered due to re-cutting in the eighteenth century, including Reach Lode and Wicken Lode. It is likely that from the time of their construction these lodes were used for waterborne trade, a practice that continued until the twentieth century.

In keeping with much of the fenland landscape much of the fen edge around Burwell was dry in the summer months and wet in winter. The need to increase pastureland, combined with increased pressure on the higher arable lands due to the expansion of the village, may have provided the catalyst for the earliest medieval drainage attempts.

Thirteenth to sixteenth century drainage

It was probably in the mid thirteenth century that any real concerted effort was made to drain the fen edge and shallower fens and turn sections of it over to either permanent pasture or arable land. Prior to this period, water emanating in springs out of the chalk formed streams that meandered westwards across the marshy fen towards the river Cam. In the thirteenth century it appears that some attempt was made to divert these small streams from flowing across the shallower marshy areas allowing them to be drained.

From the fen edge near Spring Close in the south to Pie Corner near The Ness in the north, a water course was made that separated the land from the fen at the fen edge. This watercourse was designed to collect the water from the many small streams and carry it generally northwards to Pie Corner where it fed into a stream. This stream, called Landwade Brook, formed the parish boundary between Burwell and Fordham and further on its course joins Wicken Lode, which forms the parish boundary between Burwell and Wicken. Like Reach Lode, the Wicken lode is thought to be of Roman origin. Today the stream running from Spring Close to Pie Corner retains the name Catchwater for part of its course and is known as The Weirs for the remainder. This possibly suggests that there was a faster flowing area of water where fish and eel traps were placed. It is probable that this was the stretch of water referred to in a document of 1353[2] as *Wydewereswater*.

The removal of water had a number of effects. Firstly it allowed for a number of shallow areas of fen to be drained along its course, in particular at The Broads and the area between the present Burwell Lode and the road to Reach.

Figure 32 *The Weirs as seen from Anchor Bridge in 2000.*

Secondly it caused Reach to increase in importance as the local trading centre. However navigable the streams leading across the fen had been, with the development of the new stream Burwell was cut off from water born traffic unless it came by the stream from the Cam to Pie Corner and then along the newly created channel. The stream from Pie Corner to Wicken was re-cut in later years and today has the name Monks Lode. This may possibly indicate its association with Ramsey Abbey in draining The Broads. However it has also been referred to as Stake Lode in some eighteenth century documents. At its western end, prior to it's joining the Wicken Lode, this watercourse is known today as New River.

That this watercourse was navigable is shown by evidence of a wharf alongside it close to the eastern end of Wicken village. This was probably the route used to transport grain milled at The Ness by boat to Ramsey Abbey and highlights the importance of the mill at The Ness to the Abbots of Ramsey.

From the documentary evidence that survives it is evident that this was not the usual route used for the transportation of goods from the manor farm. While the abbey had associations with its manor in Burwell, namely a tithe barn (Tyceshous) and a Hythe (Tytheshythe)[3] from which the produce was transported to Ramsey, records also show that Reach was a destination for the carriage of goods to be transported to the Abbey. That a hythe existed, probably sited somewhere near The Hall or Parsonage Farm, suggests that some items may have been transported directly from the farm presumably via Wicken or by cart to Reach and from there by boat. That the document of 1423 refers to 'Tytheshythe' as opposed to a 'Great Hythe' or a 'Common Hythe' suggests the existence of a separate hythe for the loading of tithes. The village common hythe was first recorded in 1486.

Documentary evidence exists which refer to ditches being dug in Le Brunde Fen, (Broads Fen) in 1294[4]. Ramsey Abbey carried out this work and in other documents of the fourteenth century The Broads is again referred to. It therefore appears likely that The Broads and possibly other fen areas were drained by about the year 1300. These drained fen areas, unlike the open fields of the parish, were enclosed as they were drained. Today, after much of the fen landscape has changed, it is still possible to distinguish these enclosed fields from those of the later fen drainage by the layout and orientation of the ditches. The fields are smaller and have a different orientation compared with areas of fen drained in later centuries.

It appears likely that this method of moving water northwards into the Monks Lode became insufficient as more drainage continued, thus necessitating the re-cutting of Monks Lode, and the cutting of a new Lode (Burwell Old Lode) from just south west of Goosehall westward into the fen to a point near Poor's Fen Farm. It is not known when this work was undertaken as no documentary evidence survives. In fact the earliest reference to a Burwell Lode is in 1604[5].

Post-Medieval Drainage

In medieval times the rights of commons extended to Burwell's fens. With the draining of the Bedford levels this right was removed.

The seventeenth century saw the first real impact of drainage on the deeper fen areas when 640 acres of fen were drained at the convergence of the Reach and Wicken Lodes.

In 1637 permission was granted to the Adventurers to drain this area, which today is still known as Adventurers Fen. The work commenced in 1651 and was completed in 1655-6. The current ditches in this area show the original allotments. When first drained the water was removed by gravity, draining off of the fen into adjacent lodes. However, as drainage continued and the peat shrank, this became no longer possible. It is likely that the present Burwell Lode was constructed at the same time as these lands were being drained, and the original lode altered so that it turned south from Poor's Fen Farm into the new lode. With the completion of this work, the right of commons in the fen enjoyed by the people of Burwell was removed and the fen divided into lots so that, by 1670, the fen had been allocated.

The three sections of the Adventurers lands comprising 160 acres, 247 acres and 293 acres were appropriated by the drainers and subdivided into lots of 40 acres or more. The remaining fens were allocated amongst those who had held commonable rights. The Manor of Burwell Ramseys and the Manor of Burwell Tiptofts were each so granted[6,7]:

Area	Ramseys	Tiptofts
The Broads	84 acres	84 acres
Western Sedge Fen	100 acres	100 acres
Turf Fen	100 acres	92 acres

Table 24 *Fen allocations to Burwell manors.*

The remaining lands were shared out between the other manors and approximately 112 commoners. At that time the smaller manors and the commoners held between them 145 commonable messuages of which 65 were owner occupied. Each house was awarded approximately 10½ acres. However 15 of these dwellings were described as 'thirty foot' cottages and only allocated 1¼ acres each. This then left 155 acres of the Turf Fen, which was divided between seven men in 1678. However this was all under the ownership of one person by 1794[8].

Altogether some 2350 acres of fen[9] were divided and allocated leaving Poor's Fen and 188 acres of the Turf Fen for the poor to dig.

By 1685 the present Burwell (new) Lode was complete and is shown on a map of the fens[10]. The digging of the lode was probably the work of the Bedford Level Commissioners, although there is no documentary evidence to support this. Where documents do exist, references to a 'Burwell Lode' refer either to the old or the new lode right up to the nineteenth century.

This new lode stretches for 2½ miles from Anchor Lane in North Street to the Reach Lode near its convergence with Wicken Lode. At its eastern end it has no retaining bank on its south-western side as it is below the level of the surrounding land. At its western end it has a retaining bank as the surrounding fen is six to eight feet below the water level. The bank is ten feet above the surrounding land.

The building of this new lode permitted a marked change in trade and prospects for North Street and Newnham, where the existing common hythe was probably extended. All along North Street small basins and canals were built from The Weirs and Catchwater drains up to the properties aligning the western side of the street. At least 20 canals are known to have existed, varying in length from 50 to 200 yards in length.

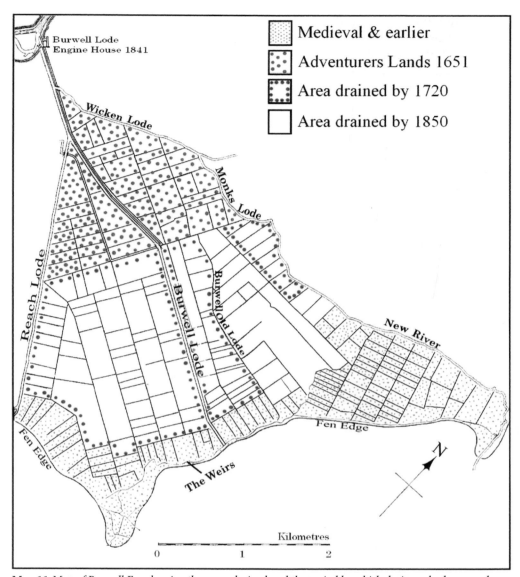

Map 11 *Map of Burwell Fen showing the areas drained and the period by which drainage had occurred.*

The width of these varied considerably, but they were usually from four to 12 feet wide and were up to six feet deep.

The Common Hythe, a public wharf, was a large basin at Newnham some 600 yards in length and 20 feet wide. This had at least one subsidiary basin at its southern side. Today, these have all but been filled in but they were originally navigable by barge and undoubtedly contributed considerably to the prosperity of this part of Burwell. The date of construction of the Hythe, the canals and basins is unknown but such a hythe is known to have been in existence by the late 1480s and may be consistent with the development of Newnham which was first recorded in 1446.

The creation of Burwell Lode permitted further fen drainage to the south-west between the lode itself and Reach Lode. It is believed that the area was drained by about 1720 although this occurred over a period of time. Hallard's Fen was completely drained by 1693 and Little Fen by 1719. A further area adjoining the Monks lode, from The Broads to the Adventurers lands was completed by 1720. The only area remaining undrained was that to the north-east of the Burwell Lode. Known as Poor's fen, this remained undrained until the nineteenth century.

Although these areas were drained they all relied on gravity for drainage and as a result were frequently inundated. Burwell's fen landowners had the opportunity to join a parliamentary scheme in 1767[11] for draining Swaffham and the neighbouring fens but refused, preferring to leave their lands in their present state.

In 1794, Charles Vancouver[12] referred to the fens of Burwell as being 'constantly inundated'. The opinion of those draining the fens was that an undrained fen was of no use. However this was contrary to the view of the people of Burwell and other fen villages who had, for centuries, been harvesting the natural produce of the fen and working alongside nature in utilising the fen as a resource. The view of the people was considered by the drainers as deluded, as can be seen from the writings of Charles Vancouver. Again in 1794 he wrote of Burwell Fen,

> 'In this most deplorable situation it is considered by the principle farmers, to be far more productive, than if it were better drained, because the water encourages the growth of reed and sedge, which is cut by the poor people and sent by water to the upper country for the purpose of drying malt. Any attempt in contemplation for the better drainage of this fen is considered as hostile to the true interests of these deluded people.'

While not as harsh in its content Gooch[13], writing in 1813, declared that any yield from an undrained fen would be less than that of a drained one. The principle yield was still mainly turf and sedge.

In 1817 the resolve of Burwellians remained strong and when new plans were drawn up to drain the fens, 53 villagers opposed them. By 1828, of the 2545 acres of fenland, 1060 acres belonged to 80 people, many of whom held 40 acres or less. Ten holdings held between 40 and 70 acres and one holding held 170 acres. The manorial estates held 715 acres[14]. By 1830 much of the fen edge alongside The Weirs, Halled Fen and The Broads were either in use as pasture or being cultivated. The remainder were being mown for sedge or used for cutting turves.

In 1819, persuaded by the charity trustees, Poor's Fen was purchased by the then vicar, Mr Baines, for the use of the poor so that they should not be a drain on the charity. Poor's Fen was the last remaining undrained area and comprised approximately 500 acres. This land had been sold off previously by the Town Lands Charity to meet unpaid drainage rates in trust for the poor. The poor agreed regulations whereby in summer they would dig turf and that any sale of land or rights could not take place with outsiders. As the turf areas became dug out the land was enclosed, some by about 1807. By 1849 the remainder of the fen was all but dug out. As a result, the Chancery ordered that the fen should be converted into one farm (Poor's Fen Farm) that would then be let out. The poor objected to this loss of their traditional rights and, after a petition failed, about 500 of them occupied the land in 1851. Initially the chancery-appointed surveyor from Ely had his way barred and as a result 12 police officers were dispatched from Scotland Yard in London. Undeterred by the arrival of the police, the protesters insisted that the land was theirs and the County Magistrate was called. After reading the riot act before a very large crowd of rowdy men the magistrate and the police withdrew. In March 1851[15] soldiers were dispatched, including a troop of hussars. The land was then retaken and the levelling and preparation for cultivation commenced. The ringleaders of the rioters were arrested and taken to Cambridge where they were imprisoned.

As noted previously, prior to 1840 the drained areas of fen had relied upon gravity to draw off water into the lodes. Shrinkage of the peat gradually made this impossible and in 1841 the Burwell Drainage Company was established. The company set up a steam engine on the Cam, just inside Wicken parish, and connected it to the fenland by excavating an engine drain that ran parallel to the north-west section of the Burwell Lode. The use of the engine proved largely unsuccessful with much of the Adventurers lands being difficult to keep drained. The engine was modified in 1884 due to the failure of the scoop wheel. The shrinkage of the peat warranted an assistant wheel to draw off water. This did not help much and in 1895 the steam engine was scrapped and replaced by an oil engine. Two years later the scoop wheel system was changed for a centrifugal pump, still with little success. At least two further engines were substituted prior to the engine being abandoned in the 1940s.

Those working the land tried to assist by constructing wind pumps to draw water from ditches into the lode, but this again had little success. At one time about eight windmills were known to be operating on Adventurers Fen. Only one of these mills survives today, taken and rebuilt at Wicken Fen. It was not until the 1940s that drainage was complete by reversing the system. The drainage was connected to the Swaffham Drainage System by means of a culvert underneath the Reach Lode.

References

1. Browne, D, 1970 'Excavations at Burwell, Cambridgeshire'. *Proceedings of the Cambridge Antiquarian Society.* **66-67**, 81 –91.
2. C.U.L., Queens College Muniments. QC 35: 39/3.
3. De Windt, E B, (Ed), 1976 *The 'Liber Gersumarum' of Ramsey Abbey: A Calendar and Index of B.L. Harley Ms. 445*, Subsidia Medievalia 7. Toronto: Pontifical Institute of Medieval Studies.
4. B.L., Add. Roll 39597.
5. British Museum. Harley Manuscript. 5011, Vol. I, folio 38v.
6. C.U.A., D.XVI.174.
7. P.R.O., C 229/6. No. 13.
8. P.R.O., C 229/6. No. 18.
9. P.R.O., C 229/6. Nos. 11, 17, 19. Also C 229/7, No. 27., C229/8, No. 35.
10. C.R.O.,. Moores Map of the Fens
11. C.R.O., R59/31/11/29. Folio 30. Also R 59/31/10/34, Folio 66v.
12. Vancouver, C, 1794 *General view of the Agriculture of the County of Cambridge.*
13. Gooch, W, 1813 *Agriculture of the County of Cambridge.*
14. C.U.A., D.XVI.172.
15. Cambridge Chronicle. 1 Feb 1851, 4.; 8 Feb 1851, 4; 8 March 1851, 4, 8; 15 March 1851, 4; 22 March 1851, 4; 14 June 1851, 8; 21 June 1851, 4, 8; 18 April 1869, 8.

Appendix 1

The Manor of Burwell (1216–1272)

A translation of an undated extent of the Manor of Burwell as part of an inquest into the holdings of Ramsey Abbey undertaken during the reign of King Henry III (1216–1272).

Borewell

This is the verdict of the jurors of Burwelle.

The church of Burwelle is in the abbot's demesne, to wit the church of Saint Mary, and in his gift. And a certain virgate of land doth pertain to the church, free from all service except foreign service.

Six hides are in the abbot's demesne, at the abbot's table. Moreover three virgates of land which are called Hinlandes, are of the abbot's demesne. Of these three virgates of land Gilbert the reeve holds fifteen acres, which Albric de Burwelle demised to him for six shillings a year for all custom, because it is of the demesne.

Geoffrey the clerk holds fifteen acres for six shillings, of the demesne in like manner, by the grant of the same Albric.

The shepherd of the sheep has in like manner fifteen acres of the demesne by the same service, but he has that now for his service and food by the year.

Edric, son of Edward, holds two acres for three shillings and performs all the customs of the vill, by the gift of Albric.

Hervey son of Everard holds five roods for two shillings, by the gift of Reginald the Cellarer.

Everard holds five roods for two shillings by the assent of Michael de Clervaus.

Robert son of Wyniat holds five roods for two shillings by the assent of Michael.

John son of Alan holds five roods for his shillings by the assent of Michael.

Simon the chaplain holds five roods by the assent of Michael.

Robert de Screcam holds two acres for two shillings.

Walter son of Justin holds one toft for two shillings, by the gift of abbot William.

Richard son of Ingard holds half an acre for six pence, by the gift of Reginald the Cellarer.

Gilbert son of Teci holds three roods towards the emendation of his toft, which Albric granted to him.

Ivo the clerk holds twelve acres for six shillings, by the gift of Albric, for all custom.

Oswy holds a certain toft in Reche for two shillings, by the gift of John son of Wuth, and all the customs of the vill.

Everard son of Gerard holds in like manner a certain toft for two shillings, by the gift of the same john. The same Everard holds one acre for twelve pence, by the gift of Reginald the cellarer, for all custom.

William Goodchild holds eighteen roods for twelve pence by the gift of Michael.

John le Bel holds one acre, towards the emendation of his land.

Robert de Clervaus and Walter de Bamville and Ralph de Osdene hold half an acre of the demesne; but they [the jurors] have never seen it in the demesne, but they have heard so.

Walter son of Averid holds nine acres of land for three shillings, for all custom, which Albric did grant to him.

Ivo the clerk holds three virgates of land, and he follows the Hundred and the County for the vill, and performs therefore foreign service.

Clariz holds three virgates of land by the same service. The same holds one virgate of land for five shillings, which was in villeinage, which abbot William did grant to him.

Alexander son of Nicholas holds one virgate of land for seven shillings for all custom, beyond foreign service. The same Alexander holds one virgate of land for thirteen shillings, which he was accustomed to plough, and reap, and mow, and the other customs which do pertain to the villeinage.

Robert de Clervaus and Ralph de Osdene and Walter de Bamville hold one hide for twenty shillings, for all customs beyond the foreign.

Henry de Nesse holds twenty four acres, and a certain mill for twenty shillings.

> *And he ought to grind the whole farm of Burwelle without toll.*

> *And to plough three acres a year.*

> *And on three days in the autumn at the bidding of the abbot to find one man. And moreover to mow one acre and a half for three loaves with companage. In all aids to participate in the villate.*

> *And one half penny towards the vine hedge, namely Wyniard.*

Walter holds twenty-four acres.

And he ought to make ready the ironwork of two ploughs from the abbot's iron.

> *And shoe one palfrey yearly throughout the whole year from his own iron.*

> *And moreover two feet.*

> *And to give two shillings for his "valda".*

> *And all the ironwork which doth pertain to the abbots court.*

> *And to participate with the villate with all aids.*

> *And one half penny towards the vine hedge, namely Wyniard.*

> *And at the abbot's biddings he will find three men.*

> *And he will mow an acre and a half and he will receive therefore loaves and companage.*

> *And he will plough in the autumn.*

The same Walter holds one croft for four shillings, but they [the jurors] know not in what manner he holds it, but he has it by the farmer.

Clariz and Robert de Clervaus and Walter de Bamville and Ralph de Osdenehold one fishery for twelve shillings.

And five acres of arable land towards the food of the fisherman. But they [the jurors] know not in what manner they hold the fishery.

Alan Rufus holds twenty four acres, with his croft.

And he ought to work from the feast of Saint Michael until Pentecost for one day each week.

And to plough one rood and a half, except twelve days at Christmas and in the Easter week, and in the Whitsun week, and this is fifteen acres.

And from Pentecost until the day of Saint Peter ad Vincula for two days each week, and to plough one rood and a half. And from the day of Saint Peter ad Vincula until the Nativity of Saint Mary he ought to work for three days in each week.

And moreover at thee biddings he ought each day to find one man.

And moreover he ought to mow three half acres; but he ought to have three loaves and companage.

And he ought to lead three cartloads of wheat, and three cart loads of oats. And he ought to collect the abbot's hay with the villate, and bring it to the court.

And from the nativity of Saint Mary until the feast of Saint Michael he ought to work for two days each week.

And at Christmas one hen and the fourth part of one quarter full of oats.

And at Easter eight eggs.

And moreover he will give yearly sixteen pence and one farthing at three terms towards fulstyngpounde, and at the fourth term six pence towards londgavel.

And he ought to lead the abbot's "valda" from one place to another place with the villate.

And he ought to harrow in Lent for the service of one day, one day with a horse, without food.

And he will perform carrying service as far as Ramsey, when he is summoned. And if he is there for three days, or four, it shall not be accounted except as one day.

And he shall make ten quarts of malt by the year.

And he shall take corn to the mill, and flour to the ship, with the villate.

And if it shall be necessary to perform carrying service, he with his two men shall find a cart, to drive wherever the abbot shall require, within the county. And in like manner he with his two men shall find a cart to carry away dung, until the court is cleared.

To each one it ought to be accounted for one day. But if he does not work, he ought to give, by the year, eight shillings for his work.

And sixteen pence and one farthing to fulstyngpounde.

And one penny towards the vine hedge, namely Wyniard.

And to plough as before.

And to all the other customs, except six pence towards landgavel

Aubrey holds twenty-four acres by the same service with his toft.

Agneta holds twenty-four acres by the same service with his toft.

Robert de Huntyngdone twenty-four acres with his toft, by the same service.

John Chaunterel holds twenty-four acre, with his toft, by the same service.

Richard Faithful servant twenty-four acres with his toft, by the same service.

Godman twenty-four acres, with his toft, by the same service.

Walter son of Justin holds twenty-four acres with his toft, by the same service.

Simon Sac holds twenty-four acres with his toft, by the same service.

Nicholas holds twenty-four acres with his toft, by the same service which Richard Ingald performs.

Richard Ingaldi holds twenty acres with his toft, for seven shillings.

> *And fourteen pence, one halfpenny to fulstyngpounde.*
>
> *And three farthings towards the vine hedge.*
>
> *And he ploughs by the year twelve acres and a half.*
>
> *And he ought to give at Christmas, the fourth part of one quart of oats.*
>
> *And six eggs at Easter.*
>
> *And he leads in the autumn five cartloads full of corn to the court.*
>
> *And he ought to mow without bidding, one acre, but he ought to have two loaves with companage.*
>
> *And other customs as Alan, if he works.*

William holds twenty acres with his toft, by the same service.

Henry son of Everard holds twenty acres with his toft, by the same service.

Ralph Newman holds twenty acres with his toft, by the same service.

Ailin widow holds twenty acres with her toft, by the same service.

Maurice holds one virgate of land and pays therefore yearly eight shillings.

> *And he will have his fold upon his land.*
>
> *And moreover he will give to fulstingpounde twenty-two pence, except a farthing.*
>
> *And one penny and a farthing towards the vine hedge, and a herring.*
>
> *And he will plough twenty acres in the year.*
>
> *And he will lead to court eight full horse loads of corn.*
>
> *And two bushels of produce at Christmas, and one hen.*
>
> *And at Easter ten eggs.*
>
> *And after reaping he will afford help in collecting the lords hay.*
>
> *And with others he will bring it home. And at the three biddings of the abbot, at each he will find men.*
>
> *And will mow two acres. And will receive for his comody for loaves and companage.*

And in all other things he will participate with the others of the vill.

Aylred holds twenty-four acres and performs therefore as Alan Rufus.

And moreover he holds eight acres for which he pays yearly.

And he ploughs twenty acres.

And he performs other customs as Alan Rufus. Except this, that he will give two bushels of produce.

And in the autumn he ought to mow two acres and he will have his food.

And he will take home four four-horse loads of corn.

Bernard holds fifteen acres and a toft.

And he ought to work one day each week from the day of Saint Michael until Pentecost.

And from Pentecost until the feast of Saint Peter ad Vincula two days a week. And in the autumn from the feast of St Peter ad Vincula in five weeks, three days each week.

And from the Nativity of Saint Mary until the feast of Saint Michael for two days.

And he shall plough ten acres in the year.

And at the abbot's bidding, he shall mow for three days and he shall receive food.

And he will mow one acre and shall receive two loaves and companage. And he will lead home four four-horse loads of corn.

And one bushel of oats.

And at Christmas one hen.

And five eggs at Easter. And he will with others, his equals, reap, collect and take home hay.

And he shall take the dung out from court with his two fellow companions, with a two wheeled cart.

And he shall perform carrying service as far as Ramsey or elsewhere in the county.

And he shall honour in Lent one day for the service of one day.

And to fulstingpounde eleven pence except a farthing. Towards the vine hedge and towards herrings, a halfpenny and half a farthing. At the feast of Saint Peter ad Vincula four pence for landgavel.

Robert son of Wymer holds fifteen acres for the same service.

Everard holds as much for the same service.

John son of Alan holds as much for the same service.

Robert de Stratham holds fifteen acres for the same service.

John the clerk holds one toft which was accustomed to render three shillings.

And John son of Wez gave to him with aforesaid croft, fifteen acres and now performs all things as others do for fifteen acres.

William son of Aldith holds fifteen acres for the same service, with his toft.

William son of Teci holds fifteen acres for the same service.

Gilbert his brother holds fifteen acres for the same service.

Thomas son of Levivae holds fifteen acres for the same service.

Walter the Wise holds fifteen acres for the same service.

Robert son of Richard holds fifteen acres for the same service.

Thomas Palmer holds fifteen acres for the same service.

Godfrey holds fifteen acres for the same service, with his toft.

Richard atte Corner holds fifteen acres for the same service, with his toft.

Gilbert Rufus holds fifteen acres for the same service, with his toft.

Avice holds fifteen acres with his toft for the same service.

Wylekin holds fifteen acres for five shillings and four pence. And he ploughs and performs all customs as the others.

Each of them, if he does not work, ought to give six shillings a year.

> And to fulstingpounde, eleven pence, less half a farthing.

> And towards the vineyard hedge, and towards herrings, one halfpenny and half a farthing.

> And he will plough ten acres.

> And at the abbot's biddings he will mow for three days and will receive food. And will perform the other things as Bernard, besides the works of the weeks. And will participate in aids.

Thomas the fisherman holds eight acres for two shillings by the year.

And he ploughs five acres by the year.

> And he gives to fulstingpounde five pence and a halfpenny.

> And towards the vineyard hedge one farthing and half a farthing.

> And half a bushel of oats and one hen and three eggs at Easter.

> And he will lead in the autumn two four-horse loads of corn.

> And will collect and carry hay.

> And will participate in aids.

Aschil holds eight acres for the same service.

Robert Scot holds eight acres for the same service.

Alger holds eight acres for the same service.

Godwy holds eight acres for the same service.

Richard German holds eight acres for the same service.

Thomas ate Place holds eight acres for the same service.

John le Bel holds twelve acres with certain land which is given towards emendation for four shillings.

> And he ploughs in the year six acres and a half.

> And at three biddings in the autumn he will find three men.

> And moreover he will mow one acre and he will have his food.

> And he will lead three four-horse loads in the autumn.

And one hen and four eggs and half a bushel of oats.

And to fulstingpounde seven pence and halfpenny.

And towards the vine hedge he gives one halfpenny.

And will carry and collect hay.

And will participate in aids.

Seger holds a certain toft for two shillings and ben and bedrype.

Edward holds a certain toft for two shillings and ben and bedrype.

Peter holds a certain toft for two shillings and ben and bedrype.

Evered holds a certain toft for two shillings and ben and bedrype.

Edward holds a certain toft for thirtytwo pence and ben and bedrype.

William Carpenter holds a certain toft thirty two pence and ben and bedrype.

Nicholas son of John holds a certain toft thirty two pence and ben and bedrype.

Thomas son of Hamonis holds a certain toft thirty two pence and ben and bedrype.

Elias the clerk for a certain will find a ship to carry the farm produce of the abbot of Ramsey.

Fulco his brother holds a certain toft for thirty two pence and ought to participate with the vill in aids.

John the Shepherd holds a certain toft for twenty pence and ben and bedrype.

Matlida holds a certain toft for two shillings and ben and bedrype.

Gilbert the Reeve holds a certain toft for two shillings and ben and bedrype.

Godwy holds a certain toft for two shillings and ben and bedrype.

Ailg'er holds a certain toft for three shillings and ben and bedrype.

Simon the Thresher holds a certain toft for two shillings and he ought to have food when he threshes.

Richard a certain toft for two shillings and ben and bedrype.

Arnold a certain toft for two shillings and ben and bedrype.

Aldwyn a certain toft for two shillings and ben and bedrype and the rest.

Richard Scot a certain toft for two shillings and ben and bedrype and the rest.

Robert Scot a certain toft for two shillings and ben and bedrype and the rest.

Alfric the merchant a certain toft for two shillings and ben and bedrype and the rest.

Alicia a certain toft for two shillings and ben and bedrype and the rest.

Aschil a certain toft for two shillings and ben and bedrype and the rest.

Ivo son of Alan a certain toft for two shillings and ben and bedrype and the rest.

John son of Muriel one toft for three shillings and ben and bedrype and the rest.

Thomas the fisherman one toft for sixteen pence and ben and bedrype and the rest.

Robert nephew of Godman one toft for three shillings and ben and bedrype and the rest.

Henry son of Alan one toft for two shillings and ben and bedrype and the rest.

Henry de Nesse holds the abbot's toft at Olive and the Mill for thirty two pence.

Hyldaiet holds one toft for two shillings.

Robert nephew of Godman one toft for two shillings.

Alun holds one toft for sixteen pence.

But neither do these two cleanse the corn at the barn doors.

Godfrey had one toft for three shillings, afterwards Ailirie gave him fifteen acres and gave him of his own money, so that he does not give now for those fifteen acres and the aforesaid toft, but six shillings with the other customs in the time of abbot William.

Ivo the clerk bought of abbot Robert Ailred for half a mark.

Walter son of Richard dwells at Finstede in another fee.

William son of Godwin dwells at Snouwelle in another fee.

Note:- in reference to the Wyniard the phrase *sepem vitis* is found. *sepem* is a later overwriting of what appears to be *septem* and this may indicate a payment for work on the vines rather than the maintenance of the enclosure hedge.

Appendix 2

The *Liber Gersumarum* of Ramsey Abbey

The *Liber Gersumarum* of Ramsey Abbey is preserved in the British Library as Harley Manuscript 445. It is a single bound volume of 256 numbered parchment folios containing Latin transcripts of land transfers, marriage licences and exodus fines from 42 manorial villages of the monastery in the counties of Huntingdon, Cambridge, Bedford, Hertford and Northampton from the third year of Abbot Thomas Butterwyk (1398) through to the twenty-seventh Year of Abbot John Stowe (1458). Included in these pages are the following entries for Burwell.

Abbot Thomas Butterwyk (1398 – 1399)

2 August 1398 – Full Manorial Court

1. William Taylor, alias Poket and John Toys: The fishpond of La Nesse, with adjoining meadows and ponds and the mill dam, previously held by Richard Fraunceys, from the previous Michaelmas for 10 years, rendering this year 10s, and each year thereafter 11s 4d at the customary times. Further they will maintain the properties both regarding ditches and all other necessities, at their own expense, with the exception that the bailiff will assign 20 *opera* of the customaries of the lord in assistance, and the customaries will be suitably rewarded by the firmarii when they come. Further the Lord will be kept free of damage regarding anyone by them during the aforesaid time. Gersumaria: excused because of a rent increase of 40d.

2. Helena, daughter of Thomas Sparwe and naif of the lord, pays 5s for the licence to marry whom ever she wishes, this time.

3. William Ideygne: one tenement of 15 acres of servile land without buildings, once held by his father, located next to Tyceshous, *ad censum* from the previous michaelmas for life, rendering annually all services and customs rendered by other tenants who hold *ad censum*.

6 October 1398 – Leet without Court

1. Richard Spencer: five acres of demesne land, of which three acres lie in Dychefeld at Galewhyll (Gallow hill) and two acres in Estfeld at Buntynges Paath, from the previous michaelmas for nine years, rendering annually 5s at the customary times. G.: excused.

2. Margaret, daughter of Simon Styward and naif of the lord, pays 5s for licence to marry whomever she wishes, this time.

3. William Westmorland pays 8d for licence to marry Agnes, daughter of Thomas Swyn and naif of the lord. And he pays no more because he is a pauper.

4. Richard Gardener: one cote with croft previously held *ad censum* by Thomas Sawyer, in *aurentatio* from michaelmas for 10 years, rendering annually 6s at the customary times. G.: 6s.

11 October 1398 – Leet with Manorial Court combined

1. Thomas Bosoun, Chaplain: eight acres of demesne land lying at Le Nesse, four acres of demesne land at "Bynnges" and "Rebynes Hanedlond", four acres of demesne land at Estfeld previously held by John Walden, two acres of demesne at Ayllyhanedlond recently held by John Walden, two acres of demesne in Dychfeld at Galowhyll and one rod of demesne in Northfeld at Braddeye touching upon Gyllescroft, and three acres of demesne in Le Braach, from the previous michaelmas for 20 years, rendering annually 20s 6d at the customary times. G.: excused by the senchal.

2. Thomas Schipwreyght; one tenement with one building and 15 acres previously held by Alexander Sparwe in *arentatio* from the previous michaelmas for 10 years, rendering annually 20s., with 4d for *capitagium*, at the customary times. G.: two capons.

3. John Rolf one tenement of 15 acres with one croft previously held by Robert Wyot, in *arentatio* from the previous michaelmas for 20 years, rendering annually 15s at the customary times. G.: one capon.

4. John Jemes: one croftland containing three acres, previously held by himself, and four acres of land lying in the fields of Reche, once held by Thomas Swasham.

21 December 1398 – Leet without court

John Sparwe: three croftlands in Reche previously held by Robert Rede, in *arentatio* from the previous michaelmas for life, rendering 10s this year and 12s each year thereafter, at the customary times. G.: excused by the senchal.

July 1399 – Leet without court

1. William Ideyne, naif of the lord, pays 2s. for licence to marry his daughter, Margaret, to Radulf Lane, Freeman, this time.

2. Richard Chapman Barkere: One plot with building with 15 acres of land once held by William Swyn, in bondage for 20 years, rendering annually 20s as rent at the customary times, and 4d. as common fine. G.: 2s.

3. John Peytour: One plot with building with 15 acres of land once held by Robert atte Brygge, in bondage for 20 years, rendering annually 16s as rent at the customary times, and in all things as did Robert. G.: 6d.

4. Naifs of Burwell (this is a list of 7 Naifs (Natives) servants of the Lord of the Manor)

Thomas Sparwe
Simon Styward
Thomas Swyne
William Ideyn
Thomas Plumbe
William Howghton
Thomas Rower

17 October Leet with Court

1. Constancia, widow of John Kyng, and her son John: half of one tenement of 24 acres once held by Edmund Poul and recently held by her husband, the other half of which is now held by John Aylwynne, in *arentatio* from the previous michaelmas for 20 years, rendering annually 11s at the customary times, as rent and 2d as common fine.

2. Same Constancia and John: one toft of one croft previously held by John Kyng and once held by John Bocher, in *arentatio* from the previous michaelmas for 20 years, rendering annually 6d at the customary times. G.: 2s.

3. John Aillesham and his wife, Maria: one cote with croft pertaining to a tenement of 20 acres, lying in Northstrete next to the tenement of John Baret, on the east, and previously held by John atte Hyll, together with the aforesaid 20 acres, in *arentatio* from the previous michaelmas for 20 years, rendering annually 5s at the customary times. G.: 6d.

4. Nicholas, son of John atte Hyll: one built up tenement of 20 acres previously held by John atte Hyll, in *arentatio* for 20 years, rendering annually 15s at the customary times. 4d as common fine, and reaping, binding and tribute of two acres of grain in the demesne land. Pledge for maintaining the property: William Poket. G:. 2s.

1404

1. Joanna Perye widow of Henry Pomeray one cote and one croft previously held by her husband and once held by John Smart, for life. Rendering annually in all things as did Henry. G.: 12d.

2. John Ayllewyn, one curtilage recently made of a furlong of the lord, at the eastern end, for life, rendering annually 10d. Also two butts ends alongside the old furlong of the lord, for life, rendering annually 4d at the customary times, with the provision that the lord can make a furlong on that land without a reduction of rent. G:. excused because of a rent increase of 4d.

1405 – Leet

John Roolee Jr, four acres of servile land lying between Estfeld and le Sowthfeld and previously held by the aforesaid John, for 20 years, rendering annually in all things as he was accustomed to render. G:. 12d

1405 – Leet with Court

John Wryght; 12 acres of servile land once held by John Frache, for 20 years, rendering annually in all things as did Frache. G:. 3s 4d.

Simon Calvesbane; pays 3s 4d to marry Cecilia Wyat widow of Nicholas Rolf, and to enter into 26 acres of servile land previously held by the aforesaid Nicholas, for the lifetime of Cecilia, rendering annually all services and customs owed therein.

1 May 1405 – Full Manorial Court

1. Radulph Calvesbane: one cote with croft and three acres of servile land previously held by Thomas Ideyngne, in bondage for 30 years, rendering annually in all things as did Thomas and suit to court

2. Same Radulph Cavesbane: eight acres of servile land once held by Thomas Higenye and once held by John Derye, in *arentatio* for 30 years, rendering annually in all things as did Thomas.

3. Same Radulph Cavesbane:eight acres of servile land once held by Thomas Ideyngne, in bondage for 30 years, rendering annually in all things as did Thomas and suit to court, with the condition that Radulph will build two houses on the property at his own expense and with his own lumber within the next two years. G:. 2s 4d and no more because of extensive repairs.

4. Same Radulph Cavesbane: 12 acres of servile land once held by Thomas Ideyngne, in bondage for 30 years, rendering annually in all things as did Thomas.

5. Thomas Stroppe: half of one messuage and 20 acres of servile land, for 20 years, rendering annually 21s at the customary times and all other services and customs owed therein. G.: 7s 8d.

There are no records for 1406.

12 November 1407 – Leet

1. Adam Alot: one cote with adjacent croft once held by Alicia Kirkeby, with one acre of land, rendering annually in all things as did Alicia. G.: 2s.

2. John Fabbe: one half messuage with 24 acres of land once held by his father Richard Fabbe, for 30 years, rendering annually all services and customs owed therein. G.: 6s 8d.

3. Robert Wilkyn: 12 acres of demesne land once held by Richard Wilkyn, for several years (unspecified), rendering annually in all things as did Richard. G.: 6s 8d.

There are no records for Burwell for 1408

4 November 1409

Thomas Paxman: One messuage and 15 acres of land once held by Andrew Morice, for life rendering annually 21s 4d., which land used to render 28s. He will render all other services and customs owed therein, and he will repair and maintain the property at his own expense, through the pledge of William Poket. G.: 6s 8d.

27 September 1410

John Barwe: Chaplain, and Robert his brother: one tenement of 15 acres of land once held by Thomas Swyn at Wakeleysmegate and once held by John Barwe, their father, for 24 years, rendering annually 17s. at the customary times and all other services and customs rendered by their father; another tenement of 15 acres once held by Robert atte Brigge and once held by their father, for life, rendering 17s annually at the customary times; one croft once held by John Sadde and adjoining Gilbertescroft, for life, rendering annually 12d. four acres of demesne in Estfeld in one piece once held by Hugo Berker, for life, rendering 4s annually; two crofts once held by Thomas Plumbe against the land of the rector, for life, rendering 4s annually. They will build a new house on the cote once held by Sawyer and also once held by Elena Helewys, at their own expense within the next 3 years, which cote is now held *per copiam* by Robert Barwe for a term of years. G:. 6s 8d.

8 January 1411 – Full Manorial Court

1. John Kent: the capital messuage of one tenement of 15 acres, for 20 years, rendering annually 8s as rent and 4d as common fine. G:. Two Capons.

2. William Houghton: naif of the Lord, pays 6s 8d for licence to marry Margaret his daughter, to Alexander Lyne.

3. Thomas Poule: 15 acres recently held by John Dyry, for 30 years, rendering annually in all things as did John. G.: 6s8d.

4. John Sperwe: One plot with building with a curtilage recently held by Thomas, his father, for life, rendering annually in all things as did Thomas. G.: 6s 8d.

1412 – Leet without Court

1. John atte Hill: 20 acres once held by Thomas Stop, for 20 years, rendering annually in all things as did stop. G.: 40d.

2. Thomas Poul: one half of one tenement of 24 acres, for 20 years, rendering annually 13s 4d and 4d as common fine. G.: 12d.

3. William Ydeigne: surrender of one built up cote, one croft, one acre of land once held by his father, which he and his wife Katerina, receive back, for the life of whomever lives longer, rendering as before. G.: two capons.

4. Richard Sowtheman: one tenement of 15 acres and two crofts with one piece of meadow, once held by Richard himself, with a half acre of land in le Nethfeld next to the land of John Prikke, in place of a third croft from Michaelmas for four years rendering annually 21s 4d., common fine, reaping of two acres of wheat and ploughing of three acres at the will of the bailiff or *firmarius*. G: 2s.

5. Richard Garyner: one built up cote with one croft once held by Edmund Waleys, next to the land of Thomas gardener, for 21 years, rendering annually 4s 4d at the customary times. G.: excused.

6. John Benet and his wife Agnes, one toft once a cotland recently held by Robert Bocher and two tofts recently in the waynage of the lord for the life of whomever lives longer.

1413 – Leet without Court

1. Robert Chapman: surrender of one tenement of 15 acres once held by William Swynedd, to the use of John Rolf Jr., for 30 years, rendering annually 23s. at the customary times and all other services and customes owed therein. G.: excused because of rent increase.

2. John Poket: all lands and tenements recently held by John Plumbe, from Michaelmas for 18 years, rendering annually as did John Plumbe, with a rent increase this year of 12d., and common fine, the reaping of one acre of wheat and one acre of Barley, and the carrying of grain. He will repair and maintain the property at his own expense. Pladges: William Poket and William Jay. G.: six capons.

3. Thomas Rower: the capital messuage of one tenement of 15 acres once held by John Kent, for 20 years, rendering annually as did John. G.: six capons

4. Laurence Skenale: the capital messuage of one tenement of 20 acres recently held by Simon Calvysbane and now held by William Gell, and one tenement of 8 acres, for 20 years, rendering annually for the capital messuage 2s and for the eight acres 8s with 2d as common fine and with obligation to rebuild the *insathous* on that messuage within the next 2 years on penalty of forfeit. G.: six good pullets.

There are no records for Burwell for 1414

1415 – Leet without Court

1. Simon Styward pays 40d for licence to marry Agnes, his daughter, to John Fuller of Milford Suffolk, the second time.

2. Thomas Rolf Jr: half of one tenement of 20 acres and half of one tenement of 15 acres for 20 years, rendering annually as did Thomas (*cut off*). G.: three capons.

3. Robert Wylkin: one tenement of eight acres recently held by Radulph Calvesbane, for 20 years, rendering annually in all things as did Radulph. G.: three capons.

4. Radulph Lyne and his wife, Margaret: half of one tenement of 15 acres *ad censum* and half of one tenement of eight acres once held by William Ideyne, *ad censum* for 20 years, rendering in all things as did William, in the time when the manor is in the lords hands. G.: 5s.

5. William Taylor (alias Poket), and his wife Margaret: one tenement of 15 acres in arentatio once held by Thomas Lyne, and one tenement of 24 acres in arentatio once held by Walter Ermyn, for 20 years, rendering annually 40s and all other services and customs rendered by Thomas and Walter. G.: 3s 4d and two capons.

6. William Ideyne and his wife Agnes: one cotland with croft and one acre *ad censa* half of one tenement of 15 acres *ad censum*, with half of one tenement of eight acres *ad censum*, and one pithel called Cheselenspightill, for life, rendering all services and customs previously rendered, in the time when the manor is in the lords hands. G.: two capons.

There are no records for Burwell for 1416

1417

and customs rendered by Thomas. G.: 2s.

1. John Clerk alias Blaunteyn: one tenement of 20 acres once held by John Wyot and before that by Swynley, with the capital messuage reserved to the lord, for 20 years, rendering annually 16s, to suit court and leet and all other services and customs rendered by Wyot.

2. John Rolf Jr and his wife, Alicia: one tenement of 15 acres once held by Simon Calvesbane, with the capital toft reserved to the lord, for 20 years, rendering annually 15s 8d, suit to court and leet, and all other services and customs rendered by Simon. G.: 2s.

3. George Hervy Bocher and his wife, Katerina: half of one tenement of 24 acres once held by Simon Calvesbane, for 20 years, rendering annually 12s, suit to court and leet, and all other services and customs rendered by Simon. G.: 2s.

4. Johanna widow of Robert Barow: one tenement of 15 acres once held by Wakelyn, and another tenement of 15 acres once held by John Barow, one cote once held by Helywys, with the croft reserved to the lord, two crofts at the land of the rector, four acres of demesne land, and one cotland at Ness called Longcroft, for 20 years, rendering annually 43s, ploughing, suit to court and leet, and all other services and customs rendered by John. For the four acres of demesne she will render as agreed with the firmarius. G.: 6s 8d.

5. Thomas Webstere, alias Arnold, and his wife Olivia: one cotland once held by Alexander Sparwe, a half croft reserved to the lord, for 30 years, rendering annually 5s suit to court and leet, and all other services and customs rendered by Alexander. G.: 12d.

6. William Crabbe and his wife, Alicia: half of one tenement of 24 acres once held by Thomas Calvesbane, for 20 years, rendering annually 13s, suit to court and leet, and all other services

7. John Benet, *firmarius*, and his wife, Agnes: half of one croft formerly held by John Sadde and one pithel at Reche once held by Baroun, one croft once held by Swynley in Burwell, half croft once held by John Sparwe next to the gate of the manor, and seven acres once held by John Jemes, for life of whomever lives longer, rendering annually all services and customs owed therein. G.: Three capons.

1418 – Leet with Court

1. Richard Wrighte and his wife, Alicia: one tenement of eight acres once held by John Bury, for 20 years, rendering annually 11s at the customary times. Common fine, suit to court and leet, and love boon, except that the lord or firmarius will have his croft in payment, or Richard will have an allowance of 8d in any year. G.: 12d and one crane.

2. John Purt and his wife, Margaret: all lands and tenements once held by John Poket, for 20 years, rendering annually in all things as did Poket. G.: 40d.

3. John Pryk Jr. and his wife, Johanna: all lands and tenements that Johanna, widow of John Barow, took up from the lord in 22 Thomas, for 20 years, rendering annually in all things as did Johanna. G.: one goose, two capons.

4. John Rolf and his wife Katerina: One tenement of 15 acres with one croft once held by John Wyet, from the previous Micaelmas for 22 years, rendering annually 15s in arentatio. G.: two capons.

5. Richard Spencer Sr. and his wife, Alicia: one tenement of 12 acres with a cotland and one and a half acres in a croft and three acres in the fields recently held by

Radulf Calvesbane, for 20 years, rendering annually in all things as did Radulf, common fine, suit to court and leet and one love boon. G.: 6s and two capons.

6. Thomas Pury and his wife, Etheldreda: one tenement of 24 acres recently held by Simon Calvesbane, for 20 years rendering annually in all things as did Simon and suit to court and leet. Pledges rent and Gersuma: William Taillor and John Pury. G.: 40d.

7. Radulf Rower: one tenement of 15 acres and one cotland called Pellams recently held by Margaret Rower, for 20 years, rendering annually in all things as did Margaret, and suit to court and leet. G.: six capons.

8. William Jay and his wife, Isabella: 24 acres with one plot once held by William Houghton, for 30 years, rendering annually 28s., customs of the vill and suit to court and leet, with the obligation to repair and maintain the property at their own expense. G.: two capons.

9. John Payntor and his wife, Agnes: one tenement of 15 acres and one cote recently held by himself, for 22 years, rendering annually in all things as he did previously, and suit to court and leet, love boon and common fine. G.: 40d and two capons.

Abbot John Tychemersch (1419–1420)

1419

1. Nicholas Lyne: one tenement of 20 acres recently held by Thomas Payer, for 30 years, rendering annually in all things as did Thomas, suit to court and leet, and one love boon. G.: two capons.

2. Thomas Payn: surrender of one plot once held by Simon Scot to the use of John Benet and his wife Margaret, for life, rendering annually in all things as did Thomas. G.: excused because of repairs.

3. Elizabeth Styward, naif of the lord by blood, pays 6s 8d for licence to marry.

4. Alicia Law: two cotes in Reche Assensum once held by Hugo Lawe, for 6 years, rendering annually in all things as did Hugo. G.: three capons.

5. John Saxtoun and his wife, Johanna: one cotland with adjacent croft once held John Pury, for 22 years, rendering annually all services and customs owed therein. G.: two capons.

6. John Wylkyn, and his wife, Olivia: one toft with adjacent croft, a parcel of one tenement of eight acres once held by Richard Berker, for 40 years, rendering annually 14d. at the customary times, with the obligation to build a grange on the toft within the next two years. Pledge, William Jay. G.: two capons.

7. Robert Wylkyn and John Wylkyn: one tenement of 24 acres, once held by John Wyott, for 30 years, rendering annually 26s at the customary times, common fine, holmsilver, when it occures, raising or stacking for one day, one ploughing *precaria*, and all other customs or services rendered by Wyott, with no allowance granted for a mowed furlong on their land. G.: 3s 4d.

1420 – Leet without Court

1. Thomas Goodynche and his wife, Cristina: one tenement of eight acres, once held by John Purye and recently held by John Jay, for 30 years, rendering annually in all things as did John Jay. G.: 3s 4d.

2. Robert Wyot and his wife, Margaret: one tenement of 20 acres, once held by John Wyot Midwyf, his father, for 30 years, rendering annually in all things as did John. G.: 3s 4d.

3. Thomas Rower, pays 3s 4d for licence to marry Alicia his daughter and naif of the lord by blood, to William Hurton this time.

4. Nicholas AtteHill and his wife, Cecilia: One tenement of 20 acres that he previously held, for 20 years, rendering annually in all things as he did previously. G.: 3s 4d.

1421 – Court

John Lyne Jr., and his wife, Agnes: one tenement of 20 acres *ad opus* recently held by Thomas Peyer, for life, rendering annually in all things as did Thomas, and suit to court and leet. G.: two capons.

19 October 1422 – Leet

1. Thomas Knoole: one tenement of 20 acres once held by John At Hill, in *arentatio* for 20 years, rendering annually in all things as did John, suit to court and leet. G.: 2s.

2. John Rolf Jr: one tenement of 15 acres once held by John Fraas, in *arentatio* rendering annually in all things as did Fraas. G.: 3s 4d.

3. John Dene: one tenement of 20 acres recently held by Thomas Pury, excluding the messuage and croft, for 20 years, rendering annually 13s 4d and all other services and customs rendered by Thomas, including suit to court. G.: 20d.

4. William Taillor half of one tenement of 24 acres once held by William Crabbe, for 20 years, rendering annually in all things as did William Crabbe, and suit to court. G.: four bushels of wheat.

1423 – Leet

1. Thomas Notewyn and his wife, Maria: the capital messuage with croft and three rods of land of one tenement of eight acres held by Robert Edrich *ad opus* and once held by Richard Fabbe, and five and a half acres of demesne land, of which two lye in Dichefeld, two acres in Estfeld, and one and a half acres in Bradweye, for 40 years, rendering annually 2s 6d for the capital messuage, and to the *firmarius* 5s 6d for the five and a half acres, at the customary times, as well as suit to court. After their deaths the *firmarius* will pay the rent of 5s 6d for the demesne land. G.: two capons.

2. Thomas Godale and his wife Elena. One tenement of eight acres ad censum once held by Margaret Plumbe, for 15 years, rendering annually in all things as did Margaret, and suit to court and leet. G.: 12d.

2 October 1424 – Leet

1. John Moleman and his wife Emma: Two cotelands ad censa and three acres of land once held by Hugo Lawe, for 20 years, rendering annually in all things as did Hugo. G.: two capons.

2. Agnes Role, one tenement of 15 acres in arentatio recently held by her husband, John Role, for 20 years, rendering annually in all things as did John and suit to court and leet, with half croft next to the manor gate reserved to the lord. G.: 2 capons.

Appendix 3

Survey of the Manor of Burwell Ramseys 1649

Transcript of a survey of the Manor of Burwell Ramseys 1649 by Parliamentary Surveyors

A survey of the manor of Burwell with the members and appurtanences thereof lying within the countie of Cambridge aforesaid late parcell of the possessions of Charles Stuart and Henrietta Maria late Kinge and Queene of England, made and taken by us whose names are hereunto subscribed in the month of January 1649. By virtue of a commission granted uppon an acte of the Commons assembled in Parliament, for sale of honours, Manors, and Landes herefore belonging to the late Kinge, Q"ueene and Prince, under the hand and seale of five or moore of the Justees in the said Acte named and approved.

The Quitt Rentes due to the Lord of the foresaid Manor of Burwell within the Towne of Burwell aforesaid and holder of the foresaid Manor in fee Soccage tenure, according to y^e custom thereof, and payable at Michelmas and Lady Day are	*lix.s ob.q^{tt}*

per annum_____

A certain Annuall rente, due and issuable out of the Rectorie of Burwell aforesaid unto the aforesaid Lord of the Manor, as Lord of the same, and payable att Michelmass only is per annum_____	*xl.s.*

The rentes of Assize due from Coppieholders within the Towne and Parishes of Burwell – aforesaid and elsewhere, due to the lord of the said Manor for their Coppiehold Landes – and Tenementes holden of the said Manor of Burwell by Fyne uncertaine, att the will of the Lord according to the custome of the said Mannor and payable att Lady Day, and Michelmas by equal pocons are per annum_____	*xlv.li.iiij.s.ij.d.ob.*

Certaine Rentes paid by sundrey coppyhold Tennentes within the Manor of Burwell – aforesaid unto the Lord thereof (called Holmesilver) that is to say according to the shiftes of the feildes. And when the Eastefeild is sowen with wheate and rie every whole holmeland payeth 6^d per annum and when the said field is sowen with barley, or lyeth fallowe then every whole holme land as aforesaid payeth to the Lord of the Manor aforesaid 4^d only, and soe according to that proporcons for every halfe holme land annually besides 4s. 4d. for every Third yeare, which is the increase of the holmesilver aforesaid. And for every two yeares it yearly amounts unto the some of 12s. 8d. And every third yeare it amountes unto the some of 16s. 10d. All of which somes communibus annis amounte unto the full some of	*Xiiij.s. j.d. q^{tt}*

The custome henns, hencorne, and eeges due from the severall copyholders hereafter named for their copyhold landes unto the Lord of the manor aforesaid, and payable att x^{tt}pinas are followeth:-	

Inprininis, from John Bridgman for henn and henncorne………	*iij.s ix. d.*

From Ann Rogers widow for a henn — vj.d.

From William Liftechild for a henne and hennecorne — j.s. iij.d.

From John Wilkin senior for henn and hennecorne — j.s. xj.d.

From Ezkell Parkin the elder for henn and hennecorne — j.s. xj.d.

From   Woodbridge for henn and henncorne — -- viij.d.

From George Clarke for a henn — . vj.d.

From Robert Cranford for henn and henncorne — j.s. iij.d.

From John Warner for henn and henncorne — j.s. x.d.

Somme totall of the hennes and henncorne amountes per annum unto the some of .... — Xiij.s. vij.d

The goodes of felons, fugitives, felloes de se, and put in exigent, condemfined and outlawed persons within the said Manor wee value to be worth communibus annis... — -- ij.s

Memorandum all the aforesaid – premises are in possession and doe amounte in toto per annum unto the some of .... — lj.li. xij.s. xj.d. ob

Leasehold. Justian Povey Presente tenante	*The Courte Barron and Court Leet, fynes Amerciannetes of Courte, wayves, estrayes, casualtyes, jusfittes, comodityes and hereditamentes whatsoever in any Courts within the said Mannor ariseinge, as perquisits of Courte there knowne accepted and reputed, and all copyhold and customary fynes, herriottes and Releifes within y* said Manor of Burwell aforesaid.*
Clayme	*Memorandum that Justian Povey esq^re auditor General to the late Queen by meane conveyances claymeth all that aforesaid premises as they are verbatim before recited from and under the Indenture dated 10th July 13th year annoque Domini 1637 made betweene Henrietta Maria late Queene, Henry Earle of Holland, and others of the one parte and Richard Miller Esqre of the other parte who granted the premises as aforesaid*
Redit v.li.vij.s. x.d.	*to the said Richard miller and his assignes for and in consideracion of a surrender of a former grante and of service donn and of the rentes reseived. To have and to hold aforesaid premises for 60^ty yeares if Thomas Povey, William Povey, and Francis Povey shall so long live yeildinge and payinge in all annuall rente of 5lib 7s. 10d. att Lady day and Michelmas by equal porcions.*

The lessee covenetes to pay the Steward of the said
Manor liij.s. iiij.d. annually for his fee, for keepinge of
Courtes with a juorisue in the said grannte that Richard
Miller aforesaid or his assignes shall give an accompte
of all excepted goodes in the said grannte, which are
thus expressed in the said grannte(except the goodes of
felons and fugitives, felons de se, and just in exigent,
condemfined and outlawed in the said Manor (which
were before valued att 2s. per annum) unto the Auditors
of the Countie of Cambridge, and Counterpartes of the
Court Rolles.

With another provisoe for the payment of the said
rente within 40ly dayes nexte after the aforesaid usuall
dayes of payment, or els the said grannte to be voide.

All the foresaid lives are in
beinge Thomas Povey is aged
20 yeares. William Povey is   or thereabouts
aged 26 yeares. Francis Povey
is aged 24 yeares

But if the said Courte Barron with the profittes
of the same as they are above recited were out of lease,
and in present possession the same were worth above
the rente received Communibus annis as were value the
same   lxxx.lv

	Acres	Roodes	Yearly Value

All the scite of th Manor of Burwell
aforesaid with the appurtanences and

Burwell Manor house.
Justinan Povey present tenante
the demesne landes with the orchards
Piscaryes fishings and yᵉ customary
works of yᵉ tenants or yᵉ prizes thereof, as
they are lett to Justinian Povey Esqʳᵉ by
the late Queen and others as followeth

Leaseholde
All that capitall messuage or
tenement commonly called Burwell Hall
or the Manor House of Burwell with the
scite thereof being an olde farmehouse
consisting of a hall, a parlor, a kitchen
and a buttery with two other rommes
for necessary use belowe stayres, and
fower chambers above staires, with a
barne and stable, and some other small
outehouses, a dovehouse and an orchard
planted with olde Appletrees and
some other fruite Trees theein with the
yeardes, wayes, casements, profittes, and
commodities thereunto belonginge now
in yᵉ occupacion of Robert Gilbert or his
assignes couleyning by estimacion

2   00   vj. li.

*Two closes of pasture ground on the
backside of the said Manor house
towards the West, and two other closes
of pasture towards the North and
East of the said Manor house, nowe
in the possession and occupation of
Robert Gilbert aforesaid or his assignes
couleyning by estimacion*   20   00   *xxviij. li.*

*All these severall parcels of land lying
dispersedly in the Common feildes of
Burwell aforesaid (vigt) in the North
feilde and in ye Easte feilde and also in
Mill field commonly called the demesne
lands belonging to the said manor of
Burwell and every parte and parcel
thereof with the said Manor were
occupied and injoyed andnowe in the
occupation of the said Robert Gilbert*

Or his assignes containing by estimacion   221   00

*All that Sheepe walke which is due
and belongs to the lord of the Manor
of Burwell aforesaid, as lord thereof,
within ye boundes and wales of the
said Mannor, as have binn ever and
constantly enjoyed and occupied
therewith worth per annum*   *xx.li.*

*Memorandum the foresaid Mannor
house and the scite thereof and all the
demesne landes and premises formalie
mencioned and recited cont 251 acres
in all, with the shepe walke thereto
belonging are by lease att present lett
unto Robert Gilbert before mencioned
an undertenante by Auditor Povey
aforesaid att the yearly rante 161 li. 13s.
12d. beinge the improved value thereof*

*All those parcels of arable land,
lyinge and beinge dispersedly in the
common fields of Burwell aforesaid
and parcel of the demesne landes of
the aforesaid Mannor of Burwell and
nowe in the occupacion of William
Speareman containing by estimacion*   39   00   *xij.li xij.s. x.d.*

*All those parcels of arable land,
lyinge and beinge dispersedly in the
common fields of Burwell aforesaid
and parcel of the demesne landes of the
aforesaid Mannor of Burwell and nowe
in the occupacion of Stephen Palmer
containing by estimacion*   39   00   *xvj. li*

All those parcels of arable land, lyinge and beinge dispersedly in the common fields of Burwell aforesaid and parcel of the demesne landes of the aforesaid Mannor of Burwell and nowe in the occupacion of John Fuller containing by estimacion	39	02	*xvj. li. ij.s.*
All those parcels of arable land, lyinge and beinge dispersedly in the common fields of Burwell aforesaid and parcel of the demesne landes of the aforesaid Mannor of Burwell and nowe in the occupacion of William Fuller containing by estimacion	18	00	*vij. li. xiiij.s*
All those parcels of arable land, lyinge and beinge dispersedly in the common fields of Burwell aforesaid and parcel of the demesne landes of the aforesaid Mannor of Burwell and nowe in the occupacion of Thomas Castborn containing by estimacion	21	00	*viij. li. viij.s*
All those parcels of arable land, lyinge and beinge dispersedly in the common fields of Burwell aforesaid and parcel of the demesne landes of the aforesaid Mannor of Burwell and nowe in the occupacion of John Clark containing by estimacion	090	00	*v. li. viij.s.*
All those parcels of arable land, lyinge and beinge dispersedly in the common fields of Burwell aforesaid and parcel of the demesne landes of the aforesaid Mannor of Burwell and nowe in the occupacion of Thomas Izatson containing by estimacion	32	03	*x. li. viij.s.*
All those parcels of arable land, lyinge and beinge dispersedly in the common fields of Burwell aforesaid and parcel of the demesne landes of the aforesaid Mannor of Burwell and nowe in the occupacion of John Flawtrer containing by estimacion	13	00	*iiil. li. xvi.s.*
All those parcels of arable land, lyinge and beinge dispersedly in the common fields of Burwell aforesaid and parcel of the demesne landes of the aforesaid Mannor of Burwell and nowe in the occupacion of Thomas Palmer containing by estimacion	13	03	*v. li. xiiij.s. iij.d.*

All those parcels of arable land, lyinge and beinge dispersedly in the common fields of Burwell aforesaid and parcel of the demesne landes of the aforesaid Mannor of Burwell and nowe in the occupacion of Steven Paine containing by estimacion	10	02	*iiij. li. ij. s.*
All those parcels of arable land, lyinge and beinge dispersedly in the common fields of Burwell aforesaid and parcel of the demesne landes of the aforesaid Mannor of Burwell and nowe in the occupacion of John Buntinge containing by estimacion	6	00	*xlviij. s.*
All those parcels of arable land, lyinge and beinge dispersedly in the common fields of Burwell aforesaid and parcel of the demesne landes of the aforesaid Mannor of Burwell and nowe in the occupacion of William Ransdell containing by estimacion	11	00	*iiij.li. ij.s. vj.d.*
All those parcels of arable land, lyinge and beinge dispersedly in the common fields of Burwell aforesaid and parcel of the demesne landes of the aforesaid Mannor of Burwell and nowe in the occupacion of Benjamyn Paine containing by estimacion	16	02	*vj.li xix.s.*
All those parcels of arable land, lyinge and beinge dispersedly in the common fields of Burwell aforesaid and parcel of the demesne landes of the aforesaid Mannor of Burwell and nowe in the occupacion of John Baron containing by estimacion	06	02	*xlviij.s.*
All those parcels of arable land, lyinge and beinge dispersedly in the common fields of Burwell aforesaid and parcel of the demesne landes of the aforesaid Mannor of Burwell and nowe in the occupacion of Amos Ginings containing by estimacion	03	00	*xxiiij. s.*
All those parcels of arable land, lyinge and beinge dispersedly in the common fields of Burwell aforesaid and parcel of the demesne landes of the aforesaid Mannor of Burwell and nowe in the occupacion of William Wilkin containing by estimacion	33	00	*xiiij.li. xj.s.ix.d.*

198

All those parcels of arable land, lyinge and beinge dispersedly in the common fields of Burwell aforesaid and parcel of the demesne landes of the aforesaid Mannor of Burwell and nowe in the occupacion of Thomas Paine containing by estimacion	25	03	*xj.li. xiiij.s.*
All those parcels of arable land, lyinge and beinge dispersedly in the common fields of Burwell aforesaid and parcel of the demesne landes of the aforesaid Mannor of Burwell and nowe in the occupacion of Barnaby Gardner containing by estimacion	01	02	*xij.s.*
Somma Totalis of the Acres and yearly value yo~	02	01	*CClxxxxvj.li. ~ xviij.s. ij.d.*

Customarie works in Lease..

The customary workes due yearly and every yeare from severall copyhold Tennantes of the said Mannor for their copyhold landes and tennementes unto the lord of the said Mannor (over and above their annual copyhold rents as aforesaid) consitinge of Plowinge of the Lordes Land, reaping of his wheate and rie, sowinge, gatheringe and takeinge of Barley ready for the carte, And for severall days workes in making of the Lordes hay are as followeth, viz

Anne Fuller vidua for her copyhold landes with customary worke unto the Lord of the Mannor aforesaid and is to reape one half acre of ye Lordes wheate every yeare and that is worth per annum — *j.s. iiij.d.*

Edmund Gardner oweth as before, and is to reape one acre of wheate worth per annum — *ij.s. viij.d.*

John Bridgman oweth as before, and is to reape 3 roodes of wheate worth per annum — *ij.s.*
The same is to plowe 6 acres of the lordes land and is worth each acre ij.s. in all per annum — *xij.s.*
The same is to worke ij dayes in making hay, and is worth viij.d. per diem and per annum — *j.s. iiij.d.*
The same is to carrie ij loades of the lordes corne in harvest tyme every yeare and is worth per annum — *ij.s.*

William Rogers oweth as before, and is to reape iij roodes of wheate worth per annum — *ij.s.*
The same is to worke ij dayes in makeinge the lordes hay and is worth per annum — *j.s. iiij.d.*

John Bridgman th elder oweth as abovesaid, and is to reape one acre of wheateand is worth per annum — *ij.s. viij.d.*
The same is to mowe one acre of barley, and to make the same ready for the carte and is worth per annum — *j.s. vj.d.*
The same is to worke ij dayes in makeinge the lordes hay and is worth per annum — *j.s. iiij.d.*

[   ] *Chapman vidua oweth as aforesaid and is to reape ½ an acre of wheate and is worthe per annum*   j.s. iiij.d.

Isaac Brooke oweth as ~~aforesaid~~ abovesaid, and is to reape 5 acres ½ of the lordes wheate, and is worth per annum   xiiij.s. viij.d.

John Casborne oweth as before and is to reape ½ an acre of wheate, and is worth per annum   j.s. iiij.d.
The same oweth as before, and is to plowe one acre of the lordes land worth per annum   ij.s.

Phillip Fyson vidua oweth as before, and is to reape one acre and one roode of wheate worth per annum   iij.s. iiij.d.
The same is to mowe and make ready for the carte one acre and one rood of barley worth per annum   j.s x.d. ob.
The same is to plowe 5 roods of the lordes land worth per annum   ij.s. vj.d.
The same is to worke one day in making hay for the lord worth per annum   viij.d.

George Carrowe oweth as before and is to plowe one acre of the lords land worth per annum   ij.s.

Thomas Paine oweth as before, and is to reape one acre of wheate worth per annum   ij.s. viij.d.
The same os to mowe onely one acre of the lords barley which is worth per annum   ix.d.

John Clarke oweth as before, and is to worke ij. dates in makeinge of the lords hay worth per annum   j.s. iiij.d.

Mary Izackson oweth as before and is to make ready iij roodes of barley for ye carte worth per annum   j.s.
The same is to worke for one day in making the lordes hay worth per annum   viij.d.

Henrie Clarke oweth as before, and is to reape iij. Roods ½ of wheate worth per annum   ij.s. iiij.d.
The same is to ,owe and make ready for the carte iij roods ½ of barley worth per annum   j.s. iij.d. ob
The same to plowe one acre ½ of the lords land and is worth per annum   iij.s.

Cornelius Pamphlyn oweth as before and is to ready for ye carte iij. Roodes of barley worth per annum   j.s. j.d. ob
The same is to plowe iij. Roodes ½ of the lords land worth per annum   j.s. ix.d.
The same is to worke ij. dayes in makeinge of the lordes hay worth per annum   j.s. iiij.d.

Danyell Wilkin oweth as before and is to reape one acre of wheate worth   ij.s. viij.d.
The same is to mowe, and make ready for the carte one acre of barley worth per annum   j.s. vj.d.
The same is to worke ij. dayes in makeinge the lordes hay worth per annum   j.s. iiij.d.

Oliver Pamphlin oweth as before, and is to reape iij. Roodes of   ij.s.
wheate worth per annum
The same is to mowe and make ready for the carte iij. Roods   j.s. j.d. ob
of barley worth per annumThe same is to worke one day in
makeinge the lords hay worth per annum   viij.d.

The Churchwardens for ye tyme beinge of Maryes parish in ye
towne of burwell aforesaid are to reape one acre of wheate for
their copyhold lands which they hold in trust for ye use of ye
parish aforesaid and is worth per annum   ij.s. viij.d.
The same Churchwardens are to mowe and make ready for the
carte j. acre of barley worth per annum   j.s. vj.d.
The same are to worke ij. dayes in makeinge the lords hay worth
per annum   j.s. iiij.d.

Ropbert Casborne for his copyhold lande in ye occupacion of
Robert Gilbert oweth as before and is to plowe j. hindale rood
that is to say ½ an acre and ½ a roode of the lords land worth
per annum   j.s. iij.d
The same is to plowe and sowe ½ an acre ½ a roode of the lordes
land worth per annum   j.s. iij.d.

William Hinde oweth as abovesaid and is to reape 5 roodes of
wheate worth per annum   iij.s. iiij.d.

Robert Wilkins oweth as before, and is to worke one day in
makeinge of hay for ye lord worth per annum   viij.d.

Robert Gilbert for landes late William Fuller oweth as
abovesaid, and is to work one day in the makeinge of the lordes
hay worth per annum   viij.d.

Summa totalis of the customary
workes due per annum   iiij.li. xix.s. j.d.

All which said severall sommes have binn
paid to the lord of the said mannor by
the said tennents annually by the space of
fifteen years last past, and are payable at
Michelmas only, and are worth in toto as
abovesaid.........................iiij.li. xix.s. j.d.

Customarie   *The Hall strawe which is to be laid into the lords Mannor*
hall strawe   *yeard by the severall Coppyhold Tennants and are for their*
in Lase.   *landes (above all the aforesaid annuall rentes of assize and*
custome worke) upon every Munday and Thursday from
Trininty Sunday to Benedictes day yearly (being usually the
11ᵗʰ day of July as followeth).

Danyele Wilkin for his copyhold lands is to bringe into
the yeard of the said Mannor house one whole or full hall
strawe upon every Munday and Thursday in the weeke from
Trinity Sunday to Benedictes day as aforesaid which said
stawe is worth per annum.........................x.s.

Thomas Pratt for his copyhold land is to bringe in one
whole or full hall strawe as before which is worth
per annum.........................x.s.

*George Clarke for his copyhold land is to bringe in one
halfe hall strawe as before which is worth
per annum..v.s.*

*Thomas Vice for his copyhold land is to bringe in one
halfe hall strawe as before which is worth
per annum..v.s.*

*Memorandum that the Hall Strawe above mentioned is the finest sedge cut
upon the playne fenns, within the said Mannor, and there bound into sheaves. And
a whole or full hall strawe is 40^{ty} sheaves, et 120^{ty} sheaves is one loade, and one loade
communibus annis is worth iij.s.*
*And soe the Total of all the whole or full hall strawe amounts communibus
annis unto the just some of ....xxx. s.*

Clayme

*Memorandum that Justinian Povey Esquire Auditor General to the late
Queen Henrietta Maria claymeth to hold the premises (viz) the scite of ye Mannor of
Burwell aforesaid with the appurtenances and the demesne landes with ye orchards,
piscaries, fyschings and the customary workes of the tennantes or the juizes thereof
as they are hereby recited by and from one indenture dated 3º January 15 Car. R_x
Annoque Domini 1639 made between the said Henrietta Maria and others on the one
parte, And the said Justinian Povey on the other parte, To have and to hold the said
premises from the date of the said indenture unto the end and tearme of 60^{ty} yeares,
yf Thomas Povey, and Francis Povey, or any of them shall soe long live yeildinge and
payinge the yearely Rente of xx.li. per annum att Lady d and Michaelmas by equal*

Redit. xx. li.   *porcions.*

*The lessee covenantes to keep ye howses and seperacions and soe to leave
them.*
*There is a covenant for ye payment of rente within 40ty dayes nexte after the
aforesaid dayes of payment with a nominee pene ti and to distraine.*
*The lives are all in beinge, Thomas Povey aged 20 yeares, William Povey aged
26 yeares, Francis Povey aged 26 years, or thereabouts.*
*But if the said Scite of the aforesaid Mannor with the appurtenances and
the demesne landes, orchards, piscaryes, fishings and the customary workes of ye
tennantes, or ye juizes thereof (as they are before recited) were out of lease, and in
present possession were worth above ye rente reseived, as in ye particulars aforesaid
doth appear per annum...........................CC. Lxxxiij.li. vij.s. iij.d.*

Reprizes.

*Steven Paine Bayliffe of the said Mannor of Burwell desinge pleasure hath
allowed him for collectinge of the lordes rentes per annum – xl.s.*

Memorandum

There is a courte Baron belonginge to the said Mannor, kept att ye Manor house aforesaid, att ye will of ye lord.

There is a courte Leete kepte att the usuall tymes.

The tennants of the said Mannor are to performe their suite and service to the Lord att the courte aforesaid.

The freeholders of the said Mannor doe always pay to the Lord of the Mannor aforesaid a Relief upon a discente one yeares Quitt Rente.

The Coppyhold landes and Tennementes within the said Mannor are Coppyholders of inheritance.

The Fynes of Coppyholders for their said Coppyholds within the said Mannor of Burwell are uncertaine and arbinable att the will of the lord who usually taketh upon a discount one yeare and a halfes Rente to the Improved value, and upon an estyemacion by purchas one yeares Rente according to the said Improved value.

The copyhold lands and Tennementes within the said Mannor of Burwell and holder of the same by coppy of Courte Roll according to the customethereof doe amount to the number of 925 acres or thereabouts. And the improved Annuall value of all the said Coppyhold lands and Tennementes as aforesaid are worth per annum 350 li. = 925 acres, 00 Roodes, CCC li. Annual value.

The Coppyholders within the said Mannor have the benefit of Common in the Fennes and Moores within the said Mannor and parish of Burwell aforesaid according to their custome. Noe Herriottes within the said Mannor.

An abstracte of the present profittes and fulure Improvementes of the said Mannor of Burwell. ____ The Rentes od assize and Royaltyes are per annum lj.li.xij. s.xj.d. ob. = The Demesnes in possession nut. The reseived Rentes upon the severall leaseholders xxv.li. vij.s. xd. Somma totalis of the present profittes are per annum – lxxvij.s. ix.d. ob. The improvement of the severall Leases within the said Mannor are per annum – CCClxiij. Li. vij.s. iij.d. Somma totalis of the fulme improvementes are per annum – ut supra. Noe woodes, underwoodes, nor Tymber Trees within the said Mannor.

Signed and subscribed by us whose names are hereunder written nominated and appointed surveyors in the Countie of Cambridge by the Justees according to the foremencioned Act this sixteenth day of January 1649. W. Blish. Tho. Fowle. Examinant per Will. Webb Supervisorem Generalem 1649. John Ward

(Parliamentary Surveys, Public Record Office, E 320/C10.)

Appendix 4

John Lawrence de Wardeboys (Warboys)

John Lawrence de Warboy's much mutilated brass monument is to be found in the chancel of St Mary's church. John was the last abbot of the Benedictine monastery of Ramsey, which held the principle manor in Burwell up to 1539.

John was the thirty-fifth and last abbot of Ramsey, and of his early life little is known except that he originated in Warboys. On entering the Benedictine order it was required that the novice dropped their worldly surname in favour of the name of their native place. Hence for most of his life John Lawrence was known as John de Wardeboys (Warboys).

In 1507, John was elected abbot of Ramsey Abbey, the tenth richest abbey in all England. His job was not an easy one. The community of about 40 monks, scholars, novices and lay brethren were mostly to be found in two communities; the abbey in Ramsey and Slepe priory in St Neot's. The fabric of both the abbey and the priory were in a poor state of repair at the time of his accession and remained so for a number of years. When, in 1518, William Atwater, Bishop of Lincoln, in whose diocese Ramsey Abbey fell, visited the abbey he found it in a dire state. Bishop Atwater describes the state of the fabric as being so bad that on wet days water poured in and onto the high altar, and that a similar situation existed at St Ive's where he found that scaffolding to repair the church roof was only partly erected as the scaffolding contractor had not been paid.

Bishop Atwater, who interviewed and recorded the testimonies of all the community, found that only the prior and one or two monks attended the conventual mass. Few of the monks rose at night for matins and the prior was frequently drunk. Surprisingly the bishop's notes appear to suggest that the abbot had little to do with the day-to-day liturgical life of the monastery. The bishop also noted the size of the community and asked John Lawrence to recruit others into it. In a tone of exasperation, he also implored John Lawrence to provide basic education for the novices, which was seriously lacking, and filed injunctions for action to be taken to correct the abuses being undertaken by the existing brothers, such as the prior.

On 30 August 1530, the abbey was visited again, this time by Bishop John Longland of Lincoln who noted many changes and improvements since the 1518 visit. However he still found much wrong, including the maintenance of the offices and liturgical hours at St Ive's (but not at Ramsey). He did note, however, that the younger monks were now being schooled in grammar.

The lack of attention from 1507 to 1518 was probably due to the periods of absence of Abbot Lawrence, who was himself was gaining his own education. In 1519 he was admitted as a Doctor of Theology to the University of Cambridge. It was only after 1519 that he became prominent as an actor in the great events of the period. Firstly in tightening up at Ramsey and St Ive's, and then turning his attention to national events.

In 1529 he was summoned to parliament with 25 other Benedictine abbots. The subject under discussion was reformation. Parliament in the sixteenth century sat infrequently, unlike now, and this discussion over reformation was to continue until 1534. In 1531 John Lawrence joined the members of the House of Lords in preparing a letter to the Pope in favour of King Henry VIII's divorce. He also appears to have been present in convocation in 1531, when nine Bishops and 62 abbots and priors acknowledged the king as supreme head of the church in England. Subsequently he and the monks of Ramsey swore an oath accepting the king's supremacy as head of the church.

In 1535 the King ordered that all monasteries be evaluated so that a new tax could be imposed on all ecclesiastical property. This visitation by the King's Surveyors was followed shortly afterwards by a visit from Thomas Bedyll, Archdeacon of London. Bedyll's visit in January 1536 was on the orders of Cromwell. He was known to be a very critical man but he came away from Ramsey impressed, stating,

"… in mine opinion the abbot and convent be as true and faithful obedientiaries to the king's grace as any religious folks in this realm…".

In addition Bedyll's letter to Cromwell tells us that Abbot Lawrence had exhibited a charter of King Edgar in the parish church at Ramsey, which Lawrence interpreted as the acceptance by the monastery of the supreme headship of King Edgar over the English church and thereby the supremacy of all kings that had followed. This was clearly a political act which was intended to impress Thomas Bedyll, which it clearly did.

In 1536 the smaller monasteries (those with an annual taxable income of less than £200) were dissolved. The larger abbeys, such as Ramsey, appear to have thought they would be allowed to continue much as before. There was much to suggest that this was to be the case, for during that year King Henry VIII founded a new abbey and re-founded another, which increased the hopefulness of the larger abbeys. 1536 was also the year in which Catherine of Aragon was buried at Peterborough Cathedral and at which Abbot John Lawrence was in attendance.

By 1538 with further visitations taking place on behalf of Cromwell, it was clear that the larger monasteries were also to be dissolved. In the case of Ramsey, the visitation took place on 15 October 1538. The visitor was Richard Williams, Cromwell's nephew, who wrote to Cromwell after visiting both Ramsey and Ely. In his letter he wrote that he found Abbot John Lawrence to be "comfortable to everything" suggesting some form of deal was being done.

When Parliament met again in 1539 Abbot John Lawrence was among the heads of 19 religious houses summoned. In this session of Parliament he was present when the bill to suppress the larger monasteries was read. During this extended stay in London he was probably arranging his affairs including a suitable pension.

Ramsey Abbey surrendered to the Crown on 22 November 1539. At the dissolution the brethren was made up of Abbot John Lawrence and 29 other monks, including one

Burwell born monk, John Bridgeman. Each monk of Ramsey was, on 29 January 1540, allowed to exchange his habit for the clothes of a secular priest and hold a benefice. Despite that they were no longer monks, they had to remain celibate. Each monk was also awarded a pension. The average was between five and eight pounds per year.

Abbot John Lawrence however was given an astounding amount, which comprised of:

£266.13s.4d

Bodsey House,

100 loads of wood yearly out of Bottnall, Buckyse grove and Warvyswood,

one hundred mark of Swans with the profit thereof,

one "bootegate called the subcellarers bote gate, with the hylke and pertinences belonging to the same"

By any measure of the time this was a very large pension. Clearly he was rewarded for his support of the dissolution.

Despite having the use of Bodsey House, a former manor house of the abbots of Ramsey at Bodsey near Ramsey, John Lawrence moved to Burwell. There, with three companions whom he referred to as 'his chaplains', he settled and set up a small community – a little Ramsey Abbey. His three companions were, John Faunte, John Pawmer and George Marshall. This was probably as much an educational community, with links into the University, as a religious one. For all were well-educated men, John Faunte for example was a Bachelor of Theology, and was appointed as the Rector of St Andrew's Church, Burwell. John Lawrence himself was drawing the pension of the rector of St Mary's church.

The community did not last long as, on 12 December 1541, John Lawrence died. On his death he was buried in St Mary's church as stated in his will, which reads

'...my body be buryed in the church of Sainte Mary at Burwell...'

In this will, probated on 7 November 1542, he made a number of bequests, including the sum of 6s 8d to each former priest of Ramsey Abbey and provision for a spire on the church at Ramsey.

It is likely that John Lawrence had something to do with the giving of the advowson of St Mary's church to the University of Cambridge. When this was ratified in 1544, three years after his death, the document states that the award of the rector's pension of 40s was to be given to the abbot of Ramsey. This suggests that either the transfer of advowson from abbey to university was arranged as part of the dissolution or as part of his pension deal. Unfortunately it did not happen in his lifetime.

Index